T0372893

ISRAEL'S NATIONAL SECURITY
TOWARDS THE 21st CENTURY

Of Related Interest

Israeli Strategy after Desert Storm
by Aharon Levran

Democratic Societies and their Armed Forces: Israel in Comparative Context
edited by Stuart A. Cohen

Revisiting the Yom Kippur War
edited by P.R. Kumaraswamy

Fighting World War Three from the Middle East:
Allied Contingency Plans, 1945–1954
by Michael J. Cohen

The British Army, Manpower and Society into the Twenty-First Century
edited by Hew Strachan

The US Military Profession into the Twenty-First Century
by Sam C. Sarkesian and Robert E. Connor Jr

Israel's National Security Towards the 21st Century

Editor

URI BAR-JOSEPH
University of Haifa

Routledge
Taylor & Francis Group

LONDON AND NEW YORK

First published by Frank Cass Publishers 2001

This edition published 2012 by Routledge
2 Park Square, Milton Park, Abingdon, Oxfordshire OX14 4RN
711 Third Avenue, New York, NY 10017

Routledge is an imprint of the Taylor & Francis Group, an informa business

Website: www.frankcass.com

Copyright © 2001 Frank Cass Publishers

British Library Cataloguing in Publication Data

Israel's national security towards the 21st century
1. National security – Israel
I. Bar-Joseph, Uri
355'.033'05694

ISBN 0-7146-5169-9 (cloth)
ISBN 0-7146-8183-0 (paper)

Library of Congress Cataloging-in-Publication Data

Israel's national security : towards the 21st Century / editor, Uri Bar-Joseph.
    p. cm.
"A special issue of the Journal of Strategic Studies on Israel's national security
conception at a crossroad".
Includes bibliographical references (p.) and index.
ISBN 0-7146-5169-9 – ISBN 0-7146-8183-0 (pbk.)
I. National security–Israel. 2. Israel–Defenses. I. Bar-Joseph, Uri.

UA853.I8 I89 2001
355'.03305694–dc21   2001028963

This group of studies first appeared in a Special Issue on
'Israel's National Security Towards the 21st Century'
of *The Journal of Strategic Studies* (ISSN 0140 2390) 24/2 (June 2001)
published by Frank Cass.

*All rights reserved. No part of this publication may be reproduced, stored in or introduced into a retrieval
system, or transmitted, in any form, or by any means, electronic, mechanical, photocopying, recording, or
otherwise, without the prior written permissionof the publisher of this book.*

In memory of
Amos Perlmutter and Michael I. Handel,
scholars and friends.

Contents

Contents

1

Introduction

URI BAR-JOSEPH

'Israeli military thinking since the 1950s' argues one of its students 'is merely a footnote to the military thinking that was crystallized then.'[1] Though there is more than a grain of truth in this statement, tracing the intellectual roots of Israel's present national security concept will bring us to an era even earlier than that. In part it is the 1930s – the establishment of the first Jewish mobile units ('*Nodedet*') by the unorthodox Haganah commander, Yitzhak Sadeh, and of the Special Night Squads (SNS) by the legendary British Captain Orde Charles Wingate in response to the Arab rebellion of 1936–39. Their most prominent students were Yigal Allon and Moshe Dayan. Both admit the impact of Sadeh and Wingate on their intellectual and military thinking and both influenced extensively Israeli approach to security problems. Allon, the 1948 War's most important general, played a major role in shaping Israeli strategic thinking between the late 1940s and the 1973 Yom Kippur War. Dayan – the Chief of Staff in the mid-1950s and Security Minister between 1967 to 1974 – was the chief architect of the Israel Defense Forces' (IDF) *esprit de corps*, and the most influential figure in security affairs in the aftermath of the Six Day War.[2]

Yet the founding father of Israel's national security concept was no soldier but a civilian. Though he saw a military service in the First World War, David Ben-Gurion was never raised beyond the rank of corporal and had no combat experience. Moreover, until the British mandate of Palestine approached its end he had hardly occupied himself with security affairs. But since early 1947, when he realized, at the age of 60, that the birth of the Jewish state was likely to involve a war with its neighbor countries, his prime concern became Israel's national security. It remained so until he left office in 1963.[3]

Ben-Gurion's belief system was shaped in Tsarist Russia before the revolution, where struggle between Russian socialism and Zionism as a panacea to the Jewish problem was so common. As a grown man and already the leader of the Jewish *Yishuv*, he witnessed the Holocaust, which proved so vividly how real was the threat to the mere existence of the undefended Jewish people. And in 1948 he lead his country through a war in which its existence was put into question. Combined, these traumatic experiences facilitated a *Weltanschauung* in which Arab destruction of the new Jewish state was not only possible but also very real. No wonder, then, that Ben-Gurion's approach to Israel's security challenges can be best typified as 'security bolshevism'. Since the early 1950s, when he concluded that Israel could not reach peace with the Arab world at a cost he deemed acceptable, he became the prominent carrier of the belief that all national resources should be mobilized for the sake of the state's security. Consequently, not only immigration absorption, education, or buildup of settlements was security in his eyes, but also his famous ideal that Israel should become 'a light unto the nations' ('*or lagoyim*'). As he explained it, besides its moralistic value, being a paragon to other nations has an important security function: without it Israel will lose the external support which is so essential to ensure her existence.[4]

Underlying Israel's security conception that was born in the early 1950s were four elements which, to a large extent, remained dominant ever since:

- The massive disproportion between Israeli and Arab national resources, chiefly in terms of territory, manpower, and GNP, prevents Israel from ending the conflict by military means, while allowing the Arabs to do so. Consequently, Israel is a territorial and political status-quo power. Hence, the only goal of the IDF, as implied by its name, is to defend the country against a revisionist Arab world.

- The most fundamental and dangerous threat to Israeli existence is an all-out coordinated Arab surprise attack. Consequently, Israel should always maintain the ability to defend herself under the conditions of such a worst case scenario, known as *mikreh hakol* ('the all-out case').

- As derived from the above, Israeli national security doctrine rests on three pillars: *deterrence* (as implied by the defensive goals of its national security conception); *strategic warning* (on any development which might endanger its national existence); and *decision* (the military ability to win a decisive victory if deterrence fails).

- The operational implications of this doctrine are chiefly two: (a) the buildup of the capability needed to provide a high quality strategic warning and a quick response to external threats. This explains why the Defense Military Intelligence (DMI), the Air Force (IAF), and the Navy are regular forces while the ground forces are based on reserve manpower. (b) Attainability to maintain operational initiative in the initiation of wars and in the battlefield, in order to be able to win a decisive victory within a short time.

At the basis of this work stands a twofold argument:

First, that in spite of 50 years of military struggle which demanded the lives of close to 20,000 Israeli civilians and soldiers, despite major changes in the structure of the Israeli society, the structure of the Arab–Israeli conflict and the structure of the international system, and in defiance of a revolution in military affairs which has reshaped the face of modern battlefield, Israel's national security conception has undergone no radical changes since the early 1950s.

Second, that this situation is about to change.

The present work aims at describing and analyzing some of the theoretical and empirical aspects of the coming changes. In order to set them in a theoretical framework, it first addresses two issues: the meaning of the concept of security in the aftermath of the Cold War, and the sources of change in national security doctrine. It, then, moves to discuss the Israeli context of national security by addressing three major issues:

- the way the IDF may adapt itself to recent changes in warfare known as the revolution in military affairs (RMA);

- possible strategies by which Israel can deal with the threat of weapons of mass destruction (WMD) which replaced, since the early 1990s, the all-out conventional offensive as the main danger to its national existence;

- and the impact of societal, political, and technological changes on Israel's future war objectives.

Since this work focuses on existential threats and the way Israel meets them, the issue of Low Intensity Conflict (LIC) is not discussed here. Certainly, the Fedayeen of the 1950s, the Palestinian guerrillas of the 1960s, 1970s, and 1980s, the Hizballah during the 1990s, the *Intifada* of 1987–93 and its current wave – all constituted, and still do, a permanent threat to lives of Israeli citizens. But none of these ever presented an actual challenge to the existence of the Jewish state. For this reason, we decided to exclude the analysis of this subject from this collection.

As Benjamin Miller of the Hebrew University maintains in his essay about the meaning of the concept of security in the aftermath of the Cold War, the last decade witnessed many calls for adopting a new conception of security and for extending the traditional concept. Confronting this approach, is a more traditional school, which persisted in defining the field of security studies exclusively in terms of 'the study of the threat, use, and control of military force'. Miller asks two questions:

First, are the new conceptions and extensions necessary or is the traditional concept the right way to address the security issue?

Second, are the re-definitions useful or do they carry heavy costs which will bring more damage than benefit to our understanding of the security concept?

In addressing the debate on the expansion of the concept of security Miller argues that the 'expanders' of the concept beyond the focus on threats of organized violence and armed conflicts are wrong because of the resultant loss of intellectual coherence of the concept and of the security field, and also because of the remaining importance of the question of war and violence under international anarchy. On the other hand, while the 'minimalists' (mostly realists who can also be called traditionalists), avoid these two potential problems, they are nevertheless wrong by de-emphasizing both peace as a central component of the security field and nonmilitary causes or means affecting national as well as regional and international security.

Miller's argument is based on a distinction between the phenomenon to be explained (or dependent variable), which defines the scope of the field and the substantive issues it addresses, and the explanations (or independent variables), which include all the relevant competing causal factors affecting the explained phenomenon. The subject matter that the security field addresses is the threat of organized inter-group violence (including inter-state and low-intensity conflict) and the ways to manage and to prevent it. Here a somewhat broadened version of the traditionalist security concept – which should treat peace as a central element of the field alongside war – is in order. At the same time, however, the door should be kept wide open to a greater variety of causal factors, theories and explanations of war and peace on the condition that they logically and empirically affect these issues.

Miller's contribution starts with a brief discussion of the relations between international anarchy and national and international security. After presenting the traditional approach to the concept of security in international relations, the essay introduces the major challenges which have emerged to the traditional conception, and which have grown immensely since the end of the Cold War. The study then discusses the limitations to these challenges and suggests an approach that will help maintain conceptual coherence through a focus on the substantive issues of war and peace. The author illustrates the discussion with aspects of the national security of Israel. The main implication of the proposed approach for Israel is that its national security debate should continue to focus on threats of organized violence (by states and non-state guerrilla and terrorist organizations) to national core values, but the complex relations between peace and such threats should be a major focus of inquiry in both the academic and policy communities.

In 'New Threats, New Identities, and New Ways of War: The Sources of Change in National Security Doctrine', Emily O. Goldman of the University of California, Davis examines the conditions under which national security doctrines change. She argues that dramatic shifts in national security doctrine are often the product of major discontinuities such as regime change, defeat in war, disappearance of a major threat, or revolutionary technological breakthroughs that alter the foundations of national power. Dramatic discontinuities in the strategic, technological, and domestic environments that render traditional planning assumptions and standard procedures obsolete frequently produce a crisis in national security identity. This requires political leaders to create a new theme, or national purpose orientation, around which domestic society can be mobilized.

Goldman uses the concept of 'national security uncertainty' to capture the strategic dilemma facing national security establishments today. She develops a typology of uncertainties orchestrated around six key categories: one's own goals, the goals of potential allies, and those of potential adversaries; one's own capabilities, the capabilities of potential allies, and those of potential adversaries. This typology deftly captures the complexities of operating in the post-Cold War, information age security environment.

Goldman then proceeds to examine the drivers of national security uncertainty, chief among them being changes in the nature of the threat, shifts in the domestic social and political milieux due to economic and demographic shifts, rapid and discontinuous technological change, and changing norms both nationally and internationally.

The question then becomes how one would expect national security doctrines to adjust to these discontinuities. While there is little well-developed theory on national security adjustment under uncertainty, Goldman mines the relevant theoretical literature – structural, domestic political, organizational, and ideational – to tease out hypotheses about how we should expect national security doctrines to adapt.

She concludes by providing a set of indicators for analyzing responses to national security uncertainty along four key dimensions: diplomatic posture, resource allocation priorities, military mission priorities, and domestic mobilization theme. Her rich analysis provides a useful starting point for debates about why and how national security conceptions are transformed.

Following Miller and Goldman's theoretical setting, the focus of the rest of this collection is on three principal dimensions of Israel's national security policy. Chris C. Demchak of the University of Arizona analyzes the difficulties involved in the adoption of Israel's conventional forces to the Revolution in Military Affairs and a possible solution to these problems. Her piece, 'Technology's Knowledge Burden, the RMA, and the IDF: Organizing the Hypertext Organization for future "Wars of Disruption"?' starts with an analysis of the manner in which the IDF modernizes for the twenty-first century. She shows how the IDF is adopting in an ad hoc fashion many of the short-term budget-reducing elements of the US-defined RMA model of a modern military, and concludes that by embracing such issues as focusing on reducing the costs of so many conscripts or minimizing reservists, the Israeli defense leaders are choosing a path of modernization highly problematical for the knowledge-conditions of their nation.

The knowledge burden of the highly integrated RMA model, Demchak maintains, is enormous and poses some daunting initial conditions to reach the organizational outcomes expected. This complexity requires carefully embedded tradeoffs in time, distance and money to provide slack in case of inevitable misjudgments when orchestrating finely tuned activities with large-scale technical systems. Even if adopted piecemeal in elements, the RMA model defined by the United States remains a socio-technical arrangement most appropriate for an expeditionary army of a relatively isolated and wealthy society.

Demchak asserts that the RMA in its emerging design is similar to the trends in the business world towards 'business process reengineering' (BPR) usually involving 'enterprise resource planning' (ERP) to produce an enterprise-wide highly integrated overall management system. The information technologies (IT)-enabled BPR and the associated ERP are integral to the RMA military being pursued by the US defense establishment and for much the same reasons: cheaper, faster, more productive (in marketplace or battle) and more control throughout the system. Like the RMA model, the ERP process engages in knowledge management (KM) intensely. It closely couples all processes, often using such processes as 'just-in-time' (JIT) logistics to keep inventory costs to a minimum.

Unfortunately for the RMA designers, the record of business experience is not encouraging. While there are some remarkably successful BPRs that integrated large corporate structures effectively, some 80 per cent of BPRs fail. This lack of success is often due to a failure to understand the firm's initial conditions across all the elements of this socio-technical system right from the outset, especially the knowledge burden.

More discouraging for military planners is that these business failures occurred in organizations that, unlike militaries, are able to operate daily in their core competencies; they were most likely to have tested all their functions frequently. Most militaries rarely actually use all of their systems because battles are simply infrequent. Hence, a direct translation of the enterprise-wide system from the commercial world to the IT-enabled modernized military is highly problematical in any event. But, as Demchak so convincingly argues, these kinds of notions lie at the heart of the RMA image being promoted by the US and being accepted in rudimentary form all over the modernizing and modernized world, including Israel.

Underlying this piece is an understanding of the knowledge burdens inherent in constructing and operating large-scale technical systems such as the one embedded in the RMA and on the experiences already demonstrated by the corporate and computer business world to explore the implications of an RMA implementation in the IDF. Israel has resources and even has some exceptional characteristics that allow a modernization into a knowledge-enhanced military. But Israel's initial conditions differ from other westernized nations in this kind of evolution. Success in orchestrating complex integrated militarized-knowledge systems is more likely if the IDF can break out along a different organizational path than the US/NATO RMA. In many respects, Demchak maintains, the IDF as an organization poised for an evolutionary leap is fortunate in the level of technical familiarity of its input population and by the social construction of both its mission and this emerging set of new tools.

Demchak's study reviews the RMA model's organizational knowledge requirements and the current knowledge conditions facing the IDF, both those that favor an RMA implementation and those that work against a successful adoption of that model. It includes a brief discussion of the RMA implications for Israel's conventional deterrence; the role of surprise in future conflicts; crisis stability; and the possible transformation of the IDF.

Given the difficulties involved in implementation of a US/NATO RMA model in the Israeli case, Demchak proposes an alternative modernization model for the IDF, one that is tailored to the strengths of its wider society and points a path to modernizing to ensure slack through knowledge-creation/ applications that are developing in any case in Israel's vibrant computer startup community. Called the 'Atrium', this model is a non-RMA knowledge-centric organization more congruent with Israeli geostrategic and internal knowledge conditions, and longer-term innovations. The uncertainties of the Israeli circumstances require a different kind of modernization of the military organization – one that recognizes a new social construction of the role of knowledge as *a player in organizational operations and deliberately seeks and fosters this development.* With such an approach, the IDF's organizational strategy can be to maintain the robustness of its technological edge, its traditional role as school of the nation, and its close ties to the burgeoning knowledge development of the surrounding society through its reserves.

To meet these aims, Demchak proposes a variant of the 'hypertext' organization described by Nonaka and Takeuchi. This refinement, which she labels the 'Atrium' form of information based organization, is a design that treats knowledge as a third and equal partner in the organization. In the original model and in her refinement, the knowledge base is not merely an overlain tool or connecting pipelines. Rather, the knowledge base of the organization is actively nurtured both in the humans and in the digitized integrated institutional structure.

This model attempts to reconcile the competing demands and benefits of both matrix and hierarchical organizational forms across three intermingling structures: a matrix structure in smaller task forces specifically focused on problems at hand and answering to senior managers, a second hierarchical structure that both supports the general operational systems but also contributes and then reabsorbs the members of task forces, and finally a large knowledge base that is intricately interwoven through the activities of both matrix and hierarchical units.

In this approach, current elements of the IDF's structure, culture and specifically successful activities are retained, including special units, conscripts and reserves, all of whom have a real role in a modernized military. As Demchak summarizes her discussion, adopting this approach the IDF is more likely to successfully modernize while accommodating the best of its own social history and its unique strategic needs.

The subject of the essay by Yiftah Shapir of the Jaffee Center for Strategic Studies at Tel Aviv University is the way Israel prepares itself to meet the rising threat of weapons of mass destruction (WMD). Titled 'Nonconventional Solutions for Nonconventional Problems', its starting point is that since the end of the 1991 Gulf War Israel perceives WMD, as repeatedly expressed by its leaders, as the greatest threat to its security. Given this focus of concern, the question addressed is: what options does Israel have to mitigate these perceived threats?

According to Shapir, Israel has five courses of action to meet the WMD threat: the use of defensive measures like shelters and protective gear to mitigate the damage caused by these weapons; the buildup of weapon systems aimed at destroying ballistic missiles once they are launched; the adoption of offensive measures designed to destroy the missile launchers in their bases, before the missiles were launched; relying on deterrence aimed at dissuading the opponent to avoid using WMD by threatening with a larger-scale retaliation; and, finally, the political option – coming to some terms with potential opponents in order to achieve agreements to prevent, or at least to limit the use of ballistic missiles or other types of WMD.

As Shapir shows, Israel's anti-WMD doctrine relies on all five options rather than one or two of them. In attempting to achieve a comprehensive and as safe as possible answer to the WMD threat, Israel developed a multi-layered doctrine which combines the nation's traditional deterrence strategy with passive defense means for civilian population (shelters and protection gear), and active defense made of a ballistic missile defense (BMD) system (primarily the Arrow system), a boost-phase intercept (BPI) system, and extensive military preparations for attacking the enemy missile launchers and their infrastructure. At the same time, most Israelis believe that the political avenue is the ultimate answer for addressing this threat. But until such a political arrangement is reached, Israel is expected to rely on its might.

Some of these five 'security belts' were criticized as expensive, ineffective or inefficient, and as compromising Israel's deterrence. Shapir's analysis shows that on a pure technical level there is more than a grain of truth in this critique. Some analyzers are probably right when arguing that the Arrow system will not be able to provide the defense it boasts it will and that the system cannot be efficient in the long-run because its cost is expected to exceed the probable damage from incoming ballistic missiles. The same is true with passive defense where, despite extensive investments, the authorities cannot provide all the population with the required level of defense. In part this is the result of a policy which spends a lot on defending sections of the public who do not live in high-risk areas.

Despite these and other defects, Shapir concludes that for Israeli decision-makers the doctrine of multi-layered defense is a sound policy. This is so because of the impact of other considerations involved. Prime among them are considerations related to the strategic relations with the USA and domestic and bureaucratic politics which dictate further investments in the various means of defense. The best example is the decision to continue investing in the Arrow system. Canceling this project is, as Shapir shows, a political decision that no Israeli Prime Minister can take without fear that he or she would be blamed for neglecting the defense of the population. It would also mean a massive damage to the high-tech defense industries and to Israel's reputation as a leader in this realm. Canceling this program, moreover, might jeopardize American interests and damage the good relations with Israel's strategic ally.

Similar considerations apply to protective measures. Once protective equipment was distributed to the population, there would always be a demand for more – a demand, which would be supported, for domestic political considerations, by the political opposition. Thus, as long as threat perceptions of the public remains the same, Israel will continue investing in these systems.

Looking at the Israeli doctrine for the coming years Shapir predicts that deterrence will remain Israel's most suitable strategy against WMD. This will certainly be the case if another state in the region becomes nuclear – a situation which would call for the development of a second-strike capability and implementation of a 'mutually assured destruction' (MAD) balance of power, as the only means (besides a political solution) to prevent a large-scale destruction in the region. Notwithstanding, according to Shapir, the offensive layers of Israel's doctrine make its deterrence strategy more effective. Deployment of a BPI system – despite its high cost and unproved technical feasibility – can convey a message of resolve. Though such systems cannot give an invincible defense, they can be counted on to control the damage in case of an attack.

As Shapir puts it, his argument borders on a paradox. While the fate of BMD systems should be decided on their technical merits, cost/effectiveness alone cannot justify their development since they are technically and economically inefficient. But other considerations, such as the contribution to the hi-tech industry, domestic politics and the effect on the strategic relations with the USA, overweigh considerations of efficiency alone and justify, for the time being, the development of such systems. Consequently, Shapir predicts that the Arrow system is here to stay, and more would be invested in it.

The same is true with passive protective measures – the sealed rooms and the gas masks, which will continue to be a part of everyone's life in Israel. On the other hand, since BPI systems (or BLPI systems), are still in their infancy, it is too early to predict their future.

The last article in this work, 'Israeli War Objectives into an Era of Negativism' by Avi Kober of Bar-Ilan University, analyzes the impact of recent political, social, and technological changes on future Israeli war objectives.

Analyzing the history of Israel's war objectives, Kober concludes that, at least to some extent, they were different from the way they were generally perceived. Not only have there existed Israeli war objectives in each of the Arab–Israeli wars, but also they have been defined by the political, rather than by the military, echelon and have even proven to be relatively dynamic in nature. The impression that Israel has failed to formulate war objectives can, to a large extent, be attributed to the relatively vague definition of its negative/'defensive' political objectives. The subordination of war to politics has been deeply rooted in Israeli civil-military and political-military relations. It has expressed itself not only in principle, but also in practice.

It is, however, true that the perceived need to achieve battlefield decision, so deeply embedded in Israeli strategic thinking, has created a strong commitment to its achievement at the expense of the commitment to achieve the war objectives. Battlefield decision has often taken on the meaning of an objective, rather than means. Due to Israel's narrow security margins, until the late-1960s, there existed a non-linear, asymmetrical relationship between its political and military war objectives – the former tending to be 'defensive' and the latter 'offensive.'

As Kober shows, from the late 1960s through the mid-1970s, a new military and political reality developed in the Middle East. A strong sense of self-confidence in Israel in the wake of the 1967 War, thanks to the so-called defensible borders, perceived superpower constraints by Israeli decision-makers, unwillingness on the part of large portions of the Israeli society to wage war by choice, and the developing reality of peace between Israel and the Arab world as of the mid-1970s have all played a significant role in the shaping a new attitude, characterized by a gradual shift to negativism: deterrence-by-denial and war objectives of a thwarting nature.

The relationship between Israeli political and military war objectives came to be more linear and symmetrical, due to political and military constraints. Both have gradually become more defensive in nature. Israel also gradually withdrew from its unequivocal commitment to the achievement of battlefield decision, putting more emphasis on victory.

The main reasons for the declining value of battlefield decision, as opposed to the rising value of victory, have been the strengthening of firepower relative to maneuver on the battlefield, the difficulty in translating battlefield decision to political achievements, and the growing political constraints on the freedom of action on the battlefield.

Since the late 1980s, in part as a result of the experience gained in the ongoing war in Lebanon, the volume of the voices calling for the introduction of more defensive elements into the Israeli security conception has amplified considerably. As Kober demonstrates, senior Israeli politicians on both sides of the political spectrum, such as Yitzhak Rabin on the one hand and Ariel Sharon or Moshe Arens on the other, have delivered themselves the view that Israel was neither interested in going to war in order to achieve positive gains from the other side as it cannot impose peace agreements on its enemies and has no need of any more land.

These trends, Kober forecasts, are only going to intensify in the foreseeable future. It will be difficult, in the future, for Israel to achieve positive war objectives for both military and political reasons. At the same time, victory, defined here in terms of the achievement of the war objectives, will become more central in Israeli strategic thinking and practice than the achievement of battlefield decision. These two seemingly contradictory trends are likely to lead Israel towards placing greater emphasis on victory which, at least in the initial stages of a future war, will take on a negative, rather than positive, meaning. Mainstream thinking on war objectives in the future is likely to be more negative than ever.

NOTES

1. Israel Tal, *National Security: A Few Against the Many* (Hebrew, Tel Aviv: Dvir 1996) p.218.
2. Amos Perlmutter, *Military and Politics in Israel* (NY: Praeger 1969) p.33. Moshe Dayan noted in his autobiography: 'The seeds of Wingate's novel ideas and tactics had already been implanted in us by Yitzhak Sadeh, the pioneer of the "emerge-from-the-defense" school.' (Moshe Dayan, *Story of My Life* (London: Sphere Books 1976) p.47). Allon's most notable strategic coin – 'active–defense' can be directly linked to the same school of 'emerge-from-the-defense' (Yigal Allon, 'Active Defense – a Guarantee to Our Existence', in *Communicating Vessels, Essays* (Hebrew, Tel Aviv: Hakibutz Hameuchad 1980) pp.101–11.
3. Michael Bar-Zohar, *Ben-Gurion: A Political Biography* (Hebrew, Tel Aviv: Am Oved 1978) pp.120–7; 645–55.
4. David Ben-Gurion, *Yihud and Yiud (Distinction and Destiny)* (Hebrew, Tel Aviv: Am Oved 1971) pp.162; 263.

2

The Concept of Security:
Should it be Redefined?

BENJAMIN MILLER

In the aftermath of the Cold War there have been many calls for adopting a new conception of security and for extending the traditional concept. Thus, the United Nations Development Program advocated in 1994 a transition 'from nuclear security to human security', or to 'the basic concept of human security', defined as safety from 'such chronic threats as hunger, disease and repression', and 'protection from sudden and hurtful disruptions'. The International Commission on Global Governance recommended in 1995 that 'Global security must be broadened from its traditional focus on the security of states to the security of people and the planet.' Clinton administration officials repeatedly referred to extended or 'human' security, including to 'a new understanding of the meaning and nature of national security and of the role of individuals and nation-states'.[1]

Among scholars Richard Ullman[2] was one of the first to advocate an extension of the security concept to include a wide range of threats from natural disasters and diseases to environmental degradation.[3] Such advocacy became much more prominent with the end of the US-Soviet rivalry because of a decline in military threats while other threats, notably to the environment and thus to human well-being, have seemed to increase in recent decades.[4]

In contrast, the traditionalist approach to security persists in defining the field of security studies exclusively in terms of 'the study of the threat, use, and control of military force'.[5] Similarly, Helga Haftendorn equates security with 'the absence of a military threat or with the protection of the nation from external overthrow or attack'.[6]

Are the new conceptions and extensions necessary or is the traditional concept the right way to address the security issue? Are the re-definitions useful or do they carry heavy costs which will bring more damage than benefit to our understanding of the security concept?

In this study I address the debate on the expansion of the concept of security which emerged especially after the end of the Cold War. I will argue that the 'expanders' of the concept beyond the focus on threats of organized violence and armed conflicts are wrong because of the resultant loss of intellectual coherence of the concept and of the security field, and also because of the remaining importance of the question of war and violence under international anarchy. But on the other hand, the 'minimalists' (who are mostly realists and can also be called traditionalists), while avoiding these two potential problems of the expanders, are also wrong by de-emphasizing both peace as a central component of the security field and nonmilitary causes or means affecting national as well as regional and international security.

My argument is based on a distinction between the phenomenon to be explained (or dependent variable), which defines the scope of a field and the substantive issues it addresses, and the explanations (or independent variables), which include all the relevant competing causal factors affecting the explained phenomenon. The subject matter that the security field addresses is the threat of organized inter-group violence (including inter-state and low-intensity conflict) and the ways to manage and to prevent it. Here a somewhat broadened version of the traditionalist security concept is in order which should treat peace as a central element of the field alongside war; in fact, as the other side of the security coin.

Yet, regarding the competing explanations of war and peace, the door should be kept wide open to a great variety of causal factors, theories and explanations, on the condition that they logically and empirically affect war and peace. Thus, environmental degradation should be part of the security field only to the extent that environmental factors affect the likelihood of armed conflict, namely, war and peace. But environmental threats which are unrelated to these issues should be excluded from the security field despite their great importance for the welfare of the human species. They obviously deserve to be addressed in a very prominent way, both academically and policy-wise, but in other contexts.

I will start with a brief discussion of the relations between international anarchy and national and international security. After presenting the traditional approach to the concept of security in international relations, the essay will introduce the major challenges which have emerged to the traditional conception, and which have grown immensely since the end of the Cold War.

I will then discuss the limitations to these challenges and suggest an approach that will help maintain conceptual coherence through a focus on the substantive issues of war and peace. I will illustrate the discussion with aspects of the national security of Israel. The main implication of the proposed approach for Israel is that its national security debate should continue to focus on threats of organized violence (by states and non-state guerrilla and terrorist organizations) to national core values, but the complex relations between peace and such threats should be a major focus of inquiry in both the academic and policy communities.

ANARCHY AND SECURITY

Due to the many threats that states have traditionally faced to their values and independence in the anarchic international system, the concept of security has long been a key concept in international relations. International anarchy means neither a war of all against all, nor a total disorder and a lack of cooperation, nor an absence of norms and rules in the international system. Rather, it means that in the absence of a global law-enforcement agency and effective global institutions to manage international conflicts, there is no automatic security provider to all states. This stands in contrast to the situation within normal states, which are sovereign, namely, constitute the ultimate and exclusive governing authority within a defined territory. Thus, states have central institutions which are in charge of keeping law and order within that territory and have a monopoly over means of violence there.[7]

Precisely because states are sovereign, there is no higher overall authority in the international system. As a result, the system is one of self-help, namely, the states must take care of their own national security.[8]

To illustrate the difference, within an ideal functioning state every citizen can dial a certain number such as '911' in order to call the police if he or she is attacked, and the police is obligated to help irrespective of the citizen's identity, income or ethnic affiliation. Thus, to the extent that there are specialized agencies which provide security to all, citizens do not have to arm themselves in order to defend their families. By not arming themselves they also do not pose threats to their neighbors and the likelihood of an arms race among citizens is low. In contrast, in the international system there is still no functionally equivalent effective agency which would respond automatically and universally to calls for help by any state that has been attacked, irrespective of its particular attributes (e.g., its resource endowment, geographical location, strategic importance, or alignments).

Anarchy, that is, the absence of a supreme reliable law-enforcement agency, may encourage wars among states in three major ways.

First, it may permit powerful aggressive or revisionist states to initiate wars, as under anarchy there is no powerful central authority to stop them. In this sense, although anarchy serves as a permissive factor,[9] the causes of specific wars lie in the aggressive intentions and attributes of the initiating state.

Second, in light of the weakness of the international institutions for conflict resolution and the absence of effective agency to enforce settlements, a resort to force remains a final arbiter of inter-state conflicts, even when the parties are not necessarily aggressive. As Waltz argues: 'in politics force is said to be the ultima ratio. In international politics force serves not only as the ultima ratio, but indeed as the first and constant one.'[10] Thus, the first road to war results from the absence of an international police force to deter aggressors, while the second stems from the lack of an effective international judicial system.

Third, anarchy may have a more direct effect on the outbreak of wars through the operation of the security dilemma. The security dilemma refers to a vicious interaction whereby measures that a state adopts to increase its own security constitute a threat to others who, as a result, take defensive steps of their own, which in turn reduce the sense of security of the first state.[11] In a self-help system, the quest of states to survive and the resultant security dilemma are sufficient to lead even status quo powers to pursue arms races, construct alliances, and occasionally even stumble into undesired and unintended wars.[12]

This understanding of international anarchy and its implications has given rise to the traditional concept of security.

THE TRADITIONAL CONCEPT OF SECURITY

The dictionary definition refers to security in the most general sense as freedom from threats, fear and dangers.[13] Thus, one is secure under two conditions. First, when no one poses a threat to previously acquired values.[14] Second, if such threats exist, one will be secure if one has the capability to defend oneself against the sources of danger at reasonable costs.[15]

The traditional conception of national security is composed of five major dimensions:[16]

1. *The origin of threats*: threats to national security are posed by other states, notably revisionist states which are dissatisfied with the status quo. Most of

the threats are posed either by proximate neighbors, which have both the opportunity (i.e., the capabilities) and the motivation due to substantive sources of conflict (i.e., territory and borders, ethnicity and nationalism) to pose a threat,[17] or by the great powers which have both global power-projection capabilities and world-wide interests.

2. *The nature of threats*: according to the traditional conception involves mostly offensive military capabilities possessed or acquired by opponents. But since in many cases it is almost impossible to make a clear-cut distinction between offensive and defensive capabilities, any military reinforcement of the opponents (neighbors in the case of regional states, great powers in the case of other great powers) is seen as a potential threat which requires a balancing reaction.[18] In addition to growth in the opponent's offensive capabilities, other moves on its part that are likely to be viewed as threatening are joining an opposing alliance, let alone a mobilization of forces, putting them on high degrees of alert and concentrating them near one's border.

3. *The response*: the only relevant and appropriate response to such military threats according to the traditional approach to security is also viewed as military – the maintenance of a deterrent posture through armament or the movement or alert of forces, or diplomatic-military– the establishment of alliances.

4. *Who is responsible for providing security?* Since there is no reliable supra-national security provider to all states, the state itself is the only body which can take care of its own security in a self-help system.

5. *Core values* for the defense of which the state is ready to go to war in the traditional conception are related to the nation-state – preserving its sovereignty and national independence, maintaining its territorial integrity and the sanctity of its boundaries and not tolerating coercive interference in its domestic affairs.

This traditional conception of security was criticized well before the end of the Cold War.[19] One major point raised by the critics was the appropriateness of exclusively military responses to security threats. Due to the working of the security dilemma[20] an accumulation of military power may jeopardize national security rather than enhance it because the opponent may regard it as a threat. In light of the security dilemma, the state should moderate its military buildup in order not to provoke others and at the same time try to reduce the opponents' incentives to use force by accommodating their key legitimate interests and demands and thus changing their *intentions* and making them more peaceful.

This strategy, if successful, may achieve the first above-mentioned condition of security: the absence of threats, rather than the capability to meet them at reasonable costs. Indeed, according to Wolfers, 'the ideal security policy is one that would lead to a distribution of values so satisfactory to all nations that the intention to attack and with it the problem of security would be minimized'.[21] Yet, such an aspiration can be utopian in many cases while, on the other hand, too much moderation and concessions may convey weakness to potential aggressors and thus tempt them to be more aggressive – an argument often based on 'the Munich analogy'.[22]

This dilemma of resolve or coercion versus accommodation and concessions has not been resolved so far in interantional relations theory.[23] Yet, the critique of the traditional approach for its exclusive focus on military means implies that the concept of security should be expanded to include diverse non-military strategies for reducing security threats such as conflict resolution and peacemaking, economic development, functional cooperation in various issue-areas, regional integration or democratization. Most important, this critique raises the need for studying under what conditions all these alternative strategies will contribute to security, and under what conditions they will be counterproductive.

THE POST-COLD WAR EXPANSION OF THE TRADITIONAL CONCEPT OF SECURITY

While the older critique of the traditional approach has focused on the issue of military versus non-military responses to security threats, the end of the Cold War has brought about a great variety of demands to expand the concept of security on all five of its dimensions. The background to this new approach is the feeling that a fundamental transformation is taking place in the international arena, and that it is moving away from the traditional world of territorial states,[24] military threats and the danger of war[25] and inter-state rivalry.[26] Instead, completely different challenges and needs have moved to the top of the global and human agenda.[27]

According to this approach, such a transformation is not only occurring empirically, but is also desirable on normative grounds in order to advance human values and needs. Thus, the traditional approach loses ground not only empirically, due to the dramatic transformation that has allegedly occurred in many arenas of world politics, but also on a normative basis.

The Origin of Threats: From External to Domestic; and from State to Global

The new approach criticizes the traditional conception of security for focusing on external challenges, most notably, military threats posed by rival states. Critics of the traditional conception argue that rather than originating from rival states, the origin of contemporary security threats is either nonstate (domestic or transnational), or, in a different conception, the state itself poses a threat to its citizens. Military conflicts result primarily from problems of domestic legitimacy, such as revolutionary challenges to the legitimacy of elites and political regimes[28] or from ethno-national challenges to the legitimacy of states and their boundaries[29] on the part of secessionists (such as Tamils, Basques, Chechens) or pan-national unionists (Serbs, pan-Arabists).

   This criticism relies on studies, especially those focusing on Third World security, which have shown that most wars in recent years have been domestic rather than inter-state.[30] Even though there is frequently external intervention in the domestic upheavals, the major form of intervention is not by armies crossing international borders but rather by guerrilla organizations and militias, insurgents, secessionist and terrorist groups and transnational crime organizations, who find shelter in neighboring states and cross borders back and forth at will.

   Moreover, many critics argue that from the point of view of numerous human beings, the major security threat is posed by the states themselves, which violate their human rights, discriminate on ethnic, racial or gender basis, jail dissidents and even carry out ethnic cleansing and mass killings.[31] On the other hand, failed states (such as Haiti, numerous African states, Afghanistan, and at times some former Yugoslav and Soviet republics, including to an extent even Russia) leave their citizens vulnerable to threats by a variety of gangs, militias, terrorists, criminals and polluters. The armaments of many states, especially in the Third World, are not designed to protect their citizens but only to secure the regime and the elite, and are often used against the population. Furthermore, many threats to humankind now originate not from specific aggressive states, but are global and transnational in nature, such as pollution, hunger, diseases, drugs, and the threat of proliferation of missiles and weapons of mass destruction to both rogue states and transnational terrorist groups.

   The Nature of Threats – from Military to Comprehensive: The critics advocate a much more comprehensive approach to security which views it as 'human security' addressing a great variety of menaces.[32] The comprehensive notion of security was introduced by Ullman[33] who viewed it as the efforts to meet human needs and protect the residents of the state against events that threaten to degrade their quality of life, such as natural disasters and environmental problems. Buzan similarly advances a comprehensive multi-dimensional view of security divided into five major dimensions: military, political, social, economic and environmental.[34]

The 'expanders' not only see nonmilitary problems as the source of military conflicts, but also argue that nonmilitary threats are much more relevant to most people than military ones, especially since the end of the Cold War. For many people in the industrialized world the most relevant threats are economic ones (job insecurity and the fear of chronic unemployment, or having to cope with low-paid jobs). There are also identity/cultural threats to established societies and to dominant groups posed by illegal immigration and refugees.[35] The problem of illegal drug trafficking by transnational crime gangs is a major problem for the US and many other industrialized states. The narcotics threat is closely related to high crime rates in urban centers posing mortal threats to many individuals in low-income neighborhoods.[36]

People in the South face grave economic threats to their well-being and even survival due to the shortage of basic necessities such as housing and foodstuff leading occasionally to mass starvation.[37] Spreading diseases like AIDS cross national borders and result in high death rates. Because of the acute threats they pose to the survival of very large segments of the human species, meeting such human needs as food, health and housing is a crucial aspect of national security.[38]

In the last two decades there has also been an enormous increase in the awareness of ecological threats as major issues of security,[39] because of environmental degradation and pollution, the depletion of the ozone layer, global warming due to a greenhouse effect, and resource scarcity coupled with population growth.[40] According to the new approach, all these threats far exceed traditional security threats in importance and relevance.

Changing Responses: from Military to Nonmilitary – A change in the conception of the problem – the diagnosis of the origins and nature of security threats – leads to a change in the prescription. Thus, if the source of the security problem is the nature of the domestic regime, an accumulation of military capabilities by the state would not be a useful solution but rather a part of the problem. Thus, military investments come at the expense of economic growth and spending on human needs such as food and health.[41] In addition, acquired armaments are likely to be used against the population. Instead, a host of nonmilitary/civilian solutions such as democratization, state-building, the development of civil society and economic growth and interdependence are much more helpful.

Since much of the new approach to security focuses on the domestic arena, domestic transformation is seen as essential to address security problems. In this context, many, including US administrations in the 1990s, prescribe democratization. This is partly because democracies tend to behave less violently to other states, especially if they are also democracies, thus creating a zone of democratic peace,[42] but also because liberal democracies adhere more to universal human rights, are much more tolerant to minorities and take care of basic human needs rather than maintaining a narrow exploitative elite in power.

Others are worried about the de-stabilizing effects of rapid democratization, especially in weak multi-ethnic states which lack a liberal tradition.[43] Thus, in order to control ethnic conflicts and rising attempts at secession, some Third World specialists prefer an initial focus on strengthening existing state institutions and maintaining their monopoly on coercive power as prerequisites to democratization at a later stage.[44] Strengthening existing states should also help them deal successfully with domestic and trans-border security threats.

While political liberalism focuses on liberal democracy as the key to peace and security, economic liberalism prescribes free and open markets that lead to rising interdependence through growing trade, the globalization of production and investment, and the free movement of people, goods, money and services. In the view of economic liberalism, this will bring about more peaceful relations among states because interdependence increases the stakes in continued trade rather than in territorial expansion, which becomes increasingly obsolete and economically irrelevant in highly developed economies.[45] Thus, economic prosperity increases the stakes in peace and decreases the motivation for war.

Globalization and interdependence constrain the ability of states to act unilaterally not only in economic matters but also in the security domain. Moreover, according to this perspective, free markets will bring increased prosperity and the fulfillment of human needs and thus will address the new security agenda much better than spending scarce resources on wasteful armies, which protect regimes rather than peoples and bring destruction rather than addressing major human problems and providing for basic necessities of the common people.

Changing Responsibility for Security – from National Security to Common Security: While the traditional conception views the state as the sole agent responsible for its national security in an anarchic self-help international system, new views underline the interdependence of security relations and thus see security as common to humankind.[46] Common security means that there are global threats to all of humanity which cannot be addressed by individual nation-states.[47] This conception leads to a focus on international cooperation rather than competition and to multilateralism rather than unilateralism in managing global security challenges.[48]

This logic suggests a key role for global agencies, most notably the UN or respective regional organizations.[49] Moreover, in acting for common security, international institutions can limit a traditional core value of states – state sovereignty – by intrusive inspection for the purposes of diminishing states' ability to initiate surprise attacks and enforcing arms control, especially nonproliferation of WMD (such as the inspection regime established in Iraq after the 1991 Gulf War which lasted until 1998). The international organizations can also go beyond traditional collective security by exercising the right to carry out 'humanitarian interventions' if universal norms are infringed upon by massive violations of human rights, most notably, ethnic cleansing and genocide.[50]

Apart from pure morality, political instability and ethnic conflict are now treated by other states as posing a threat to their key interests in more ways than before[51] notably by creating mass flows of immigrants and spreading instability. This brings about a growing perception of 'strategic interdependence' among all the actors in the international system.[52] As a result, domestic as well as local conflicts are seen as major international security issues which have to be addressed by joint actions of the international community.

Core Values: from National to Global; from the State to the Individual

In contrast to the traditional concept of national security, which focused on defending the key core values of national independence, sovereignty and territorial integrity, the challengers of the traditional approach argue that a process of value change is under way and that it is desirable that this process continue and accelerate. The new values, which are supposedly replacing the centrality of the nation-state, are located at both the individual and global levels. On the individual level, the new values are associated with human rights and needs. On the global level, the focus is on transnational values common to all humanity: on the one hand, the spreading of democracy and free markets, and on the other, ensuring the well-being of the human race against common threats through the protection of the environment and fighting transborder pollution, diseases, drugs and crime and the proliferation of non-conventional weapons.

At the same time, the former core value of state sovereignty is in decline both as a result of the emerging new values and of rising transborder technological and socio-economic forces, which undermine state power and government control and make states much more penetrable in key areas (the information revolution reaching its climax with the Internet, instant massive financial transactions, mounting volumes of commerce in goods and services, and the spread of ideas across boundaries).

Thus, the 'expanders' present a comprehensive view of common security which poses serious challenges to the traditional-minimalist conception on all its dimensions (see Figure 1).

LIMITATIONS AND DISADVANTAGES OF THE EXPANDED CONCEPTION OF SECURITY

Despite some significant and persuasive arguments, the expanded view of security has at least four important problems, both substantive and methodological.

1. *Empirical Overstatement*

The critics of the traditional approach to security tend to overstate the changes that have taken place in international politics, and underrate the

FIGURE 1

THE TRADITIONAL/MINIMALIST VERSUS THE POST-COLD WAR/COMPREHENSIVE CONCEPTIONS OF SECURITY

	Traditional	Post-Cold War
Origin of threats	Rival states (neighbors/great powers)	Nonstate: domestic/transborder; The state versus its citizens
Nature of threats	Military capabilities	Nonmilitary: economic, domestic political; Transnational/global (Immigration, drugs, diseases, environment, proliferation of WMD, crime, terrorism)
The Responses	Military (arms and alliances)	Nonmilitary: free/global markets, democratization, state-building.
The Responsibility for providing security	The state	International institutions; multilateral interventions
Core Values	National independence, territorial integrity, sovereignty and sanctity of boundaries	Human rights and needs, economic prosperity, environmental protection

persistence of international anarchy and traditional security concerns. This overstatement concerns the decline in state power and sovereignty, the decline in inter-state rivalries and war and the relevance of military power, and the rise of international institutions.

One source of the critics' misconception is the view which identifies the end of the Cold War with the end of the phenomenon of international war in general.[53] Unfortunately this is not the case either logically or empirically. Although the end of the Cold War terminated the East–West division in Europe and brought about a decline in some regional conflicts in the Third World (Southern Africa, Southeast Asia, Central America, and the Arab–Israeli conflict), it did not end all regional disputes (India–Pakistan, China–Taiwan, the two Koreas) and even made possible the eruption of some new violent conflicts in the Balkans, among former Soviet republics, and in some cases in Africa.

More fundamentally, in the absence of effective collective security organizations, there are still threats of armed conflict and organized violence as a last resort in case of sharp disagreements on important values and interests. Indeed, states continue to behave as if physical safety is the core of security.[54] Thus, even the wealthiest and most secure states – the Western allies – have recently adopted self-help security measures: the US is planning a national missile defense to cover its territory against 'rogue' states. The European Union is drawing up its own autonomous military force. Japan is launching its own reconnaissance satellites instead of depending on American intelligence in response to the North Korean, and potentially future Chinese, missile threats.[55]

The threats that these measures are intended to address (at least in the cases of the US and Japan) stem from traditional inter-state conflicts. Yet, the critics are right in arguing that contemporary security threats include also domestic violence which poses threats to neighboring states and may involve them also in hostilities. As a result, ethnic violence, especially when it involves irredenta or secession, should be regarded as an issue of international security because of its likely transboder effects: creating opportunities for external intervention, generating fears of instability and security dilemmas among neighbors and creating problems of refugees, transborder guerrilla groups and terrorism. It is primarily the threat of ethnic violence (as in the former Yugoslavia) that the EU hopes to address by creating its own army.

Israel's national security also continues to deal with threats of armed conflict and of organized violence against the state and its population, even though the type of threats is changing from the conventional threat posed by the armies of proximate states (Egypt and Syria) to the acquisition of weapons of mass destruction by more distant opponents (Iran and Iraq) and to low-intensity conflicts (terrorism and guerrilla warfare) in Israel's more immediate environment. These changes are related to the on-going peace process with Israel's proximate neighbors which is partly related to the change that has taken place in the international environment with the disintegration of the Soviet Union and the rise of US hegemony.

Potential long-term changes in the international system (the formation of a countervailing coalition to US hegemony, the rise and strategic involvement in the region of new great powers like China, India, a united Europe, or a resurgent Russia, and US decline or disengagement from the region) may affect the Middle East security environment and result in a renewal of conventional threats to Israel in addition to the non-conventional ones, for example, through a resurgent alliance between Syria and Russia.

In the economic sphere state power may have weakened considerably vis-à-vis nonstate actors. Yet, although states do not possess a complete monopoly over means of violence – organized crime gangs, secessionist ethnic groups, rebels, terrorists, and revolutionaries also possess a considerable amount of weapons and challenge state monopoly – states still remain by far the strongest military actors and control the most powerful means of violence. Thus, states continue to play the central role in international security.

Although the UN has become much more visible in the post-Cold War era than previously, notably in sponsoring peacekeeping operations around the globe, key elements of the anarchic international system have not changed. The UN, whose role is supposedly to take care of threats to international security, does not have independent capacity and resources (that is, its own troops and independent financial revenues) for carrying out peace-enforcement and peacekeeping operations, and thus fully depends on states' cooperation. This severely limits its ability to act against the interests of its member states, especially the permanent members of the Security Council, namely, the major powers, who also have the right to veto any Council decision. Thus, even though the Council is authorized to use force against an aggressor state, its ability to do so depends on the good will and cooperation of the powers. That means that there is little chance for effective collective action when the major powers disagree, as is the case more often than not.

Even the 1999 humanitarian intervention in Kosovo was not authorized by the relevant international organization – the UN Security Council. Rather, it was a unilateral decision by NATO which was opposed politically and legally by Russia and China and other Third World states. The intervention could be carried out for an extended period with low costs to NATO only due to the balance of power between NATO and the other major powers, notably Russia. Russia is both weak militarily (as was manifested in the failure of the military campaign in Chechnya in 1994–96) and is economically highly dependent on the West. Thus it could not deter the Western intervention and eventually had to cooperate in bringing about a ceasefire and the withdrawal of Serb forces from Kosovo in June 1999. At the same time, a nuclear-armed Russia is too dangerous for NATO to consider a humanitarian intervention against the Russian human rights violations in Chechnia, which accelerated drastically just a short time after the cessation of hostilities in Kosovo.

Although states continue to be central players in the security field, two types of states should be distinguished according to their degree of coherence, in the sense of identification of the populations with the existing states and their territorial identities. Whereas in coherent states the main security threats are external, incoherent states (which are common in Africa, parts of Asia and the Middle East, and former Soviet republics and in the Balkans) face both external and domestic threats.[56] The implication is that in the relatively benign post-Cold War international environment under US hegemony, the incoherent states produce a large share of international security problems, which involve primarily these incoherent states and their neighbors.[57]

2. *Loss of Conceptual Clarity*: For a concept to be helpful, it should tell us what it excludes. If one 'stretches' a concept to include everything, it loses its analytic utility and explanatory value.[58] Thus, too much conceptual comprehensiveness results in confusion rather than clarity. The comprehensive notion of security does not make clear what important human domain is *not* security. But if security is everything, then it ceases to be a useful concept. As a result, expanding the 'security studies' field would destroy its intellectual coherence.[59] A good example are the calls to expand or re-define the concept of national security to include environmental degradation.[60] As Deudney argues:

> national-security-from-violence and environmental habitability have little in common. Given these differences, the rising fashion of linking them risks creating a conceptual muddle rather than a paradigm or world view shift – a de-definition rather than a re-definition of security. If we begin to speak about all the forces and events that threaten life, property and well-being (on a large scale) as threats to our national security, we shall soon drain the term of any meaning. All large-scale evils will become threats to national security... [61]

3. *Inability to Evaluate Trade-Offs*: A related implication of concept 'streching' is that the concept then becomes useless for making distinctions that are necessary both for theory building and prioritizing for policy purposes. If everything is security, how can we appreciate such tradeoffs as guns versus butter? Security should be seen as one important value among many. In a world in which there is a scarcity of resources, there is a need to allocate them among competing objectives, and thus one cannot avoid the question how much security is enough.[62] The pursuit of security always comes at the expense of other values that could have been pursued with the resources allocated to security. Thus, a specification of the concept of security makes possible an informed debate on how much to allocate to this domain relative to competing objectives.[63]

4. *Confusion between Empirical Analysis and Normative Advocacy*: There is a difference between arguing on an empirical basis that elites in the Third World care largely about regime security and that they often threaten the well-being of their citizens,[64] and the liberal-idealist advocacy of putting individual human rights at the center of the international security concept on normative grounds. Rather than simply asserting the importance of humanitarian interventions, analysts still have to investigate whether and under what conditions such interventions are becoming a major pattern and norm of behavior by major states and multilateral coalitions in the post-Cold War era.[65]

The linkage of security and environmental issues is also made for polemical-political purposes[66] in order to show that these new issues are as important as traditional security ones and thus deserve as much money, manpower and prestige. Yet, that legitimate desire does not make the environment issue a security issue on substantive grounds and on the merit of the case. Moreover, a manipulation of the concept of security for polemical-political purposes, for example through the so called 'securitization' of potentially any conceivable issue[67] can be dangerous because politicians can abuse it for their narrow goals as they have done numerous times in the past. A coherent and consistent conception of security can make it possible to challenge such abuses and to show that political manipulations do not enhance national security.

Defining the Security Domain: The Need to Distinguish Between the Phenomenon to be Explained and its Competing Explanations

Based on the above critique of the expanders, my response to the debate between the expanders and the minimalists is a distinction between the subject matter of the security field and its explanations. In order to make clear what is included – and what should be excluded – from the security field, we need to differentiate between the phenomenon to be explained (i.e., the dependent variable) and its competing explanations (i.e., the independent variables). The dependent variable defines the scope of the field and its subject area, namely, organized inter-group violence. Yet, contrary to the traditionalist/realist conception, the field should also include efforts to eliminate threats of such violence by peacemaking.

Thus, the dependent variable of security studies deals with the outbreak, threat, management and prevention of organized violence among groups (notably, but not exclusively, states), that is, issues of war and peace.[68] More specifically, security issues include threats of resort to force, the eruption of wars, the management of wars and the means of violence, conflict prevention, and peacemaking.

The independent variables refer to any cause or source which affects the likelihood of wars and organized violence. They concern the explanations, causes and sources of variations in the onset of wars, the management of the use of force or the decline in the likelihood of violence, that is, the emergence of peace. These sources can be realist or military, such as questions of power (power maximization as a policy objective,[69] or the distribution of capabilities or polarity as a causal variable)[70] and security, (notably the security dilemma and the offense/defense balance).[71]

But the independent variables can also be nonmilitary: nationalism,[72] nation-to-state imbalance,[73] ethnic conflict, territory, culture (such as a clash of civilizations), ideology, domestic regimes (that may produce diversionary wars) and elite security.

Environmental factors should be included to the extent that they affect the likelihood of violence (like water or energy shortages or other environmental scarcities)[74] but not if they are ecological developments that threaten all of humanity but do not affect (for better of worse) the question of war and peace.

Similarly, a humanitarian distribution of food to hungry people in Africa is not a security issue unless it becomes entangled with organized violence and an armed conflict. Thus, even if the initial intention of President George Bush in late 1992 was a purely humanitarian intervention in Somalia, it became a major security issue once US troops began to get involved in continuous hostilities with Somali gangs.

Sources of peace should also be included in the security field: both realist causes (deterrence, balance of power, hegemony, alliances) and liberal explanations (the democratic peace theory, economic interdependence, international institutions), and also the effects on peace of the following factors and policies: state-building,[75] the growth of civil society, the promotion of human rights and humanitarian interventions, peacekeeping, peace-enforcement and peacemaking.

Thus, since peace is a core component of security, the Arab-Israeli peace process should be evaluated as a road to national and regional security and not only as a moral issue or a question of economic prosperity and social welfare. The connection between peace and security should be manifested in the reduction of threats of organized violence against Israel as the peace process progresses. For example, while the return of the Golan Heights to Syria may weaken Israel's security by reducing its defensive capabilities and by making a potential Syrian attack easier, the withdrawal from the Golan may also enhance security to the extent that it reduces the Syrian threat to Israel due to the combined effect of the mitigation of the Syrian motive to attack Israel and the stabilizing role of the proposed security arrangements between Israel and Syria. Thus, the relations between the peace process and Israeli security have to be carefully investigated for both theoretical and policy purposes.

DEVELOPING THE SECURITY CONCEPT

The distinction between independent and dependent variables allows to develop the security concept further. As noted above, a state is secure under the following two conditions:

1. If threats of violence against the core values of the state are present, the state can be secure to the extent that it possesses the capabilities to defend its key values at reasonable costs.

2. In the absence of threats of violence against the state's major values.

The focus on one of these two conditions allows to distinguish between two major schools of thought in International Relations and their competing approaches to security issues: realists on the one hand, and liberals on the other.[76]

In contrast to liberals, realists are skeptical that it can ever be possible for states not to face threats for an extended period so long as the international system is anarchic, that is, while states have to provide for their own security. Thus, for realists, since some level of external threats of violence is given over time, the key to state security lies in possessing the capabilities essential to cope with such threats. Realists argue that it is difficult to plan one's security according to the estimation of the intentions of other states, both because it is very difficult to know others' intentions and because intentions can change easily. Therefore, the assessment of intentions should be based on a cautious worst-case analysis. In contrast, there can be a greater confidence in identifying capabilities, and it is also less easy to change capabilities overnight. Indeed, for realists the key to security is the balance of capabilities and this balance shapes intentions: an imbalance of power creates a temptation for aggression; thus, a powerful state which faces weak opponents will abuse and coerce them. At the same time, equal or superior capabilities induce moderation in a rival because of the expected high costs of aggression. In other words, capabilities produce intentions.

Realists differ in whether equal or superior capabilities (relative to rivals) are more desirable in providing security. While offensive realists[77] argue that superior capabilities that are able to overwhelm the rival are generally a better guarantee of security, defensive realists[78] advance a more nuanced conception based on the security dilemma. According to this view, superior capabilities are perceived by rivals as threatening and encourage them to develop their capabilities further, thus becoming a source of insecurity. As a result, defensive realists recommend a more equal balance of capabilities that is sufficient for deterring rivals.

An Israeli security issue that may illustrate the different approaches of defensive and offensive realists is the question of Israel's alliance with Turkey. Thus, offensive realists advocate the enhancement of Israel's alliance with Turkey, and in the future potentially also with Iran, in order to maximize Israel's capabilities vis-à-vis its proximate Arab opponents (primarily Syria). Offensive realists are skeptical regarding the possibility for a lasting peace among neighbors with a long history of violent disputes. Thus, their policy recommendation is to ally with the neighbors of the neighbors since the 'enemy of my enemy is my friend', and the neighbors themselves are usually enemies.

Defensive realists, on the other hand, regard the alliance with Turkey as dangerous and destabilizing because it increases the Arabs' security dilemma due to their fear of the Israeli-Turkish axis which might be directed against them in future. Thus, defensive realists recommend lowering the profile of this bilateral relationship, especially in the strategic field, in order not to frighten the Arabs and not to compel them to respond by countervailing moves such as armament and the formation of a balancing coalition. The result of such moves could be the escalation of Middle East tensions and a growing danger of regional war.

An important component of security according to the logic of defensive realism are security arrangements and confidence-building measures which enhance transparency and reduce the ability to conduct a surprise attack, and thus mitigate mutual fears about being attacked. These fears are a major source of insecurity, especially if offensive capabilities have an advantage over defensive ones (and consequently there are advantages to preempting the opponent by attacking first), or if it is impossible to distinguish between offensive and defensive capabilities.[79] The purpose of arms control, in this view, is to decrease the offensive capabilities of states while enhancing defensive ones in nonprovocative ways, and thus to reduce the security dilemma and provide mutual reassurance by making as sharp a distinction as possible between offensive and defensive capabilities.

Thus, according to this perspective, such security arrangements as demilitarized zones, areas of force reduction and early warning stations in the Golan Heights will enhance Israel's security vis-à-vis Syria. This is because they will minimize the gravest security danger to Israel – that of a strategic surprise by an attacking Arab army or a coalition of such armies, and as a result Israel's security fears and its consequent aggressive behavior will decline as well. Moreover, the current proximity of the Israeli forces in the Golan Heights to the Syrian capital aggravates the Syrian security dilemma as well, and thus creates a permanent danger of an inadvertent escalation, even if currently the Syrian army is relatively weak. Thus, removing the Israeli forces away from Damascus while at the same time removing the Syrian army from the Israeli border and creating a large buffer between them will reduce drastically the danger of an uncontrolled escalation.

Defensive realists view the nuclear revolution as the ultimate guarantor of security that provided states with the ability to deter each other by having a capacity to inflict unacceptable damage on their opponents. Yet, mutual security is enhanced only in a situation of Mutual Assured Destruction (MAD) in which all parties have a secure second-strike capability, that is, can absorb a massive surprise attack and still inflict unacceptable damage on the opponent, and thus none of the parties has incentives to preempt and to strike first.[80]

Thus, the security implications of Israel's monopoly over nuclear weapons in the Middle East are complex. On the one hand, they compensate for Israel's basic inferiority in manpower and strategic depth and therefore provide the most effective deterrence against a potential attack by a grand Arab coalition and against the use of non-conventional weapons by Israel's opponents. Israel's nuclear deterrence might even have encouraged the Arabs to desert the war option by making victory infeasible and to join the peace process. At the same time, in the view of defensive realists the Israeli nuclear option might increase Arab insecurity and thus the security dilemma in the region, provide incentives for Arab states and Iran to acquire their own weapons of mass destruction, and result in an arms race and potentially less stable multipolar deterrence than was the case in the bipolar superpower relations.[81]

A related conceptual and policy question concerns the potential trade-offs between deterrence and defense: will the deployment of a defensive anti-missile system like the Arrow reinforce Israel's security or jeopardize it? Defensive realists, who tend to be deterrence purists, argue that a defensive build-up, which makes the state less vulnerable to attack and therefore more capable of preemption, increases the opponents' security dilemma, thus leading to an arms race and growing mutual insecurity. Thus, Israel should avoid the Arrow and related defensive systems. In contrast, defense advocates assert that deterrence can fail and then the absence of defense can lead to a catastrophe. Accordingly, they recommend the deployment of missile defense. The logic of offensive realism suggests that the combined effect of Israel's deterrence, anti-missile defense and strong conventional capabilities will ensure Israel's military superiority, which, in their eyes, is the best guarantee of its national security.

In contrast to realists, who take the existence of some level of security threats for granted and therefore concentrate on the capabilities to meet them, liberals focus on state intentions as the major factor affecting international security. Liberals strongly believe in the independent effects of intentions, namely, that given benign intentions, states will not develop offensive capabilities, and thus according to this view intentions generate capabilities.[82]

According to the most prevalent liberal theory of peace – the democratic/liberal peace theory– liberal democracies do not fight each other.[83] As a result, liberals believe in the feasibility of enhancing peace and security through democratization. This theory has inspired the Clinton administration's policy of 'enlargement', designed to enlarge the world's 'community of market democracies'.[84] President Clinton asserted that this strategy serves US interests because 'democracies rarely wage war on one another'.[85]

Other major liberal peacemaking mechanisms include creating economic interdependence among states so that they will prefer 'to trade than to invade'. In the liberal view, trading states are not interested in building invading armies.[86] Liberals also believe that enhancing the power of international institutions or regimes will increase the incentives of states to cooperate with each other and will thus produce more benign state intentions.[87]

In the area of security, the most relevant institution is a collective security system under which all peace-loving states are committed to come automatically to the defense of any state attacked by an aggressor irrespective of previous particularistic ties, affiliations and alliances with the victim state. It is a system based on the universal norm of 'one for all and all for one'.[88]

Despite their general focus on state intentions, liberals agree that capabilities are a key to security to the extent that their various prescriptions for violence-avoidance are not carried out, that is, among states at least some of whom are non-democracies, are not economically interdependent or are not members of international institutions. Thus, democracies facing illiberal states, who are likely to produce offensive capabilities, will have to respond by building comparable capabilities.

The competing approaches of realism and liberalism to the security field may clarify a major policy issue facing Israel, namely the question of separation versus integration with the Palestinians, especially in the economic domain, following the expected establishment of a Palestinian state as a part of the final-status peace agreement.

Liberals prescribe economic integration in order to increase mutual prosperity and thus mutual satisfaction and lower the incentives for a resort to violence. Economic interdependence in the liberal view is a recipe for avoiding violence also because the costs of the use of force rise while its benefits decline. Economic interdependence is thus helpful for creating common interests and for enhancing cooperation in other fields including the diplomatic and security ones.

In contrast, realists see integration and the resultant growing contact and entanglement among neighbors as providing many areas of disagreement among them, and therefore as a recipe for continuing conflict with an ever-present danger of escalation to violence. Integration which involves open borders might also enhance the capabilities to inflict damage (for example, by terrorist incursions). Thus, while liberals prescribe Israeli-Palestinian economic integration, realists recommend a separation between the two ex-enemies based on the idea that 'high fences make good neighbors'– the lesser the contact, the lower the potential for violent conflict.

Figure 2 presents a typology of four ideal type situations of different levels of national security based on the combination of the two factors discussed above – the presence of threats to the state and its capabilities of defending against them. The presence of threats is itself a function of the capabilities and aggressive intentions of rival states.[89]

FIGURE 2
LEVELS OF SECURITY ACCORDING TO THE PRESENCE OF THREATS AND THE
CAPACITY TO DEFEND AGAINST THEM

Presence of External Security Threats

	High	Low
High	1 Balance of Power Deterrence (Cold war or cold peace)	4 Hegemony Emergence of non-traditional security agenda
Low	2 Small states faced by major rivals: insecurity and vulnerability	3 'Warm peace' among democracies Isolated small states

Capacity to Defend Against Threats

In situation no. 1 the state faces external security threats, derived from
the hostile intentions and offensive capabilities of rival states, but it is able
to defend against them at affordable costs. The outcome is a balance of
power and deterrence, often manifested in an arms race and the formation
of countervailing coalitions. Even if a hot war does not erupt, the outcome
is a cold war.[90] This is a situation of 'negative peace'[91] – a mere absence of
hot war in which hostilities may break out in the near future. It is
characterized by recurrent military crises and a considerable likelihood of
escalation to war in either a premeditated or an inadvertent manner.[92] The
parties succeed at best in managing the crises, that is, in avoiding an
escalation to war while protecting their vital interests,[93] but they do not
attempt seriously to resolve the fundamental issues in dispute between
them. Such a conception of a cold war fits nicely with Hobbes' idea of the
'state of war' as not necessarily consisting of 'actual fighting but in the
known disposition thereto during all the time there is no assurance to the
contrary. All other time is peace.'[94] An example is the acute periods of the
Cold War in superpower relations.

To the extent that the balance of power or deterrence situation stabilizes
and the parties also manage to reduce some of the sources of tension and

conflict among them, their relations may progress to cold peace, in which the threat of war is substantially mitigated, although it does not disappear for the long run. An example is détente periods in US-Soviet relations during the Cold War.

In world no. 2 the state is in the worst possible situation: it faces external security threats, caused by the offensive intentions and capabilities of adversaries, but is unable to defend against them because it has neither the resources nor the external allies for mounting an effective defense at affordable costs. That makes the state very vulnerable and insecure and as a result likely to submit to external pressures and even lose its independence. The Munich agreement of 1938 is the classical example after Czechoslovakia was deserted by its Western allies and thus became vulnerable to Nazi Germany.[95] Such is the context for the establishment of great power spheres of influence like the Soviet sphere in Eastern Europe after 1945 and the American one in the Caribbean Basin during the entire twentieth century.[96]

In the third situation the state faces no external threats despite its weakness relative to potential rivals. This situation may describe a warm and stable peace among the members of a 'pluralistic security community'.[97] Warm peace is a situation in which war is virtually unthinkable. Even if some issues are in dispute among the states, the use of force is completely out of the question and is ruled out as an option for addressing them. This high level of peace is characterized by extensive transnational relations and a high degree of regional interdependence. This type of relations is most likely in a region populated by liberal democracies,[98] as in the North Atlantic region after 1945. The security community that has emerged in this region allows even small states such as the Scandinavian and Benelux states to feel secure despite their weakness relative to major powers such as the US or Germany. The combination of low capabilities and low threats may also characterize small states who are sufficiently removed from potential strong opponents so as not to be threatened – for example, the small island nations of Oceania.

World 4 is a hegemonic world. The hegemon does not face any serious great power rival and thus it does not have to cope with major strategic threats to its core values. At the same time, the hegemon possesses a large repertoire of military means at its disposal. As a result, threats which are considered minor during an era of great power rivalry move to the top of the security agenda in a hegemonic period. This upgrading includes issues such as transnational organized crime, terrorism and the proliferation of weapons of mass destruction. Moreover, since a great variety of military means is available to the hegemon and it has no use against the targets for which it was designed originally, there is a growing pressure to employ them against the new non-traditional threats. This situation has emerged with the end of Cold War, the disappearance of the Soviet threat and the great military superiority of the US. To a large extent, this is the background for the much greater prominence of the demands to expand the security concept.[99]

Israel is situated in world 1 (high threats/high defensive capabilities). Since its independence in 1948 it faced a situation of cold war with all its neighbors, punctuated by hot wars. Since the last major Arab–Israeli war in 1973 the relations have stabilized and evolved toward cold peace. Major landmarks in this process have been the formal conclusion of peace with Egypt (in the Camp David accords of 1978) and with Jordan (in 1994) as well as the Oslo interim agreements with the Palestinians (1993–95). Yet, neither of these relations has so far progressed beyond cold peace. Moreover, the achievement of cold peace and its endurance depend heavily on the US role as the honest broker and the referee, and also the provider of financial aid and security guarantees in the regional peace process.[100]

Stabilizing the regional Arab-Israeli peace depends first of all on resolving all the outstanding issues which are still in dispute: boundaries, security arrangements, Palestinian statehood, Palestinian refugees, Jewish settlements and the status of Jerusalem. 'Warming' the regional Arab-Israeli peace in the longer run so that neither Israel nor its opponents will feel threatened depends on major domestic changes within the regional states, especially a growing identification of the key national groups in the region with the states in which they reside and the related decline of revisionist/irredentist and secessionist claims, followed by liberalization and democratization in the Arab world and Iran.[101] However, since these processes may take some time while democratization can be de-stabilizing, at least for the short term,[102] the hegemonic role of the US as a stabilizing force will be essential during the period of transition to democracy. Only if this domestic transformation is successfully completed, will a liberal-democratic Middle East be able to pursue economic integration, the building of regional institutions and the promotion of human and minority rights, producing a full-blown warm peace.

CONCLUSIONS

This contribution contrasted two major competing approaches to the concept of security following the end of the Cold War. The traditional/realist school argues that since the anarchic nature of international politics did not fundamentally change with the end of the Cold War, there is no need for a significant redefinition or expansion of the security concept. In contrast, those who call for the expansion of the concept assert that the world has changed dramatically in the recent decade and thus it is imperative to redefine the security concept to reflect both empirical and normative changes.

I suggest that both approaches face major problems. The realists overlook the nonmilitary factors affecting security and especially the connection between peace and security. The expanders, for their part, ignore the remaining importance of armed conflict under international anarchy, and also undermine the coherence of the concept of security by stretching it almost endlessly.

My argument is that the security field should continue to deal with questions of violence and armed conflicts at different levels of intensity, but with a growing focus on both nonmilitary causes of war and on the factors and conditions which affect peacemaking as a major security strategy.

The Israeli case, discussed at length in the other essays in this collection, is a major example of a state which still faces a great number of threats of violence, ranging from low-intensity conflict through conventional inter-state war to nonconventional weapons, and thus it has to provide for its own national defense against these threats. At the same time, Israel is engaged in a potentially very promising, although risky, regional peace process which can considerably enhance its national security as well as the security of its neighbors and of the region as a whole.

NOTES

The author is grateful for the generous financial assistance of Israel Science Foundation (founded by the Israel Academy of Sciences and Humanities). The author would like to acknowledge the useful advice and comments on earlier drafts of Avi Kober, Uri Bar-Joseph, Ram Erez, Uri Reznick, Adi Miller, and especially Korina Kagan.

1. These citations are in Emma Rothschild, 'What is Security?', *Daedalus* 124/3 (Summer 1995) pp.53–98 at pp.55–6.
2. Richard Ullman, 'Redefining Security', *International Security* 8/1 (Summer 1983).
3. Cited in Barry Buzan, *People, States & Fear: An Agenda for international security studies in the post-Cold War era* (Chapel Hill: UNC 1991) p.17; and in Marc Levy, 'Is the Environment a National Security Issue?', *International Security* 20/2 (Fall 1995) pp.35–62 at p.40. See also the citations of new definitions of the concept security in Daniel Deudney, 'The Case against Linking Environmental Degradation and National Security', *Millennium* 19/3 (Winter 1990) pp.461–76 at p.462; and the review in Levy (note 3) and the long list of references in Peter Katzenstein (ed.) *The Culture of National Security: Norms and Identity in World Politics* (NY: Columbia UP 1996) p.9, n.20.
4. Levy (note 3) p.61; Keith Krause and Michael C. Williams, 'Broadening the Agenda of Security Studies: Politics and Methods', *Mershon International Studies Review* 40/2 (Oct. 1996) pp.229–54 at p.233.
5. See Stephen Walt, 'The Renaissance of Security Studies', *International Studies Quarterly* 35/2 (1991) pp.211–40 at p.212. See also Deudney (note 3); and Levy (note 3). For a

critique of Walt, see Edward A. Kolodziej, 'Renaissance in Security Studies? Caveat lector!' *International Studies Quarterly* 36/4 (Dec. 1992).

6. Helga Haftendorn, 'The Security Puzzle: Theory Building and Discipline Building in International Security', *International Studies Quarterly* 35/1 (1991) pp.3–17 cited in Levy (note 3) p.39. See also the useful discussion by Patrick M. Morgan 'Regional Security Complexes and Regional Orders', in David A. Lake and Patrick M. Morgan (eds.) *Regional Orders: Building Security in a New World* (University Park: Pennsylvania State UP 1997) pp.22–4.

7. This refers to normally functioning states. In the case of 'weak', and especially 'failed' or collapsed states, the state is unable to maintain a monopoly over means of violence and provide security to its citizens. The result is instability and insecurity similar, in principle, to the anarchic international system. In practice, the level of violence in these failed states might far exceed the situation in a particular international system, especially if various stabilizing mechanisms operate effectively in that system, as discussed below. On weak and collapsed or failed states, see Buzan (note 3) pp.99–103; Mohammed Ayoob, *The Third World Security Predicament* (Boulder, CO: Lynne Rienner 1995); William Zartman, *Collapsed States: The Disintegration and Restoration of Legitimate Authority* (Boulder, CO: Lynne Rienner 1995); K.J. Holsti, *War, The State, and the State of War* (Cambridge: CUP 1996); and Barry Buzan and Ole Waever and Jaap de Wilde, *Security: A New Famework for Analysis* (Boulder, CO: Lynne Rienner 1998).

8. On international anarchy, see Robert Jervis, 'Cooperation Under the Security Dilemma', *World Politics* 30/2 (Jan. 1978) pp.167–214; Kenneth Waltz, *Theory of International Politics* (Reading, MA: Addison-Wesley 1979); Hedley Bull, *The Anarchical Society: A Study of Order in World Politics* (NY: Columbia UP 1977); and Buzan (note 3) p.21.

   For critiques of the realist conception of anarchy, see Helen Milner, 'The assumption of anarchy in international relations theory: a critique', *Review of International Studies* 17 (1991) pp.67–85; and Alexander Wendt, 'Anarchy is what states make of it', *International Organization* 46 (Spring 1992). See also Robert Stuart, 'Anarchy in international relations theory: the neorealist-neoliberal debate', ibid. 48/2 (Spring 1994) pp.313–44; James Fearon, 'Rationalist explanations for war', ibid. 49/3 (Summer 1995) pp.379–414; and Jonathan Mercer, 'Anarchy and identity', ibid. 49/2 (Spring 1995) pp.229–52.

9. Kenneth Waltz, *Man, the State and War* (NY: Columbia UP 1959).

10. Waltz (note 8) pp.112–13.

11. On the security dilemma, see John H. Herz, 'Idealist Internationalism and the Security Dilemma', *World Politics* 2/2 (Jan. 1950) pp.157–80; Robert Jervis, *Perception and Misperception in International Politics* (Princeton UP 1976); Jervis (note 8); Robert Jervis, 'Security Regimes', in Stephen Krasner (ed.) *International Regimes* (Ithaca, NY: Cornell UP 1983); idem, 'From Balance of Power to Concert: A Study of International Security Cooperation', *World Politics* 38/1 (Oct. 1985) pp.58–79; Alexander George, 'Factors Influencing Security Cooperation', in idem, Philip Farley, and Alexander Dallin (eds.) *U.S.-Soviet Security Cooperation: Achievements, Failures, Lessons* (NY: OUP 1988) Ch.27, pp.656–8; and Benjamin Miller, 'Polarity, Nuclear Weapons, and Major War', *Security Studies* 4/3 (Summer 1994).

12. Waltz (note 9) p.234; Jervis (note 11, 1976) pp.67, 94; Jervis (note 8); Robert Jervis, 'Systems Theories and Diplomatic History', in Lauren G. Paul (ed.) *Diplomacy: New Approaches in History, Theory, and Policy* (NY: Free Press 1979) pp.213, 217; Jervis (note 11, 1985); Alexander George, 'Ideology and International Relations: A Conceptual Analysis', Draft of a paper prepared for a conference on *Ideology and its Influence on International Politics* (Hebrew Univ. of Jerusalem 1984) pp.4–5; Benjamin Miller, *When Opponents Cooperate: Great Power Conflict and Collaboration in World Politics* (Ann Arbor: U. of Michigan Press 1995) Ch.3; and Charles Glaser, 'The Security Dilemma Revisited', *World Politics* 50/1 (Oct. 1997).

13. See Ayoob (note 7) pp.4–12.

14. Arnold Wolfers, *Discord and Collaboration* (Baltimore: Johns Hopkins UP 1962) p.150. See also the refinement in David A. Baldwin 'The Concept of Security', *Review of International Studies* 23 (1997) pp.5–26 at p.13: 'a low probability of damage to acquired values'.

15. See Lippmann's definition, cited in Ayoob (note 7) p.5.
16. These five components constitute an ideal type and there are differences on some of these points among different traditionalist scholars.
17. A considerable amount of research shows that most wars take place between neighboring states. For a review of these findings, see John A. Vasquez, 'Why do Neighbors Fight? Proximity, Interaction or Territoriality', *Journal of Peace Research* 32/3 (1995) pp.277–93 at pp.278–9.
18. The balance of power school (overviewed in Benjamin Miller, 'Competing Realist Approaches to Great Power Crisis Behavior', *Security Studies* 5/2, Spring l996) underlines the prevalence under anarchy of states preserving their security by balancing either the power of the strong states in the international system (Waltz, note 8) or particularly the power of threatening states (Stephen Walt, *The Origins of Alliances* (Ithaca, NY: Cornell UP 1987)). The balancing is done either internally (armament) or externally (alliances).
19. The best critique is Wolfers' classic essay: Arnold Wolfers, 'National Security as an Ambiguous Symbol', in Wolfers (note 14) pp.147–65.
20. Wolfers (note 19) p.159.
21. Ibid. p.161.
22. On the Munich analogy, see Yuen Foong Khong, *Analogies at War* (Princeton UP 1992) Ch.7.
23. The classic discussion is Jervis (note 11, l976) Ch.3. For an overview, see Martin Patchen, *Resolving Disputes between Nations: Coercion or Conciliation?* (Durham, NC: Duke UP 1988). The dilemma is implied as a major point of contention in the current debate between defensive and offensive realists. For overviews of the debate, see Sean M. Lynn-Jones and Steven Miller, 'Preface', in Michael E. Brown, Sean M. Lynn-Jones and Steven E. Miller (eds.) *The Perils of Anarchy: Contemporary Realism and International Security* (Cambridge: MIT Press 1995); Benjamin Frankel, 'Restating the Realist Case: An Introduction', *Security Studies* 5/3 (Spring 1996); Sean M. Lynn-Jones, 'Realism and America's Rise: A Review Essay', *International Security* 23 (Fall 1998) pp.157–82; and Jeffrey W. Taliaferro, 'Security-Seeking Under Anarchy: Defensive Realism Reconsidered', Paper presented at the Annual Meeting of the *International Studies Association* (Washington DC, Feb. l999).
24. Richard Rosecrance, *The Rise of the Trading State: Commerce and Conquest in the Modern World* (NY: Basic Books 1986).
25. John Mueller, *Retreat from Doomsday: The Obsolescence of Major War* (NY: Basic Books 1989) pp.3–62, 217–65.
26. Francis Fukuyama, 'The End of History?' *The National Interest* 16 (Summer l989) pp.3–18.
27. Krause and Williams (note 4).
28. Ayoob (note 7); J. Ann Tickner, 'Re-visioning Security', in Ken Booth and Steve Smith (eds.) *International Relations Theory Today* (Oxford: OUP 1995) pp.175–97 at p.179.
29. James Mayall, *Nationalism and International Society* (Cambridge: CUP 1990); Buzan, Waever and de Wilde (note 7) p.53.
30. Ayoob (note 7); K.J. Holsti, 'International Theory and War in the Third World', in Brian Job (ed.) *The Insecurity Dilemma: National Security of Third World States* (Boulder, CO: Lynne Rienner 1992) pp.37–62 at pp.37–8; Holsti (note 7); Morgan (note 6) p.23 and the citations he cites.
31. Nicole Ball, *Security and Economy in the Third World* (Princeton UP 1988); Buzan (note 3) pp.43–50.
32. See Rothschild (note 1).
33. Ullman (note 2); see also Tickner (note 28) p.182.
34. See Buzan (note 3); for further development of this conception of security, see Buzan, Waever and de Wilde (note 7).
35. E. Azar and C. Moon (eds.) *National Security in the Third World* (London: Edward Elgar 1988); Myron Weiner, 'Security, Stability, and International Migration', *International Security* 17/3 (Winter 1992–93); Samuel Huntington, *The Clash of Civilizations and the Remaking of World Order* (NY: Simon & Schuster 1996).
36. Buzan (note 3).
37. Ball (note 31).
38. C. Thomas, *In Search of Security: The Third World in International Relations* (Boulder, CO:

Lynne Rienner 1987); Seyom Brown, 'World Interests and the Changing Dimensions of Security', in Michael T. Klare and Yogesh Chandrani, *World Security: Challenges for New Security* (NY: St Martin's Press 1998); additional citations in Tickner (note 28) pp.180–2.
39. Buzan, Waever and de Wilde (note 7) pp.71–94.
40. Jessica Mathews, 'Redefining Security', *Foreign Affairs* 68/2 (Spring 1989) pp.162–77. For additional citations see Duedney (note 3) p.462 and Levy (note 3).
41. Ball (note 31).
42. Kant cited in Michael Doyle, 'Liberalism and World Politics', *American Political Science Review* 80 (Dec. 1986) pp.1151–69; Zeev Maoz and Bruce Russett, 'Structural and Normative causes of Peace between Democracies', *American Political Science Review* 87/3 (Sept. 1993) pp.624–38.
43. Edward Mansfield and Jack Snyder 'Democratization and War', *Foreign Affairs* 74/3 (May/June 1995) pp.79–97.
44. Ayoob (note 7); Holsti (note 7).
45. Rosecrance (note 24); Carl Kaysen, 'Is War Obsolete? A Review Essay', *International Security* 14/4 (Spring 1990); reprinted in Sean M. Lynn-Jones (ed.) *The Cold War and After: Prospects for Peace* (Cambridge, MA: MIT Press 1990) pp.81–103.
46. See Buzan (note 3) p.13, n.35.
47. Tickner (note 28) pp.181–2.
48. On cooperative security and multilateralism, see Janne E. Nolan (ed.) *Global Engagement: Cooperation and Security in the 21st Century* (Washington DC: Brookings 1994); John G. Ruggie (ed.) *Multilateralism Matters: The Theory and Praxis of an Institutional Form* (NY: Columbia UP 1993); and the citations in Barry R. Posen and Andrew L. Ross 'Competing Visions for U.S. Grand Strategy', *International Security* 21/3 (Winter 1996–97) pp.5–53 at pp.23–32.
49. For the institutionalist perspective in International Relations, see R. Keohane, *After Hegemony: Cooperation and Discord in the World Political Economy* (Princeton UP 1984); R. Keohane, *International Institutions and State Power: Essays in International Relations Theory* (Boulder, CO: Westview Press 1989).
50. On state sovereignty and international intervention, see Gene M. Lyons and Michael Mastanduno (eds.) *Beyond Westphalia? State Sovereignty and International Intervention* (Baltimore: Johns Hopkins UP 1995).
51. Patrick M. Morgan, 'Regional Security Complexes and Regional Orders', in David A. Lake and Patrick M. Morgan (eds.) *Regional Orders: Building Security in a New World* (University Park: Pennsylvania State UP 1997) pp.20–44 at p.24.
52. Posen and Ross (note 48) pp.25–9.
53. Fukuyama (note 26); Mueller (note 25); Samuel Huntington, 'No Exit: The Errors of Endism', *The National Interest* 17 (Fall 1989).
54. Morgan (note 51) pp.22–3.
55. See Jim Hoagland, 'In New Millennium, the World is Confronted by a Tableau of Contradictions', *International Herald Tribune* (3 Jan. 2000) pp.1, 5.
56. Buzan (note 3); Ayoob (note 7); Stephen Van Evera, 'Hypotheses on Nationalism and War', *International Security* 18 (Spring 1994) pp.5–39; Holsti (note 7).
57. See Benjamin Miller, 'Explaining Regional War-Propensity: The Middle East in a Comparative Perspective', Paper presented at the meeting of the International Studies Association, Washington DC (1999a); idem, 'Between War and Peace: Systemic Effects on the Transition of the Middle East and the Balkans from the Cold War to the Post-Cold War Era', Paper presented at the annual meeting of the American Political Science Association, Atlanta (1999b); idem, 'The Sources of Regional War and Peace: Integrating the Effects of Nationalism, Liberalism and the International System', Paper presented at the annual meeting of the American Political Science Association, Atlanta (1999c); idem, 'Hot War, Cold Peace: International-Regional Synthesis', in Zeev Maoz and Azar Gat (eds.) *War in a Changing World* (Ann Arbor: U.of Michigan Press, forthcoming).
58. On concept 'stretching', see Giovanni Sartori, 'Concept Misinformation in Comparative Politics', *American Political Science Review* 64 (Dec. 1970) pp.1033–53.
59. Walt (note 5) pp.212–3; Katzenstein (note 3) p.11.

60. Brown and Matthews cited in Deudney (note 3) p.462, n.2.
61. Deudney (note 3) p.465.
62. Baldwin (note 14) p.15; Morgan (note 51) p.22.
63. Baldwin (note 14) pp.16–7, 21–2.
64. Ayoob (note 7); Holsti (note 7).
65. See Benjamin Miller, 'The Logic of US Military Interventions in the post-Cold War Era', *Contemporary Security Policy* 19/3 (Dec. 1998) pp.72–109.
66. Deudney (note 3) p.465; Levy (note 3) p.44.
67. Buzan, Waever and de Wilde (note 7).
68. The proposed definition of inter-group violence excludes personal or gang violence and occasional strikes or riots from the security domain, but includes armed inter-state and low-intensity conflict 'ranging from guerrilla and partisan war, insurgence and counter-insurgency, unconventional war and protracted conflict'. Edwin G. Corr and Stephen Sloan (eds.) *Low-Intensity Conflict* (Boulder, CO: Westview 1992) p.7.
69. Hans J. Morgenthau, *Politics Among Nations* 5th ed. (NY: Knopf 1978); Fareed Zakaria, *From Wealth to Power: The Unusual Origins of America's World Role* (Princeton UP 1998).
70. Waltz (note 8).
71. Jervis (note 8); Glaser (note 12).
72. Stephen Van Evera, 'Hypotheses on Nationalism and War', *International Security* 18 (Spring 1994) pp.5–39.
73. Benjamin Miller, 'The Sources of Regional War and Peace: Integrating the Effects of Nationalism, Liberalism and the International System', Paper presented at the annual meeting of the American Political Science Association, Atlanta (1999c).
74. Thomas F. Homer-Dixon, 'Environmental Scarcities and Violent Conflict: Evidence from Cases', *International Security* 19/1 (Summer 1994); Peter H. Gleick, 'Water and Conflict: Fresh Water Resources and International Security', *International Security* 18 (1993) pp.79–112; and Miriam R. Lowi, 'Bridging the Divide: Transboundary Resource Disputes and the Case of West Bank Water', *International Security* 18 (1993) pp.113–38.
75. Ayoob (note 7); Holsti (note 7).
76. On various aspects of the realist-liberal debate, see Joseph Nye, 'Neorealism and Neoliberalism', *World Politics* 40/2 (Jan. 1988) pp.235–51; David A. Baldwin (ed.) *Neorealism and Neoliberralism: The Contemporary Debate* (NY: Columbia UP 1993); Charles W. Kegley Jr (ed.) *Controversies in International Relations Theory: Realism and the Neoliberal Challenge* (NY: St Martin's Press 1995); and Michael Doyle, *Ways of War and Peace* (NY: Norton 1997).
77. See John Mearsheimer, 'Back to the Future: Instability in Europe after the Cold War', *International Security* 15/1 (Summer 1990) pp.5–56; John Mearsheimer, 'The False Promise of International Institutions', in Michael Brown, Sean M. Lynn-Jones and Steven E. Miller (eds.) *The Perils of Anarchy: Contemporary Realism and International Security* (Cambridge: MIT Press 1995); Zakaria (note 69).
78. Jervis (note 8); Barry R. Posen, *The Sources of Military Doctrine* (Ithaca, NY: Cornell UP 1984); Walt (note 18); Charles Glaser, 'Realists as Optimists: Cooperation as Self-Help', *International Security* 19/3 (Winter 1994–95); Glaser (note 12); Stephen Van Evera, *The Causes of War* (Ithaca, NY: Cornell UP 1999).
79. On the offense-defense balance as a key factor in affecting the likelihood of war in defensive realism, see Jervis (note 8); Glaser (note 12); Stephen Van Evera, 'Offense, Defense, and the Causes of War', *International Security* 22/4 (Spring 1998); Sean M. Lynn-Jones, 'Offense-defense theory and its critics', *Security Studies* 4/3 (Summer 1995); Charles Glaser and Chaim Kaufmann, 'What is the Offense-Defense Balance and How can We Measure It?' *International Security* 22/4 (Spring 1998).
80. Jervis (note 8); Kenneth Waltz, 'Nuclear Myths and Political Realities', *American Political Science Review* 84/3 (Sept. 1990) pp.731–46; Glaser (note 78).
81. On the distinctive effects of polarity and nuclear weapons on the occurrence of war, see Miller (note 11).
82. At the same time, classical and neoclassical realists (unlike neorealists) also accept the independent role of intentions through a key distinction between revisionist and status quo

states. See Morgenthau (note 69); Henry Kissinger, *A World Restored* (NY: The Universal Library 1964); Randall Schweller, *Deadly Imbalances: Tripolarity and Hitler's Strategy of World Conquest* (NY: Columbia UP 1997).

83. Doyle (note 42); Maoz and Russett (note 42). For critiques, see Michael Brown, Sean Lynn-Jones, and Steven E. Miller (eds.) *Debating the Democratic Peace* (Cambridge: MIT Press 1996).

84. Lake cited in Joanne Gowa, 'Democratic States and International Disputes', *International Organization* 49/3 (Summer 1995) pp.511–22, at p.511, n.1.

85. Clinton cited in Gowa (note 84) p.511, n.2.

86. Rosecrance (note 24); Robert Keohane and Joseph Nye, *Power and Interpendence: World Politics in Transition* (Boston: Little Brown, 1977). For a critique, see Norrin M. Ripsman and Jean Marc F. Blanchard'Commercial liberalism under fire: evidence from 1914 and 1936', *Security Studies* 6/2 (Winter 1996–97) pp.5–50.

87. Keohane (note 49); Stephen Krasner (ed.), *International Regimes* (Ithaca, NY: Cornell UP 1983). For critiques, see John Mearsheimer, 'The False Promise of International Institutions', in Michael Brown, Sean Lynn-Johns and Steven E. Miller (eds.) *The Perils of Anarchy: Contemporary Realism and International Security* (Cambridge: MIT Press 1995), and Korina Kagan, 'The Myth of the European Concert: The Realist-Institutionalist Debate and Great Power Behavior in the Eastern Question, 1821–41', *Security Studies* (Winter 1997–98) pp.1–57.

88. Inis Claude, *Power and International Relations* (NY: Random House 1962); Charles Kupchan and Clifford Kupchan, 'Concerts, Collective Security, and the Future of Europe', *International Security* 16/1 (Summer 1991) pp.114–61. For a critique, see Richard Betts, 'Systems for Peace or Causes of War? Collective Security, Arms Control, and the New Europe', *International Security* 17/1 (Summer 1992) pp.5–43.

89. On the balance of threats, see Walt (note 18).

90. The typology of hot war, cold war, cold peace and warm peace is based on Miller, 'The Sources of Regional War and Peace' (note 57, 1999c).

91. On this concept, see Arie M. Kacowicz, 'Explaining Zones of Peace: Democracies as Satisfied Powers?' *Journal of Peace Research* 32/3 (Aug. 1995) pp.265–76 at p.268.

92. On inadvertent wars, see Alexander George, *Avoiding War: Problems of Crisis Management* (Boulder, CO: Westview Press 1991); and Miller (note 11).

93. On crisis management, see Alexander George, David Hall and William Simons, *The Limits of Coercive Diplomacy* (Boston: Little, Brown 1971) pp.8–11 and others cited in Miller (note 12) p.93, n.34.

94. Cited in Stephen R. Rock, *Why Peace Breaks Out: Great Power Rapprochement in Historical Perspective* (Chapel Hill: UNC Press 1989) p.2.

95. David Vital, *The Survival of Small States: Studies in Small Power/Great Power Conflict* (London: Oxford UP 1971).

96. Korina Kagan, 'Authoritarian and Democratic Great Powers and their Proximate Spheres of Influence', PhD Dissertation (Hebrew Univ. of Jerusalem 2000).

97. Karl Deutsch *et al.*, *Political Community and the North Atlantic Area: International Organization in the Light of Historical Experience* (Princeton UP 1957); Emanuel Adler and Michael Barnett, *Pluralistic security communities* (Cambridge: CUP 1998).

98. Benjamin Miller, 'When regions become peaceful: Explaining transitions from war to peace', Paper presented at the annual meeting of the International Studies Association, Los Angeles (March 2000).

99. While there are other on-going processes conducive to the re-examination of the security concept, such as democratization and a growing concern about human rights, the technological/information revolution and the globalization of markets, all these processes are facilitated by US hegemony, thus highlighting how crucial this variable is with regard to the concept of security.

100. See Miller (note 57, 1999b).

101. On the strategies and conditions for achieving warm regional peace, see Miller (note 57, 1999c), Miller (note 98).

102. Mansfield and Snyder (note 43).

3

New Threats, New Identities and New Ways of War: The Sources of Change in National Security Doctrine

EMILY O. GOLDMAN

National security, whether understood as a process or as an objective, refers to the protection of core national interests from external threats. There tends to be little dispute over the nature of core national interests: physical security, economic prosperity, and preservation of national values, institutions, and political autonomy. Core national security interests are highly stable, though a growth in power may affect how expansively a nation defines those interests. For example, imperial expansion broadens the definition of physical security by increasing the extent to which others can impinge upon a nation's territorial interests.

National security doctrines, on the other hand, do change. National security doctrine refers to the instrumental goals through which national security interests are protected (such as containment or democratic enlargement) and to the means (military, diplomatic, economic, domestic mobilization themes, etc.) employed to serve those instrumental goals. Incremental adaptations in national security doctrines should be expected as part of the normal course of events. Change usually occurs slowly as the result of repeated interactions. Rarer are instances when states dramatically alter their national security doctrines, adopt a new national security identity, or reorder the salience of existing identities.[1]

Dramatic shifts in national security doctrine are often the product of major discontinuities such as regime change, defeat in war, disappearance of a major threat, or revolutionary technological breakthroughs that alter the foundations of national power. France's expansive tendencies in Europe followed in the wake of the major regime change brought on by the French

Revolution. With the emergence of democratic regimes in post-World War II Germany and Japan, economic competition replaced military aggression as the core national security paradigm and in each, a traditional military-political identity was usurped by an economic-political identity.[2]

Despite significant differences in power, position, and domestic imperatives, Americans and Israelis face a remarkably similar set of national security challenges today. Both have experienced dramatic discontinuities in their strategic, technological, and domestic environments. Both are struggling to anticipate and prepare for a future security environment that is highly uncertain. In each, there is widespread consensus that the foundations of long-standing national security doctrines have changed yet little agreement on what precepts and policies should replace them.

Discontinuities that render traditional planning assumptions and standard procedures obsolete are often associated with crises in national security identity. Such a crisis faces Americans and Israelis today and derives from the confluence of two major discontinuities, one strategic and the other technological. For each, the nature of the external imperative has been transformed, in one case because a long-standing adversary (the Soviet Union) collapsed, in the other case due to a tumultuous process of reconciliation with long-standing enemies (the Arab-Israeli peace process).

The defining external problems that shaped the national security doctrines of each for decades no longer operate as lodestones. At the same time, an information technology revolution in military affairs is underway. Advanced technologies such as micro-electronics, computers and software, and precision guided munitions promise to shift the technological basis of military power, affect the means of military competition and advantage, and alter the essence of world power.

Leaders in both the United States and Israel face a great deal of uncertainty as they attempt to anticipate the future security environment, establish a new psychological basis for security policy, develop principles to guide diplomatic, economic, and force structure choices, and resolve dilemmas involving the resort to military force.[3] The challenge of managing extreme uncertainty in the national security environment is not new. It has confronted leaders and publics in earlier eras when long-standing power rivalries changed course, or when the security dilemma was dampened, or when dramatic military transformations altered the foundations of national power.

This essay provides a framework and set of core concepts for understanding the nature of the post-Cold War, information age environment and the security challenges it presents. The concept of 'national security uncertainty' is developed and its key drivers are examined. The implications of this uncertainty for national security doctrine are explored in light of relevant theoretical literatures. The study concludes by providing a set of indicators for analyzing responses to national security uncertainty along four key dimensions: diplomatic posture, resource allocation priorities, military mission priorities, and domestic mobilization.

NATIONAL SECURITY UNCERTAINTY

The nature of the current national security environment can be captured best by a typology of uncertainties. At any one time, uncertainty need not exist in all its forms. At other times, several types of uncertainty may exist simultaneously. In some cases, different dimensions of uncertainty are logically inter-related.

At its core, national security uncertainty implies ambiguity about the nature of threats.[4] National security strategy, as distinct from foreign policy more generally, 'is conducted against an opponent. ... [It] implies an opponent, a conflict, a competition, a situation where an individual or a group is trying to achieve a goal against somebody else.'[5] Threat uncertainty can result from the disappearance of the prior, traditional, or familiar threat pattern. Historically, this has occurred in the wake of major wars, but this is not always the case. A rival may simply implode, as did the Soviet Union, or peaceful reconciliation might transform an enemy into a partner. Instead of a clearly defined enemy, a state may face several potential threats over the horizon; novel, diffuse, or unfamiliar threats in the near-term; or no threats even at a distance. Ambiguity surrounds the identity and goals of potential adversaries, the timeframe within which threats are likely to arise, and the contingencies that might be imposed on the state by others.

With uncertainty over the identity of future adversaries comes ambiguity in the capabilities against which one must prepare, particularly whether one should prepare for an adversary with similar or dissimilar capabilities. Peer competitors possess roughly similar capabilities across the board and tend to compete symmetrically. Symmetry can facilitate planning. A competitor that cannot match a set of superior capabilities, however, may opt to inhibit or constrain the superior power by developing niche capabilities, or asymmetric responses, designed to offset superior strengths. A niche competitor need not acquire the capabilities to defeat the superior power, but simply to deny it the ability to exploit its superior capability.

Asymmetries always exist among rivals and inferior powers invariably seek ways to avoid the strengths, exploit the vulnerabilities, and degrade the capabilities of their superiors. Today, the relative cheapness and accessibility of new technologies, many of which do not require the infrastructure needed for developing and operating more complicated systems, mean that more technologically advanced societies do not command the advantage they once might have.

Nor is warfare in the information age a sphere exclusive to states, as it was during the industrial age. The key question is the extent to which adversaries emulate or offset the capabilities of each other, in the latter case producing highly asymmetrical military arsenals that create significant problems for military planners. Uncertainty about the capabilities of future adversaries is exacerbated when the criteria for assessing the relative distribution of power are unclear, which tends to be the case during periods of rapid military transformation.

With the disappearance of the traditional threat, long-standing alliance patterns can become strained. Alliance uncertainty captures the ambiguity that surrounds the desirable and/or possible composition of future alliances and coalitions. Beyond the question of whom to ally with, uncertainty about whether one's security is served best by permanent alliances, ad hoc coalitions, or some form of collective security also arises. Collective security historically has enjoyed a resurgence when threats are ambiguous, precisely because it is not oriented toward deterring a specific adversary but rather, as Richard Betts notes, establishes obligations in terms of hypothetical enemies.[6] Ad hoc coalitions permit greater unilateralism in preparing for unforeseen contingencies, though this can be a more costly strategy.

Absent a clear and present danger, uncertainty arises over how best to manage the economy to preserve the ability to prevail in future conflicts. The natural political inclination is to divert resources from defense toward social and domestic policy initiatives. Without an identifiable threat, it can be difficult to sell defense spending to wary politicians and publics. Leaders must always balance the military risks facing the state, for which defense assets provide insurance, against the opportunity costs of devoting scarce economic resources to unproductive armaments. The difficulty of balancing those concerns rises when threats subside because financial risks are perceived to overwhelm military risks, and strategic insurance appears to depend disproportionately upon economic strength at the expense of military strength.

Uncertainty in the security environment also alters the time horizon with which states calculate their interests, forcing a choice between minimizing short-term disadvantages and maximizing long-run advantages. Current spending to retain the capability and readiness to meet unanticipated threats in the short run competes with long-term economic growth and recapitalization to meet unanticipated threats in the more distant future. If potential near-term threats appear serious or if current expenditure will have little harm for the long run, it makes sense to maintain capable forces in being. However, if potential long-run threats loom greater than short-run threats, or if the costs of failing to invest are high, it becomes more sensible to trim forces in being and channel resources into long-term economic growth and research and development for the future. Today, the alternatives of near-term readiness, modernization (e.g., producing new generations of old weapons systems and introducing some new technological advances), and aggressive transformation (e.g., shifting resources into research and development to leverage the information technology revolution) compete for scarce defense resources.

While resource uncertainty concerns the allocation of scarce national assets in order to respond to unforeseen contingencies, both now and in the future, inter-operability uncertainty involves managing and coordinating assets with potential alliance and coalition partners to enhance preparedness. Several issues arise: which partners to rely on; how extensively to rely on them; how to divide responsibility for various roles and missions across multiple states; and how to ensure interface standards across multiple partners. The problem of interface standards always exists, but is aggravated under conditions of military transformation when states are likely to be adapting their military forces to new technologies at different rates.

Uncertainty about the goals, interests, and capabilities of others collectively enhances the difficulty of deciding what type of conflict to prepare for (e.g., major war, small-scale interventions, peacekeeping operations, etc.). Operational uncertainty grows with the diversification of threat types, particularly during periods of acute financial stringency when competing threats often translate into conflicting military mission priorities. Today, operational uncertainty has taken on added dimensions given the range of threat types pervasive in the global security arena such as small weak states armed with weapons of mass destruction, as well as unconventional challenges from narco-terrorists, religious fundamentalist movements, and ethnic and nationalist violence. Moreover, to the extent that militaries worldwide are being called upon today to do things 'other than combat', such as peacekeeping, requirements for these new missions must be balanced against the primary defense need for a first class fighting force.

Particularly when there is downward pressure on defense budgets, political and military decision-makers must constantly review the balance between warfighting and non-warfighting capabilities built into the force structure.

The most dramatic manifestation of operational uncertainty involves coming to terms with shifts in war-making paradigms, typified by what have come to be called 'revolutions in military affairs' or RMAs. While change in the ways of making war is an evolutionary process, periodically a state will succeed in exploiting an integrated set of military inventions and demonstrating clear superiority over older techniques of battle. Such events mark a fundamental discontinuity with the status quo. RMAs have important implications for managing resource uncertainty because they imply that resources be channeled into research and development and away from current programs and forces in being. RMAs also have important implications for threat uncertainty by either reducing or increasing the effective geographic distance among potential adversaries, and thereby expanding or shrinking the number of actors that can pose a serious threat. Even when political threats are absent or negligible, changes in technology can enhance the vulnerability of interests. Air power, nuclear weapons, and the information age have all reduced the space between states, slowly negating the benefits traditionally derived from insularity.

Turning our gaze within the state, when no external imperative exists to function as a strategic anchor, uncertainty over the meaning of international developments for the nation's security and well-being rise and national security doctrines are more vigorously contested. Accordingly, societal support, what Sir Michael Howard calls the 'forgotten dimension of strategy', is more uncertain.[7] Prospect theory sheds light on the reasons why it becomes increasingly difficult to mobilize public support in the pursuit of security when threats are absent and uncertainty about the nation's role in the world is high. A core tenet of prospect theory is that people react differently to the prospect of losses than they do to the chance of reaping gains. People are risk-acceptant for losses and risk-averse for gains. They will pay a higher price and accept greater risks when faced with the prospect of losses, which threats imply, but are reluctant to take advantage of opportunities to reap gains at some risk.[8] Thus, it is easier to mobilize support for negative goals, defined in terms of minimizing losses in the face of threats, than for positive goals, defined in terms of reaping gains. It is always easier to imagine what *will* be lost than what *might* be gained.

The loss of a threat thus requires creation of a new theme, or national purpose orientation, around which domestic society can be mobilized. A national purpose expresses a people's orientation toward the international environment and understanding of their society's role in the world. The key issue is the purpose for engagement abroad, not the means (e.g., unilateralism, selective engagement, cooperative security), though the choice of means is not unrelated to ends. With the demise of the Soviet threat, America's balance of power purpose, manifest in the strategy of containment, no longer provided a compelling rationale for engaging in the world. President George Bush (the senior) tried to sell the US public on a hegemonic purpose with his 'New World Order'. Security was couched in terms of regulating the international system to stave off chaos, instability, and disorder. One implication was that peripheral conflicts and commitments took on greater importance.

Challenging Bush's vision were 'neo-isolationists,' who promoted either a regional/local purpose, giving greatest prominence to geographic contiguity and security concerns at the nation's borders, or a domestic purpose, defining security in terms of the economic and social health of the nation. President Clinton tried unsuccessfully to promote 'Democratic Enlargement' as the purpose for US involvement in the world, an orientation that defines security in ideational terms, as promoting one's own national values and dislodging antithetical ones.[9] In sum, as major discontinuities upset domestic coalitions, they create new expectations among the populace and compel leaders to make new promises that may impose new constraints.

We can capture an ontology of national security uncertainties in a matrix (Figure 1), orchestrated around six key categories: one's own goals, the goals of potential allies, and those of potential adversaries; one's own capabilities, the capabilities of potential allies, and those of potential adversaries. Operational uncertainty may best be understood as the resultant of all the categories.

FIGURE 1

UNCERTAINTY MATRIX

	Goals	**Capabilities**
Self	National purpose uncertainty; Mobilization uncertainty	Resource uncertainty
Allies	Alliance uncertainty	Inter-operability uncertainty ⇨ Operational
Adversaries	Threat uncertainty	Peer-niche uncertainty uncertainty
Conflict	Operational uncertainty	

DRIVERS OF NATIONAL SECURITY UNCERTAINTY

National security uncertainty is a complex phenomenon with multiple dimensions. Its causes are also complex and multiple. Uncertainty can stem from shifts in the strategic, domestic, technological, or ideational environments. Shifts in one area, moreover, can produce cascading effects in other areas. For example, technological changes, such as those heralded by developments in information technologies, alter the strategic environment by empowering new actors that can pose novel threats and challenges. Separately and in combination, these changes can alter the material and social foundations of national security doctrine, thereby affecting how leaders and publics conceive of their national security requirements, envisage the nation's identity and role in the world, and select the means to promote security.

The most obvious shifts in a state's strategic environment that would cause a dramatic reorientation of national security doctrine are changes in the nature of the threat and changes in the distribution of power, whether due to defeat in war or relative decline. By the mid-twentieth century, for example, the British had transformed themselves from a global imperial power to a European power. The British realized by 1943 that the United States would thereafter be the senior partner in any trans-Atlantic relationship. Britain's economic decline was undeniable after two world wars, and was further magnified during the Suez crisis of 1956, after which the British accepted that they could no longer influence or intervene unilaterally without the support of the United States. These developments led to a tightening of Britain's relationship with America. Moreover, while Great Britain still had an Army of 700,000 and was spending 10 per cent of its GDP on defense in 1956, by 1968 it had withdrawn from East of Suez, surrendered its military presence outside Europe, and divested the Empire. Today the British spend only 2 per cent of GDP on defense. Britain's strategic reorientation had cascading effects. After World War II, the Australians shifted their reliance from Britain to the United States, recognizing the change in power status between the two. More recently, the economic decline of the Soviet Union, and its eventual collapse, resulted in the divestment of its empire in similar fashion, with cascading effects for national security globally, and for North America and Europe in particular.

Failed policies can also produce shifts in national security doctrine, as was the case with many of the 'neutrals' after World War II. The Dutch learned that security depended on alliance relations, that neutrality was no guarantee they would be kept out of a European war. Likewise, the

Norwegians, traditionally neutral, opted to join the NATO alliance in a dramatic departure from their long-standing national security precepts.

Shifts in the domestic environment include demographic, social, cultural and political changes that alter the nation's social and political milieu, affecting the ability of national leaders to mobilize resources and popular will in pursuit of security. These shifts create incentives to alter national security doctrine in response to domestic imperatives.[10] Edward Rhodes, for example, attributes the dramatic change in US national security doctrine in the late nineteenth century, characterized by the rise of navalism, to a crisis in national identity. Rapid industrialization and urbanization, immigration, the closing of the national frontier, and the post-Reconstruction integration of the South into the body politic produced a cultural change of such magnitude that it required a new definition of '"Americanness" and new institutions to bridge class, ethnic, religious, economic and regional fissures' in society. Rhodes contends that creating a new socially unifying image of America 'necessitated a new account of America's relationship to the world, the role of the state, and the nature of war'.[11] Change in national security doctrine in this case stemmed from the need to forge a new myth of national identity to consolidate society in the face of social and cultural dislocation.

This need resonates in contemporary Russia where social and economic experiments with democracy and capitalism have produced dramatic social, cultural and economic dislocation in society. Russia's identity as the vanguard of communism, bulwark against the capitalist West, and strategic superpower in a global bipolar competition has disintegrated yet no new identity has yet been forged.

Similarly, Israel today faces a crisis of national unity and the melting pot of Zionism no longer provides a cohesive force. Ethnic cleavages were once suppressed in the interest of fending off the external threat. But now the Zionist project of nation building is complete and the external threat has waned. At the same time, demographic changes have reshaped the political landscape, most vividly seen in the large wave of immigrants from the former Soviet Union, more than 700,000 since 1989, amounting to more than 15 per cent of the population. The new Russian immigrants are eager to preserve their own identity separate from the host society, producing a politics of 'hyphenated identities'.[12] They resist social integration, like Israel's large Arab population, further fractionalizing a polity torn between secular and religious goals both at home and abroad.

Rapid and discontinuous technological change can also stimulate changes in national security doctrine by creating new threats and opportunities.[13] Historically, changes in military technology (both hardware and software) have altered the international security environment in significant ways and resulted in changes in the instrumental goals and means of national security.[14] Today, there is much debate and fervor about a revolution in military affairs that is underway. Improvements in core technologies like precision guided munitions, surveillance satellites, and remote sensing, combined with advances in the speed, memory capacity, and networking capabilities of computers, form the foundation for a fundamentally new way of war. Equally important advances may also be occurring in genetic engineering and the biological sciences that could revolutionize biological warfare.

The spread of these new technologies promises to empower traditionally weak states and non-state actors in unprecedented ways. Cruise missiles, mines, diesel-electric submarines, and unmanned aerial vehicles, can be coupled with improved civilian C^3I capabilities and navigational enhancements like GPS-based guidance systems and commercial space assets.[15] With Differential Global Positioning System products that increase the accuracy of long-range stand-off munitions, older, less capable platforms can deliver high-tech smart firepower. Weaker states can then project power more accurately, offset superior conventional forces, and deter intervention by technologically superior states.[16]

The spread of information warfare capabilities poses new types of threats for the most technologically advanced military forces and societies who rely on network connectivity to function. Connectivity dramatically enhances the lethality of military forces, but also increases their vulnerability to 'cyberwar' attacks: electronic warfare (jamming, deception, disinformation, destruction) that deny and disrupt information flows; to software viruses that destroy, degrade, exploit, or compromise information systems; and to destruction of sensing equipment.[17] High-technology forces that rely on information dominance are also more vulnerable to preemptive information warfare attacks, like covert sabotage of computer systems.[18] Moreover, an adversary need not be information-dependent to disrupt the information lifeline of high-tech forces.[19]

Information-dependent societies are similarly vulnerable to the infiltration of their computer networks, databases, and the media for the purposes of deception, subversion, and promotion of dissident and opposition movements.[20] Attacks on societal connectivity target the linkages upon which modern societies rely to function: communication, financial transaction, transportation, and energy resource networks. While the loss of connectivity is not likely to be prohibitive for a low-tech society, it can be for high-tech networked societies.

Nor is it necessary to be a high-tech networked society to have access to information warfare capabilities.[21] Terrorist organizations and organized crime groups can launch attacks on societal connectivity because information technologies are available in ways that cutting-edge capabilities were not in the past.

Shifts in the ideational environment, such as changes in global and domestic norms that define what is appropriate and legitimate behavior (e.g., what defines a modern military; constraints on the use of weapons of mass destruction), can also alter the foundations of national security doctrines. The spread of democracy has brought with it a decline in the legitimacy of lethality. To the extent that war is a social institution, democratic publics with a distaste for casualties are less likely to support conflicts unless leaders can promise they will be relatively 'sanitary'. As Chris Demchak argues, 'The ability of late twentieth century military technologies to mow down multi-thousands instantaneously has become illegitimate. In the process, the definition of innocents has also expanded to include non-military members of the enemy's society. ... Together these make anything other than extremely accurate killing – i.e., only the guilty – increasingly unacceptable in western societies. Unless it can be sanitary with few deaths, war as a legitimate institution is undermined.'[22] Stand-off precision weapons aided by information superiority may be the only way casualty-sensitive publics will allow their political leaders to use military force abroad.

The intolerance of democratic publics for casualties, indiscriminate destruction, and attacks on innocents, coupled with technological changes such as the speed and accuracy of information warfare (IW), have raised the attractiveness of IW-enabled militaries worldwide. We may be witnessing a process of global convergence of military form and practice as militaries attempt to emulate the American model of what a 'modern' military force should be.[23] The implications go well beyond force structure decisions to the way wars is conducted, the norms for waging it, and the very definitions of war and peace. According to Demchak, the US-defined notion of a modern military 'explicitly includes the concept of operating legitimately without the declaration of hostilities'.[24] Though disruption can be as great a security threat as destruction, computer software operators disrupting other computers are not seen as dangerous, let alone as acts of war. The information age holds out the prospect that the Clausewitzian industrial-era model of destructive war will be supplanted by an information-era model of war centered on disruption and paralysis with vast implications for the meaning of victory and defeat, the peace-war boundary, the conduct of war, and thus the pursuit of national security worldwide.

IMPLICATIONS OF NATIONAL SECURITY UNCERTAINTY

There is little well-developed theory on national security adjustment under uncertainty. Few scholars have systematically examined security strategy during lengthy periods of uncertainty and flux when no major adversaries or conflicts loom on the horizon. The work that does exist tends to focus on periods immediately preceding conflict when significant threats coalesce.[25] Nevertheless, several bodies of theory shed some light on how we should expect national security doctrines to adjust in the face of the uncertainties created by the dramatic discontinuities enumerated above.

Structural Approaches

Traditional security studies analysis, informed by the lens of neo-realist theory, focuses on material power, changes in its distribution, and external threats. Shifts in national security doctrine stem from shifts in the international distribution of power that alter the state's relative position. Neo-realists acknowledge that the theory has greatest explanatory power in a highly constrained international environment, when external threats to national interests and values are high. When objective external threats are absent or sufficiently distant in the future, the international environment provides far fewer constraints and imperatives.

Neo-realism is indeterminate on responses to threat uncertainty. It directs attention to the role that power and capabilities play in constructing national security, but it is difficult to deduce security posture from capabilities (e.g., population, territory, resource endowment, economic capacity, military strength, political stability and competence). For example, following World War I, the United States was practically invulnerable, faced no military threats, and enjoyed overwhelming economic superiority.[26] Yet US security policy did not exploit the potential of the nation's relative power.

Neo-realism does make clear predictions about how national security doctrine should adapt to dramatic technological change. Neo-realist analysis is premised on the constant pressure of competition in the international system and the unrelenting demands states face to adjust in order to compete effectively. Periods of military transformation produce a technologically induced insecurity, wholly independent of the level of amity and enmity among states. In response to such dramatic technological change, neo-realists argue states face powerful incentives to adopt new military methods, particularly the most successful forms and practices demonstrated, in order to remain competitive. States are like firms that 'emulate successful innovations of others out of fear of the disadvantages that arise from being less competitively organized and equipped. These disadvantages are particularly dangerous where military capabilities are concerned, and so improvements in military organizations and technology are quickly imitated.'[27]

In Kenneth Waltz's words, 'The possibility that conflict will be conducted by force leads to competition in the arts and instruments of force. ... Contending states imitate the military innovations contrived by the country of greatest capability and ingenuity. And so the weapons of the major contenders, even their military strategies, begin to look much the same all over the world.'[28] Threats are assessed in terms of capabilities, as opposed to intentions, for 'fear that an international competitor might use a fleeting technological advantage to spring a surprise attack'.[29]

Offense-defense theory comprises a series of related observations about how the balance of military capabilities affects national security. It is a structural theory that focuses on the constraints and opportunities presented by external environmental factors, particularly geography and available technology.[30] The offense-defense balance is defined as the amount of resources that a state must invest in offense to offset an adversary's investment in defense.[31] Most analysts agree that the system's more powerful states benefit when the offense has the advantage and that the system's weaker states benefit when the defense is ascendant.[32] When the offense is dominant (e.g., it is easier to take territory than to defend it) the system's stronger states and their strategies of political expansion should benefit because larger and wealthier states can more effectively exploit offensive technologies. When the defense is dominant (e.g., it is more difficult to take territory than to defend it) the system's weaker members and their strategies of local defense should benefit. All else being equal, when the defense is dominant, the security dilemma will be dampened. 'Defense dominance allows states to react more slowly and with greater restraint to the capabilities-enhancing efforts and gains of their neighbors.'[33] Conversely, offense-dominance, or anticipated offense-dominance, aggravates the security dilemma and increases pressures to quickly respond to the efforts of others.

Since geographic features are fixed, real shifts in the balance are produced by technological and organizational changes.[34] During periods of technological asymmetry, precisely the conditions that exist during periods of military transformation or revolution, the impact of the offense-defense balance and anticipated shifts in the balance on national security doctrines depends on whether a state is defensively *advantaged* or *disadvantaged*.

The defensively disadvantaged state finds it difficult to defend its national territory given geographic liabilities, the nature of existing technology, and anticipated changes in technology and is therefore more likely to devote attention to efforts to improve military technology and organization. The defensively advantaged state will display a more tentative approach and be more likely to neglect military reform.[35]

It is still unclear how the innovations associated with the information revolution will affect the global balance of power. On the one hand, the integration of information technologies confers significant advantages on superior military powers, the way offensive innovations have in the past. The combat value of fighting forces can be multiplied through information superiority. Connecting remote sensors, soldiers in the field, commanders, and weapon platforms allows the military to locate, target, engage, assess, and reengage with speed and efficiency. Total battlespace awareness combined with speedy and precise systems confers the ability to close-out enemy options and overwhelm an opponent's capacity to take decisive actions in combat.

Yet information technologies are available in ways that cutting-edge capabilities were not in the past, empowering traditionally weak states and non-state actors with unprecedented offensive capabilities. Information warfare capabilities pose novel threats for the most technologically advanced military forces and societies who rely on network connectivity to function. Connectivity enhances both the lethality and vulnerability of military forces. Because shared battlespace awareness provides such critical advantages, opponents will find this a highly valuable target and try to contaminate or disrupt information flows. Iraqi leaders did not fully appreciate the significance of surveillance planes such as AWACS (Airborne Warning and Control System) and JSTARS (Joint Surveillance and Target Attack Radar System) and networked computer communications in the 1991 Persian Gulf War, but future combatants undoubtedly will. A recent study of information warfare points out, 'the issue is not whether it is possible to defend information operations, but whether it can be done without undermining the network. Opponents need not gain ascendancy over the information system in order to challenge the superiority of the system's owner; all they have to do is persist long enough and force the creation of so many firewalls that the system no longer functions as designed.'[36] Every step toward defending some information is a step away from true shared awareness.

While offense-defense theory focuses on shifts in technology, theories of geopolitics focus on how perceptions, beliefs, and long-stranding traditions about geography shape national security doctrine. As Nicholas Spykman wrote, 'it is the geographic location of a country and its relation to centers of military power that define its problem of security.'[37] Arnold Wolfers added an important nuance. 'To say that insularity leads countries to neglect their military defenses can mean only that decision-makers are more likely to consider their country safe if it enjoys an insular position and that they will tend, as a result, to become more complacent in matters of military preparedness.'[38] Michael Handel contends that 'Nations must adapt to their environments by devising strategies calculated to capitalize on geographic assets and compensate for vulnerabilities.' Even though modern technology has made geographic factors less important than in the past – by shrinking space, accelerating time, and increasing firepower – 'national strategies are still mainly the product of a long evolutionary process shaped by generations of strategic thinkers and perpetuated through national political traditions'.[39]

Geography, or a state's position in space, can influence national security doctrine under uncertainty in several ways.

First, powers that are insular should respond to uncertainty differently than those that face intense 'border pressure'. Because they enjoy the luxury of broad oceanic borders and greater distance from powerful and potentially hostile neighbors, insular powers can more easily withdraw politically and militarily, an option foreclosed to land powers, particularly those with little territorial depth. Insular states are less likely to face a balance of power imperative, and more likely to face a broader range of strategic choices than non-insular states.

Second, global powers should respond to uncertainty differently than regional powers because they face a broader range of *potential* threats. Because the global power possesses a broader set of security interests while the security purview of regional powers is more narrowly circumscribed, the locus of potential threats for the global power is more diffuse. This only means that it is more difficult to predict the national security orientations of global powers than it is of regional powers. Consider the distinctly different orientations of the global, maritime power Great Britain and the continental power France immediately after World War I. As D. C. Watt recounts, 'French military thought was obsessed with the single, potentially more powerful enemy. British thinking, by contrast, was distracted, literally, by commitments all over the world.'[40]

Position can also refers to where a state exists at a point in time. The important factor here is the effect of the accumulated weight of the past and the nation's experience. One great difference between the United States and Great Britain after World War I lay in the fact that Britain was deeply mired in overstretched imperial commitments. Though the United States was economically stronger, it had few extra-hemispheric interests, the Philippines being the sole exception. Britain's security posture, on the other hand, was shaped by a long-standing imperial legacy, which implied an inherently broader definition of security.

Domestic Political and Organizational Approaches

Structural pressures often operate through political and organizational processes to effect change in national security doctrines. The emergence of a new enemy or defeat in war may generate pressures on military organizations to adapt, or may cause civilians to intervene to undertake major change.[41] Pushing the argument further, outside realist circles it has virtually become conventional wisdom that the actual sources, rather than simply the mediating processes, of national security doctrine are as much internal as external. National security doctrine responds to internal needs and values as much as to international circumstances, serving domestic political and social goals as much as responding to international threats.[42] The key point is not simply that national security doctrine is affected by domestic constraints, such as the amount of effort a society will devote to the national security effort, which even neo-realists would acknowledge. Rather, national security means and ends may be fashioned to serve domestic imperatives rather than strategic necessity.

Peter Trubowitz provides one explanation of the way national security doctrine is fashioned to manage and solve domestic problems. Politicians think about foreign policy the same way they think about domestic policy, as an instrument for consolidating political power internally. In the 1890s, he contends, US naval expansion was part of a Republican electoral strategy to divide the Populist movement and consolidate control over the national government.[43] Trubowitz argues that national security policy at the end of the nineteenth century was shaped by a larger set of debates: how to restore domestic prosperity and social stability; how large a role the federal government should play in promoting US interests abroad; which sectors of the economy to subsidize; and ultimately who would win and who would lose. Foreign policy was domestic policy because, as Trubowitz shows, the impact of international forces varies internally, advantaging some regions and sectors at the expense of others. Accordingly, a complex and competitive political process shapes national security policy, and during periods of transition in particular, it produces bitter struggles over what is strategically necessary, politically feasible, and at a deeper level, over the very meaning of the national interest.[44]

In similar fashion, Edward Rhodes also traces the rise of the doctrine of navalism in nineteenth century America to an attempt to solve a domestic problem but one of a different sort. Political leaders had to forge national cohesion in the face of deep cultural, ethnic, and economic divisions in society that threatened the ability of the state to act decisively.[45]

More generally, the social origins of strategic behavior emphasizes how state leaders are susceptible to societal pressure when defining strategic interests, setting priorities, and determining the availability of resources for the pursuit of security. Leaders must always attend to the need for public support, but when there is great uncertainty about security threats and objectives, domestic and social political calculations play a larger role in strategic planning. As Miroslav Nincic, Roger Rose and Gerard Gorski argue, 'the clearer the cues provided by the international environment, the slighter the domestic dissension concerning their interpretation'. By contrast the more uncertain and ambiguous the external threat, the 'more domestic social and political calculations dominate the thinking of policymakers',[46] particularly in democracies where there is likely to be greater public pressure to tailor strategic priorities to domestic preferences. As social calculations weigh in more heavily, the saliency of threats from the public's perspective should become more important. Threats to domestic well-being and those more proximate to the state should garner greater public support. Hence, national security doctrines framed in response to domestic and regional problems should be preferred by leaders and publics over more far-reaching grandiose hegemonial or ideational security doctrines. In the latter cases, the threat is amorphous, the costs potentially very high, and the domestic benefits unclear.

Organizational approaches attribute shifts in national security doctrine to politics among and within bureaucracies, focusing in particular on the role of military organizations in shaping security doctrine. Organization theories offer insights into the biases that result when organizations face uncertainty, and when military organizations face the loss of their main enemies. The conventional view of organizational politics views organizations as natural systems driven by the need to survive given budgetary constraints and inter-service-rivalry. In this view, organizations are presumed to be excessively rigid, resistant to change, incrementally adaptive,[47] and offensively biased.[48]

Though the conventional view has been challenged by professional,[49] cultural,[50] strategic choice,[51] and ideational[52] interpretations, it remains firmly entrenched in scholarly discourse.[53] This paradigm posits that when external threats are low, organizational dynamics will flourish and national security doctrine will respond to the military's institutional self-interests for bigger budgets, more prestige, and greater autonomy.[54] It predicts biases in how organizations respond to uncertainty – chiefly by privileging their own parochial interests. This tends to produce incoherent and disjointed national security policies.

The extent of military influence over national security doctrine depends on the state of civil-military relations. If military elites are well represented in the ruling coalition, or if over time civilians have delegated more authority to military leaders for security policy, service perspectives are likely to hold more sway. In Israel, a high percentage of former senior military officers serve in senior government positions. According to Michael Handel, this has traditionally produced a narrow military view of national security that downplays the role of diplomacy and economics, and that sees diplomacy as an instrument to support military goals, rather than vice versa.[55] Absent a compelling external threat, however, there is likely to be greater divergence between the strategic inclinations of civilian politicians responding to societal pressures, and military elites responding to professional incentives. The United States after World War I is a case in point. Civilian leaders, responding to public sentiment, believed that economic concerns had assumed a position of primacy in national and international affairs and that war had become too costly. They emphasized economic and diplomatic dimensions of national security, and neglected to align military policy with the broader contours of national security policy. As a result, 'the architects of national policy and makers of military strategy traveled their separate ways along paths that seemed sometimes to lead in opposite directions'.[56]

Ideational Approaches

Ideational approaches encompass a wide range of explanations at various levels of analysis, yet all focus on the role of ideas, whether in society at large, within institutions, or of individuals. At the broadest level, national security doctrine must be consistent with societal beliefs about the nature of the world and the state's relationship to and role in the world. Beliefs shape how interests are defined, how threats are perceived, the range of options considered, and how costs are weighed.[57] Societal beliefs, however, are not static. They change as social identity evolves. Social dislocation, demographic change and rising ethnic diversity can undermine the cohesiveness of society and the very idea of a 'national' identity. James Kurth argues that America has never been an ethnically homogeneous society but in the past, large influxes of immigrants were subjected to a process of massive and systematic Americanization.[58] Today, however, an ideology of the 'multicultural society' championed by a powerful political and intellectual elite is challenging America's long-standing identity as a leader of Western civilization. While this is not likely to threaten national survival, it certainly weakens the ability of the nation to act with purpose in the world.

Social identity is also linked to external relations and images of the 'other'.[59] Kal Holsti identified 17 different national role conceptions, many of which (e.g., protector, ally, imperialist) make sense only as responses to other states.[60] Similarly, Richard Herrmann and Michael Fischerkeller proposed five national role images (enemy, ally, degenerate, imperialist, and colony) that are chiefly external identities.[61] When dramatic change occurs in the external world, the moorings of social identity weaken. The collapse of its ideological adversary for the United States has called into question the nation's approach to the world. In this view, national security doctrine can be understood as a response to evolving beliefs as a society struggles to redefine itself in terms of a new 'other'.

An ideational perspective on organizations views them as open systems, embedded in and constituted by their environments.[62] The open systems view privileges the role of ideas, beliefs, and culture. Open systems approaches have gained increasing saliency among organization theorists who recognize the distinctive problems raised by uncertainty. Alternative futures cannot be specified, let alone values and risks of occurrence attached to them. Research highlights limitations on rational calculation and planning when the past is also uncertain.[63] James March and Johan Olsen posit that organizational intelligence, like individual intelligence, is built upon two fundamental processes: rational calculation and learning from experience.[64] Because rational calculation is severely constrained by uncertainty, they shift their focus to the potential for organizational learning.[65] Learning involves changing beliefs, skills, or procedures based on observations and interpretations of experience.[66] While certain properties of interpretation stem from features of individual inference and judgement[67] as suggested by cognitive theory discussed below, other properties stem from the frames[68] organizations use to develop collective understandings of history.[69] Frames reflect assumptions and knowledge about the world, and about organizational purpose. Frames contain different understandings of threat, imply different missions, and rely on different capacities.

Dominant interpretive frames that exist in an organization, often forged by the experience of war or by demanding peacetime military endeavors such as empire management or frontier defense, create biases in how military organizations think about their roles under uncertainty. This is because frames tend to persist long after they serve any rational, 'external' purpose. Yet frames can evolve absent a clear and present danger, defeat in war, or civilian intervention provided the right sorts of pressures and resources exist to reduce uncertainty (e.g., if credible knowledge is accumulated to augment the organization's experiential base and if resources and opportunities for experimentation are present). Just as societal beliefs are not static, institutional beliefs can evolve non-incrementally as organizations learn, generate new intellectual frameworks, and mold new responses to the outside world when faced with the loss of their traditional adversary.[70]

Cognitive psychology offers an ideational perspective at the individual level. Cognitive explanations focus on individual beliefs, both what we know based on past experience, and how we extract and create cues from limited information. Given a limited capacity to process information and cope with uncertainty, individuals are prone to rely on decision-making shortcuts, or cognitive heuristics, when judging the likelihood of future events under uncertainty.[71] Heuristics often result in biased judgments. The availability heuristic is a procedure for assessing the likelihood of an event by the ease with which instances are constructed and retrieved. Because availability is affected by factors other than frequency, use of this heuristic leads to predictable biases. Easily retrievable or more familiar instances, recent occurrences, and highly salient experiences are judged to occur more frequently. The availability heuristic highlights the vital role experience plays in determining perceived risk. If one's experiences are biased, than one's perceptions of risks and assessments of probability are likely to be inaccurate.

Cognitive theory leads us to expect predictable biases in the ways civilian and military leaders interpret the external environment, set priorities, and assign risk under uncertainty. Familiar, recent, and highly salient experiences should receive higher priority, and direct experience should enhance the level of perceived risk associated with similar situations. This may account for the purported tendency to prepare for the 'last war'. We should expect a state's national security doctrine to be shaped by recent events, particularly when recent events are *perceived* to resemble past events that are highly salient to leaders because of personal experience and/or the costs associated with those past events.

At the system level, ideational explanations focus on how global norms can stimulate changes in national security doctrine. These explanations attribute change to the quest for legitimacy and identity within the international system at large. Meiji Japan provides an excellent example of how a state dramatically reoriented its national security identity (in the nineteenth century by adopting modern European military institutions) in order to be accepted as a full and equal member of (Western-dominated) international society.[72] Japanese views of international affairs were shaped by contact with the West during a period of European expansionism in the 1870s. Thus, expansionism became integral to Japan's development in a world defined by the major European powers.[73] A vigorous and expansionist foreign policy was a sign of internal health and power, that Japan had joined the ranks of the great powers and could cope with the power of the West.[74] At that time, the European powers were constantly competing with each other for national strength, rarely through outright conflict but certainly by preparing for such conflict and augmenting national strength to prevail in conflict should it occur. In the 1880s, it was taken for granted by the Japanese that they must engage in this 'peacetime war'. Akire Iriye writes, 'Imperialism ... characterized part of the external behavior of modern states in the late nineteenth and early twentieth centuries. It expressed the energies, orientations, and interests of a modern state at that particular period....'[75] All modern states were imperialist. They also had huge armaments programs and elaborate war plans.

Sociology's new institutionalism focuses on the cultural and institutional foundations of world society and the way that institutional pressures stimulate the spread of legitimated forms and practices across societies and professions. Organizations, like states, adapt to attain legitimacy, not just to increase efficiency. International norms exert a powerful influence[76] and the fact that a particular security practice is normatively sanctioned abroad increases the likelihood that it will be adopted.[77]

Socialization also encourages the spread of practices. Through professional networks, organizations share norms of appropriate behavior and information on how to best structure the organization. Chris Demchak attributes the spread of the information technology-based military model to the emergence of a global military community, fed by newly available information through vehicles such as international trade shows, increasing openness and interaction among military organizations worldwide, and common sources of formal education. Each has contributed to the strengthening and widening of professional networks, and the development of mutual awareness among military organizations that they are all involved in a common enterprise.[78]

Paul DiMaggio and Walter Powell hypothesize that the more professionalized a field, the greater the convergence in organizational form as members come to share norms of appropriate behavior (regulative norms) and identity (constitutive norms).[79] Reliance on professional standards makes normative pressures high for military organizations.

Sociology's new institutionalists examine local practices and international norms (e.g., defined as normal or prevailing practices), and the relationship between them in order to assess changes in security practices. The legitimacy of certain practices abroad creates pressures for diffusion, while local values and institutions may pose barriers to change. A new practice may conflict with indigenous practices; the organizational set – necessary supporting organizations and institutions, e.g., schools, industry – may be inadequately developed to support the change;[80] or reformers may lack authority to institute change in the face of pressures to conform to existing social institutions and practices.

Neo-institutionalists expect no direct relationship between security practices and strategic necessity. Thus, the approach has much to offer when attempting to explain national security doctrine when threats are low and when dramatic military change is in the process of establishing new meanings about the nature of war and pursuit of security. Change results from normative pressures for legitimacy within a particular social system, and from socialization pressures within a particular profession. An excellent example is provided by Theo Farrell's analysis of post-revolutionary Ireland. The Irish Army abandoned its guerrilla warfare heritage and began to model itself on the British Army, even when the British model held little strategic utility. Farrell summarizes, 'The Irish Army did this because it acted according to worldwide professional norms of appropriate organizational form and action. ... [I]ts officer corps viewed themselves as professional soldiers and believed that guerilla warfare was not the business of professional armies.'[81]

NATIONAL SECURITY RESPONSES TO UNCERTAINTY

When orchestrating national security doctrine under uncertainty, political and military leaders must attend to a variety of dimensions: the nation's diplomatic posture, its economic strategy and resource allocation priorities, military missions and force posture, and domestic preferences and public support. Diplomatic considerations include whom to ally with, levels of commitment to potential alliance and coalition partners, as well as whether permanent alliances, ad hoc coalitions, or collective security are favored. Resource allocation priorities reflect important strategic decisions about how to manage the economy. They involve making trade-offs between current spending to retain the capability to meet unanticipated threats in the short run, and long-term economic growth to meet unanticipated threats in the more distant future. Military strategy includes choices about the balance of resources to be devoted to the different Services, the roles and missions that should be privileged, the paradigm of war that should serve as the basis for planning, and priorities and conditions for the use of force. Domestic mobilization requires leaders to decide to what extent to lead or be led by public opinion, and to develop a rationale for mobilizing popular support.

Often in the scholarly literature, one dimension serves as a surrogate for national security doctrine as a whole. This raises conceptual and methodological problems because national security under uncertainty is likely to be less integrated than when threats are high or compelling. In democratic polities, the disintegrative tendencies are likely to be particularly high. The difficulty democracies have in harmonizing their military and diplomatic strategies under uncertainty has been a hallmark of US policy from its very beginnings. In 1823, when the Monroe Doctrine was advanced, the Navy had virtually no capability to prevent European involvement in hemispheric affairs, making the entire strategy hostage to tacit British cooperation. At the turn of the nineteenth century, American diplomatic and economic strategy staked out the position of maintaining an 'open door' policy toward China, yet the US Navy was in no position to use or threaten force as a means of upholding the policy.[82]

In many respects, the problem deepened after World War I. In the 1920s, military policy was not aligned with the broader contours of the nation's diplomatic and economic strategies. In the Far East, diplomats aggressively pursued naval arms control while assuming diplomatic obligations there that US forces were inadequate to meet. In Europe, US leaders spurned diplomatic involvement in Europe and refused to ratify the Versailles Treaty and join the League of Nations. Yet Americans remained actively involved through financial leverage and private capital in order to stabilize European affairs and resolve the problem of German reparations.[83]

By privileging one dimension of national security doctrine, we risk adopting a partial and potentially misleading view of the phenomenon of interest. We need to examine sub-components, and consider whether and how those various components support each other in an overarching vision, or operate at cross-purposes. One way to capture national security responses to uncertainty is to examine how four dimensions of national security doctrine – diplomatic posture, resource allocation priorities, military mission priorities, and domestic mobilization theme – vary along a set of key parameters.

Intensity refers to the level of conflict prepared for, specifically whether planning scenarios, force posture, and investment reflect preparation for high-intensity conflict, low-intensity conflict, peacetime non-combat activities, or some combination.

Geographic concentration refers to the geographic breadth or concentration of strategic focus, and the degree of contiguity or distance of potential threats that underlie planning assumptions. Policies designed for power projection and global presence indicate a broad geographic focus while selective engagement and homeland defense suggest a more limited geographic focus.

Range refers to the breadth of contingencies prepared for, spanning a broad spectrum of conflict to specific localized scenarios. It also captures whether resource allocation priorities are designed for hedging against a range of conflict scenarios, or are shaped by more targeted investment strategies.

Time frame refers to the time horizon leaders use when weighing the military risks facing the state, for which defense assets provide insurance, against the opportunity costs of devoting scarce economic resources to unproductive armaments. Downsizing assumes long-run threats are greater than short-run threats, and the pay-off to reinvestment is high; maintaining capable forces in being assumes short-run threats are serious, and current expenditure will have little long-run impact. A short horizon investment strategy supports force readiness and allocation of resources to defense sectors to preserve the defense industrial base. A long horizon investment strategy supports force modernization and allocation of resources to non-defense sectors to promote economic growth.[84] Time frame also captures whether military mission priorities are designed chiefly for long-term deterrence, mid-term threats, or near-term contingency response.

Flexibility refers to the flexibility or firmness of commitments. Policies of unilateralism, support for ad hoc coalitions and informal alliances reflect a preference for flexibility; formal alliances and commitment to multilateral policies like collective security reflect a preference for a firm diplomatic posture.[85]

An additional parameter, *coherence*, captures the degree to which the constituent parts reflect a clear and logically consistent theory about how a state can best provide security for itself. Incoherence refers to the incompatibility among component parts, and may be characterized by accumulation of various political initiatives, strategic objectives, operational concepts, and capabilities that are incompatible at best and self-defeating at worst.

Finally, national security responses to uncertainty can be expressed in terms of how the nation conceives its role in the world and its relationship toward others. Several national purpose orientations are offered below as *ideal* types. In the real world, actual national purpose orientations are likely to be hybrids. These orientations are designed foremost around how threats are anticipated and how the threat environment, benign though it may be, is interpreted.[86] They serve as themes around which domestic society can be mobilized. Moreover, they logically imply particular diplomatic postures, resource allocation priorities, and military mission priorities.

A balance of power orientation is capability centric. Probable threats are linked to actors who possess the industrial, financial, and technological capabilities to shift the distribution of power, either globally or regionally. Because of their greater capabilities, warfare it is presumed, will be high-intensity in nature, requiring that resources be channeled into defense investment to preserve the defense industrial base for warfare that will either require a high-tech edge or large-scale resources. Two types of alliance strategies are consistent with a balance of power orientation. If the identity of long-term partners is possible, firm alliances will most effectively maintain those highly institutionalized structures that provide the infrastructure for waging major war. If, on the other hand, the identity of long-term partners is more fluid as it was during the eighteenth and nineteenth century in Europe where allies one day easily became enemies the next, flexible partnerships are the preferred diplomatic posture for managing national security uncertainty.

A hegemonial orientation is global centric. The threat is perceived to reside in the chaos, instability, and disorder of the international system. As then President George Bush articulated US strategy even before the Persian Gulf War, 'As the world's most powerful democracy, we are inescapably the leader, the connecting link in a global alliance of democracies. The pivotal responsibility for ensuring stability of the international balance remains ours.'[87] A hegemonial orientation is concerned with shaping the future international environment. Least explicit in articulating specific threats, it emphasizes hedging against the unknown and preparing for a range of conflict types. Because unilateral diplomatic strategies are least constraining and offer the greatest flexibility for planning for a range of contingencies, states adopting a hegemonial orientation should prefer unilateralism and ad hoc coalitions over participation in collective security arrangements as the primary approach to managing uncertainty.

A regional or local orientation is area centric, giving greatest prominence to geographic contiguity. For the United States, hemispheric defense is the more traditional label associated with this national purpose orientation. Threats of concern are located at or near the nation's borders.

For the United States today, this would include the dangers of illegal and uncontrolled immigration and narcotics trafficking. It is also an orientation that resounds with many Western Europeans confronting strong migration pressures from Eastern Europe. For the United States today, operational uncertainty would be managed by preparing for low-intensity conflicts and small 'Panama-type' wars that may arise in Central America and the Caribbean, for policing and border patrol functions to stem illegal immigration and narcotics flows, and for humanitarian and rescue operations associated with refugee crises. For Western Europe, the emphasis would be on peace support operations in the areas to the east ravaged by ethnic conflict. Because the focus is a regional one, diplomatic strategies are designed in conjunction with other actors in the area in an effort to deal with threats and challenges that are specific to the region. A state adopting a regional orientation is more likely to welcome the presence of other regional hegemons that can take the lead when crises emerge in their respective regions. Accordingly, Bosnia would be viewed as a European problem first, demanding leadership from Europe and its regional organizations. Haiti would be viewed as a crisis demanding leadership from the United States and its regional organizations.

An imperial orientation is peripheral centric. The challenges to national security privileged are those in and around the periphery of an empire. An imperial strategy focuses on maintaining and preserving an empire to guarantee access to the markets and resources the empire provides. With attention diverted from the prospect of great power war, multilateralism and flexibility are the preferred methods for coping with alliance uncertainty in extra-imperial matters. Given that future challenges are deemed to reside in the periphery where the requirements of warfare are assumed to be less demanding than against another great power, less investment need be devoted to sophisticated defense technologies. The more benign threat environment also reduces the urgency for weapons modernization. The military services can prepare for peacetime missions and low-intensity conflict contingencies.

A domestic orientation is state centric. Threats to national security lay foremost in the domestic economic and social conditions of the nation. A domestic orientation gains greater salience when risks from threats abroad are perceived to be slight, making possible a reduction in the costs associated with the nation's foreign policy in order to invest greater resources in domestic development. Improving economic performance and international competitiveness receive top priority as resources are shifted from defense investment into non-defense areas. Select elements of the defense sector may be protected. However, the impetus is not for military security reasons per se, but rather to preserve jobs and stabilize the economy. While a domestic strategy has traditionally been associated with isolationism, detachment, neutrality, and other inward-looking approaches to strategy, it does not imply non-involvement. A domestic strategy is consistent with close bilateral ties to key economic actors essential to the world economy.[88] It also favors multilateralism, followership, and dependence on international institutions when responding to crises in the international arena. A domestic strategy, however, does not preclude selective unilateralism in military operations, like the US bombing of Iraq's intelligence headquarters in mid-1993 in retaliation for a terrorist plot to assassinate former President Bush.

An ideational orientation is value centric. Threats and challenges stem from other state and non-state actors whose values are antithetical to the values of one's own nation. For the United States, authoritarianism, political repression, command economies, and human rights abuses are perceived to threaten democracy, freedom, and prosperity. An ideational strategy is most effectively pursued through multilateral diplomatic strategies and collective security organizations because the weight of world opinion can play a critical role in meeting the threat. By operating through multilateral fora, the state can also reduce its resource uncertainty by emphasizing its comparative advantages. An ideational strategy is not an exclusive category, and most leaders pledge to support national values, at least rhetorically. The ideological rivalry that became the hallmark of the Cold War illustrates how threats are often couched in ideational terms. However, ideational goals are often subordinated in actuality to the imperatives of other national security orientations. The United States supported authoritarian regimes during the Cold War to serve its balance of power orientation, while the Clinton administration granted most-favored nation trade status to China despite its record on human rights to serve its domestic orientation.

In all polities, competing national security conceptions exist. These conceptions are based fundamentally on different definitions of threat. They imply distinct diplomatic postures, resource allocation priorities, and military strategies. Which national security conception prevails will most likely be the result of protracted and divisive debate over the meaning of international developments for the nation's security and well-being and over how the nation's interests can most effectively be promoted and secured. It will also hinge on which conception appears most compelling to the public.

Planning for the future is always a process beset by uncertainty. In the national security arena, it becomes progressively more uncertain when the identity and nature of future opponents is unclear, when rapid military-technological change is underway, and when social dislocation at home undermines national unity. When it comes to addressing the question of whether or not one's forces will be sufficient to cope with future national security contingencies (i.e., are we preparing for the 'right kind' of war and against the right adversary), often the best one can do is to reduce the range of uncertainty. It is often too expensive to hedge against a range of possibilities by building a 'balanced' force that can cope with a spectrum of national security futures. Rarely have militaries in the past predicted accurately who the opponent would be and what kind of military changes would occur.

When deciding whether to engage or withdraw, pursue firm alliances or flexible coalitions, invest in defense or non-defense sectors, privilege force readiness, modernization, or research and development, and how to forge a societal consensus to ensure public support for the pursuit of security, inevitably priorities must be set and resources allocated under great uncertainty about the future. The hope is that new definitions of the future, whether shaped by simple projection of the present, technological innovation, change in perception of an enemy, institutional strengths, internal political concerns, shifts in military conceptions, or transformation in the nation's social and cultural milieu, will not be too far afield. For as Paul Kennedy reminds us, with the United States in mind:

> [S]ince it is not humanly possible to prepare for everything that may happen in the unpredictable and turbulent world of the early twenty-first century, the task is to structure the armed forces, and the economy and society upon which they rest, to be in a good position to meet contingencies. In other words, the United States ought, while seeking to fulfill its people's peacetime desires, to maintain a reservoir of productive financial and technological and educational strength – so that if a '1920s' world unfortunately turned into a '1930s' world at some point in the future, the nation would not then discover that its grand strategy was crippled by a whole series of defense 'deficiencies' which a faltering economy could not easily correct.[89]

NOTES

1. See Glenn Chavetz, Michael Spirtas, and Benjamin Frankel, 'Introduction: Tracing the Influence of Identity on Foreign Policy', *Security Studies* 8/2-3 (Winter 1998/99–Spring 1999) p.xiii.

2. See for example, Peter J. Katzenstein, *Cultural Norms and National Security: Police and Military in Postwar Japan* (Ithaca, NY: Cornell UP 1996).

3. As one study of Israel's national security puts it, 'If the old Israeli security environment was dangerous and unforgiving, it at least offered the advantages of relative clarity and predictability. Israelis knew who and what they were up against.The peace process has proved to be a mixed blessing for Israel. It has spawned new, sometimes deadly threats while simultaneously fostering higher expectations among Israeli citizens regarding peace and security. In the new environment, danger remains, but clarity and predictability have given way to ambiguity, uncertainty and a sense that the geopolitical setting in which Israeli military planners must operate remains highly unstable.' Eliot A. Cohen, Michael J. Eisenstadt and Andrew J. Bacevich, 'Israel's Revolution in Security Affairs', *Survival* 40/1 (Spring 1998) p.52.

4. How one identifies threats is often taken for granted by international relations theorists. Stephen Walt's notion of balancing against threats begs this important question. Stephen M. Walt, *The Origins of Alliances* (Ithaca, NY: Cornell UP 1987).

5. Samuel P. Huntington, 'The Evolution of U.S. National Strategy', in Daniel J. Kaufman *et al.* (eds.) *US National Security for the 1990s* (Baltimore, MD: Johns Hopkins UP 1991) pp.11–12.

6. Richard K. Betts, 'Systems for Peace or Causes of War? Collective Security, Arms Control, and the New Europe', *International Security* 17/1 (Summer 1992) p.34.

7. 'The Forgotten Dimension of Strategy', in Michael Howard (ed.) *The Causes of War and Other Essays* (Cambridge, MA: Harvard UP 1983) pp.101–15.

8. For an overview of prospect theory, see Jack S. Levy, 'Introduction to Prospect Theory', *Political Psychology* 13/2 (1992) pp.171–86; Robert Jervis, 'Political Implications of Loss Aversion', *Political Psychology* 13/2 (1992) pp.187–204; and Jack S. Levy, 'Prospect Theory and International Relations: Theoretical Applications and Analytical Problems', *Political Psychology* 13/2 (1992) pp.283–310. For an application of prospect theory to US post-Cold War strategy and foreign policy, see Emily O. Goldman and Larry Berman, 'Engaging the World: First Impressions of the Clinton Foreign Policy Legacy', in Colin Campbell and Bert A. Rockman (eds.) *The Clinton Legacy* (NY: Chatham House Publishers 2000) pp.238–42.

9. See Goldman and Berman (note 8) pp.233–38 for a discussion of Clinton's enlargement strategy.

10. Peter Trubowitz and Edward Rhodes, 'Explaining American Strategic Adjustment', in Peter Trubowitz, Emily O. Goldman, and Edward Rhodes (eds.) *The Politics of Strategic Adjustment: Ideas, Institutions and Interests* (NY: Columbia UP 1999) p.8.

11. Edward Rhodes, 'Constructing Power: Cultural Transformation and Strategic Adjustment in the 1890s', in Trubowitz *et al.* (note 10) pp.29–78.

12. 'Israel at 50', *The Economist* (25 April–1 May 1998) p.7.

13. The literature on revolutions in military affairs, both historical and contemporary, is a broad one. See Clifford J. Rogers (ed.) *The Military Revolution Debate: Readings on the Military Transformation of Early Modern Europe* (Boulder, CO: Westview 1995); Andrew Krepinevich, 'Cavalry to Computer: The Pattern of Military Revolutions', *The National Interest* (Fall 1994) pp.10–42; Eliot A. Cohen, 'A Revolution in Warfare', *Foreign Affairs* 75/2 (March/April 1996) pp.37–54; John Arquilla and David Ronfeldt, 'Cyberwar is Coming!' *Comparative Strategy* 12/2 (April–June 1993) pp.141–65; Alvin and Heidi Toffler, *War and Anti-War* (NY: Warner 1993).

14. For a discussion of the cascading effects of revolutionary military change, see Emily O. Goldman and Leslie C. Eliason (eds.) *Adaptive Enemies, Reluctant Friends: The Impact of Diffusion on Military Practice*, manuscript under review.

15. Thomas G. Mahnken, 'Why Third World Space Systems Matter', *Orbis* 35/4 (Fall 1991) pp.563–79.
16. Gregorian (see below) pp.142–7 argues Third World countries have a strong incentive to introduce new innovative systems, like GPS, that will significantly enhance their military capabilities. Moreover, GPS eliminates two major obstacles Third World countries have faced: incompatibility with existing systems and dependence on suppliers. GPS is easy to integrate into current systems and can be bought commercially, eliminating any major obstacle to technology acquisition. Finally, targeting for GPS-guided munitions though satellite reconnaissance is an avenue now open to many developing states. Raffi Gregorian, 'Global Positioning Systems: A Military Revolution for the Third World?' *SAIS Review* 13/1 (Winter-Spring 1993) pp.133–48.
17. Richard J. Harknett, 'The Information Technology Network and the Ability to Deter: The Impact of Organizational Change on 21st Century Conflict', Paper prepared for the JCISS/*Security Studies* Conference on the Revolution in Military Affairs, Monterey, CA, 26–29 Aug. 1996, pp.32–4; Arquilla and Ronfeldt (note 13).
18. Cohen (note 13) pp.45–6; Winn Schwartau, *Information Warfare: Chaos on the Electronic Superhighway* (NY: Thunder's Mouth Press 1996).
19. Donald E. Ryan Jr, 'Implications of Information-Based Warfare', *Joint Forces Quarterly* (Autumn/Winter 1994–95) p.115.
20. Arquilla and Ronfeldt (note 13) pp.144–6.
21. Harknett (note 17) p.37 notes while 'the United States may have required an advanced technological infrastructure to produce the global positioning satellite system ... ... now all one has to do is go down to Radio Shack to purchase a GPS monitor to access the system.'
22. Chris C. Demchak, 'Watersheds in Perception and Knowledge: Twenty Years of Military Technology', draft manuscript (June 1999) p.15.
23. Chris C. Demchak, 'Creating the Enemy: Global Diffusion of the IT-Based Military Model', in Goldman and Eliason, (note 14).
24. Chris C. Demchak, 'RMA in Developing States: Botswana, Chile and Thailand; Dilemmas of Image, Operations and Democracy', paper prepared for National Security Studies Quarterly Conference, 'Buck Rogers or Rock Throwers? Technology Diffusion, International Military Modernization, and the International Response to the Revolution in Military Affairs', 14 Oct. 1999, Washington DC, p.5.
25. Barry Posen, *The Sources of Military Doctrine: France, Britain, and Germany Between the World Wars* (Ithaca, NY: Cornell UP 1984); Paul Kennedy (ed.) *Grand Strategies in War and Peace* (New Haven, CT: Yale UP 1991); Richard Rosecrance and Arthur A. Stein (eds.) *The Domestic Bases of Grand Strategy* (Ithaca, NY: Cornell UP 1993).
26. John Braeman, 'Power and Diplomacy: The 1920s Reappraised', *Review of Politics* 44 (July 1982) p.345.
27. Joao Resende-Santos, 'Anarchy and Emulation of Military Systems: Military Organizations and Technology in South America, 1870–1930', *Security Studies* 5/3 (Spring 1996) p.196.
28. Kenneth N. Waltz, *Theory of International Politics* (Reading, MA: Addison-Wesley 1979) p.127.
29. Jan S. Breemer, 'Technological Change and the New Calculus of War: The United States Builds a New Navy', in Turbowitz *et al.* (note 10) p.218.
30. Chaim Kaufman and Charles L. Glaser, 'Establishing the Foundations of Offense-Defense Theory', paper presented at the NATO Symposium on 'Military Stability', 12–14 June, 1995, Brussels, pp.12–13.
31. This definition is adopted from Kaufman and Glaser (note 30) p.20. For similar definitions, see Robert Jervis, 'Cooperation Under the Security Dilemma', *World Politics* 30/2 (Jan. 1978) p.188; Charles L. Glaser, 'Realists as Optimists: Cooperation as Self-Help', *International Security* 19/3 (Winter 1994/95) pp.61–2. Jack S. Levy, 'The Offensive/Defensive Balance of Military Technology: A Theoretical and Historical Analysis', *International Studies Quarterly* 28 (1984) pp.222–30 lists other definitions. Most depend upon territorial conquest. For Jervis (p.187), an offensive advantage means that 'it is easier to destroy the other's army and take its territory than it is to defend one's own' and a defensive advantage means that 'it

is easier to protect and hold than it is to move forward, destroy, and take'. George Quester, *Offense and Defense in the International System* (NY: Wiley 1977) p.15, writes 'the territorial fixation logically establishes our distinction between offense and defense.'

32. One common critique of the offense-defense approach is the difficulty of classifying different technologies as offensive or defensive.This may not be a problem for our purposes since the critical issue is how weapons are incorporated into an overall military strategy. At this level, it is possible to distinguish offensive from defensive strategies and to determine which bundles of weapons favor a strategy of political consolidation and which favor a strategy of local defense.See Kaufman and Glaser (note 30) pp.69–75.

33. Resende-Santos (note 27) p.218.

34. Ibid. p.217.

35. Ibid. pp.219–20.

36. Richard J. Harknett and the JCISS Study Group, 'The Risks of a Networked Military', *Orbis* 44 (Winter 2000) p.132.

37. Nicholas J. Spykman, *America's Strategy in World Politics* (NY: Harcourt, Brace, and World 1942) p.447.

38. Arnold Wolfers, 'The Determinants of Foreign Policy', in idem, *Discord and Collaboration: Essays on International Politics* (Baltimore, MD: Johns Hopkins Press 1962) p.42.

39. Michael I. Handel, 'The Evolution of Israeli Strategy: The Psychology of Insecurity in the Quest for Absolute Security', in Williamson Murray, MacGregor Knox, and Alvin Bernstein (eds.) *The Making of Strategy: Rulers, States, and War* (NY: Cambridge UP 1994) pp.534–35.

40. Donald Cameron Watt, *Too Serious a Business: European Armed Forces and the Approach to the Second World War* (Berkeley: U. of California Press 1975) p.95.

41. See Posen (note 25); Stephen Peter Rosen, *Winning the Next War: Innovation and the Modern Military* (Ithaca, NY: Cornell UP 1991); Kimberly Martin Zisk, *Engaging the Enemy: Organization Theory and Soviet Military Innovation, 1955–1991* (Princeton UP 1993).

42. See for example Rosecrance and Stein (note 25).

43. Peter Trubowitz, 'Geography and Strategy: The Politics of American Naval Expansion', in Trubowitz *et al.* (note 10) pp.105–29.

44. Ibid. pp.126–29.

45. Rhodes (note 11).

46. Miroslav Nincic, Roger Rose, and Gerard Gorski, 'The Social Foundations of Strategic Adjustment', in Trubowitz *et al.* (note 10) p.179.

47. See Posen (note 25); Richard Betts, *Soldiers, Statesmen, and Cold War Crises* (Cambridge, MA: Harvard UP, 1977); Timothy David Moy, 'Hitting the Beaches and Bombing the Cities: Doctrine and Technology for Two New Militaries, 1920–1940', (PhD Dissertation, U. of California at Berkeley 1987); Graham T. Allison, *Essence of Decision* (Boston: Little, Brown 1971); Edward L. Katzenbach Jr, 'The Horse Cavalry in the Twentieth Century: A Study in Policy Response', *Public Policy* 7 (1958) pp.120–49; and Herbert Kaufman, *The Limits of Organizational Change* (University: U. of Alabama Press 1971).

48. Posen (note 25); Stephen Van Evera, 'The Cult of the Offensive and the Origins of the First World War', *International Security* 9/1 (Summer 1984) pp.58–107; Jack Snyder, 'Civil-Military Relations and the Cult of the Offensive, 1914 and 1984', *International Security* 9/1 (Summer 1984) pp.108–46; Jack Snyder, *The Ideology of the Offensive: Military Decision Making and the Disasters of 1914* (Ithaca, NY: Cornell UP 1984).

49. Samuel P. Huntington, *The Soldier and the State* (Cambridge, MA: Harvard UP 1957).

50. Jeffrey W. Legro, *Cooperation Under Fire: Anglo-German Restraint During World War II* (Ithaca, NY: Cornell UP 1995); Elizabeth Kier, 'Culture and Military Doctrine: France Between the Wars', *International Security* 19/4 (Spring 1995); Stephen Peter Rosen, *Societies and Military Power: India and Its Armies* (Ithaca, NY: Cornell UP 1996).

51. John Child, 'Organizational Structure, Environment, and Performance: The Role of Strategic Choice', *Sociology* 6/1 (1972) pp.1–22; Stewart Ranson, Bob Hinings, and Royster Greenwood, 'The Structuring of Organizational Structures', *Administrative Science Quarterly* 25/1 (1980) pp.1–17; Rosen, *Winning the Next War* (note 41).

52. Christopher M. Gacek, *The Logic of Force: The Dilemma of Limited War in American Foreign Policy* (NY: Columbia UP 1994).
53. It is interesting that despite some provocative recent scholarship that casts serious doubt on bureaucratic interpretations of the military (see in particular Edward Rhodes, 'Do Bureaucratic Politics Matter? Some Disconfirming Findings From the Case of the US Navy', *World Politics* 47/1 (Oct. 1994), this model continues to hold tremendous sway in the academic and policy communities. A survey of recent writings on military behavior reveals that scholars always feel the need to engage the bureaucratic interpretation, regardless of what particular perspective they are championing. Rhodes discusses some of the reasons why this may be so.
54. Posen (note 25).
55. Handel (note 39) pp.555, 563.
56. Louis Morton, 'Interservice Cooperation and Political-Military Collaboration', in Harry L. Coles (ed.) *Total War and Cold War: Problems in Civilian Control of the Military* (Columbus: Ohio State UP 1962) p.149; Ernest R. May, 'The Development of Political-Military Consultation in the United States', *Political Science Quarterly* 70 (June 1955) pp.161–80.
57. Judith Goldstein and Robert O. Keohane (eds.) *Ideas and Foreign Policy: Beliefs, Institutions, and Political Change* (Ithaca, NY: Cornell UP 1993).
58. James Kurth, 'The *Real* Clash', *The National Interest* 37 (Fall 1994) p.13.
59. Jonathan Mercer, 'Anarchy and Identity', *International Organization* 49/2 (Spring 1995) pp.229–52.
60. Kal J. Holsti, 'National Role Conceptions in the Study of Foreign Policy', *International Studies Quarterly* 14/3 (Sept. 1970) pp.233–309.
61. Richard Hermann and Michael P. Fischerkeller, 'Beyond the Enemy Image and Spiral Model', *International Organization* 49/3 (Summer 1995) pp.415–50.
62. The rational-natural-open systems typology of organizations is presented in W. Richard Scott, *Organizations: Rational, Natural and Open Systems*, 3rd ed. (NJ: Prentice Hall 1992), and adopted by Theo Farrell in his fine review of the literature on military innovation.Theo Farrell, 'Figuring Out Fighting Organizations: The New Organisational Analysis In Strategic Studies', *Journal of Strategic Studies* 19/1 (March 1996) pp.122–35.
63. James G. March and Johan P. Olsen, 'The Uncertainty of the Past: Organizational Learning Under Ambiguity', *European Journal of Political Research* 3 (1975) pp.147–71.
64. Ibid. pp.147–8.
65. Ibid. p.168. There have been attempts to examine military organizations from an open systems perspective, but little work that takes an organizational learning perspective. See Emily O. Goldman, 'The US Military in Uncertain Times: Organizations, Ambiguity, and Strategic Adjustment', *Journal of Strategic Studies* 20/2 (Spring 1997) pp.41–74 for an organizational learning perspective on military innovation.
66. Jack S. Levy, 'Learning and Foreign Policy: Sweeping a Conceptual Minefield', *International Organization* 48/2 (Spring 1994) p.296.
67. Daniel Kahneman, Paul Slovic, and Amos Tversky (eds.) *Judgment Under Uncertainty: Heuristics and Biases* (Cambridge, UK: CUP 1982).
68. Lynn Eden defines frames as 'ways of knowing and doing by those in an organization, coherent sets of organizing ideas and social practices, that structure how actors in organizations identify problems and find solutions. Frames incorporate assumptions and knowledge about the world, articulate or assume purpose, define problems, and shape the search for solutions.' Lynn Eden, 'Constructing Destruction: The Making of Organizational Knowledge about the Effects of US Nuclear Weapons', (1995) draft manuscript cited in Theo Farrell, 'Innovation in Military Organizations Without Enemies', paper presented at the International Studies Association Annual Convention, San Diego, CA, 16–20 April 1996, pp.6–7.
69. Barbara Levitt and James G. March, 'Organizational Learning', *Annual Review of Sociology* 14 (1988) p.324.
70. Goldman, 'The US Military in Uncertain Times' (note 64).

71. Shelley Taylor, 'The Availability Bias in Social Perception and Interaction', in Kahneman *et al., Judgment Under Uncertainty*, (note 67) pp.190–200; Amos Tversky and Daniel Kahneman, 'Availability: A Heuristic for Judging Frequency and Probability', *Cognitive Psychology* 5 (1973) pp.207–32; idem, 'Judgment Under Uncertainty', *Science* 185 (1974) pp.1124–31.

72. H. Suganami, 'Japan's Entry into International Society', in Peter Kornicki (ed.) *Meiji Japan: Political, Economic and Social History 1868–1912*, Vol.1 (London: Routledge 1998) p.9; Emily O. Goldman, 'The Spread of Western Military Models to Ottoman Turkey and Meiji Japan', in Theo Farrell and Terry Terriff (eds.) *The Sources of Military Change: Military Organizations and Their Changing Environments* (forthcoming, Lynne Rienner).

73. Akira Iriye, 'Japan's Drive to Great-Power Status', in Kornicki (note 72) p.48.

74. Ibid. pp.48, 57–8.

75. Ibid. pp.60–1.

76. See Demchak, 'Creating the Enemy' (note 23); Dana P. Eyre and Mark C. Suchman, 'Status, Norms, and the Proliferation of Conventional Weapons: An Institutional Theory Approach', in Peter J. Katzenstein (ed.) *The Culture of National Security: Norms and Identity in World Politics* (NY: Cornell UP 1996) pp.79–113.

77. Paul J. DiMaggio and Walter W. Powell, 'The Iron Cage Revisited: Institutional Isomorphism and Collective Rationality in Organizational Fields', *American Sociological Review* 48 (April 1983) p.148.

78. Demchak, 'Creating the Enemy' (note 23).

79. DiMaggio and Powell (note 77).

80. D. Eleanor Westney, *Imitation and Innovation: The Transfer of Western Organizational Patterns to Meiji Japan* (Cambridge, MA: Harvard UP 1987) pp.28–31.

81. Theo Farrell, 'World Culture and Military Change in Post-Revolutionary Ireland', in Farrell and Terriff, *The Sources of Military Change* (note 72) p.30.

82. See George F. Kennan, *American Diplomacy* (U. of Chicago Press 1951) esp. pp.23–37.

83. Melvyn Leffler, 'Political Isolationism, Economic Expansion or Diplomatic Realism? American Policy Toward Western Europe, 1921–1933', *Perspectives in American History* 8 (1974) pp.413–61.

84. It is important to have several ways to assess these distinctions in resource allocation priorities because technological changes may render some of the characterizations obsolete over time. In particular, in the information age, distinguishing between civilian and military technologies has become very difficult because commercial technologies increasingly have military applications. Moreover, information technologies are driven as much by the civilian commercial economy as by government-sponsored military research and development.

85. This continuum challenges the characterization of diplomatic posture as isolationist or interventionist.The isolationist-interventionist continuum obscures important variation in the nature of intervention or engagement.

86. One scholar studying the relationship between strategic choice and strategic culture recently argued the benefits of examining a limited, ranked set of grand strategic preferences instead of the menu of strategic options approach that I adopt. Johnston contends that using ranked preferences eases cross-societal analysis because one can more easily compare the weights assigned to different choices across societies.The use of ranked preferences as the empirical referent should, he argues, also yield more explicit predictions about choice than an unranked menu of choices.Toward this end, Johnston develops a central paradigm of strategic culture, which consists of assumptions about the role of war (inevitable or aberrant), the nature of the threat (zero-sum or variable sum), and the efficacy of force.These three dimensions are designed to capture the nature of the strategic environment.They produce a continuum spanning from hard realpolitik to soft idealpolitik. Strategic options, or actual grand strategy, should flow logically from a state's strategic paradigm, spanning offensive, militaristic strategies to accommodationist, diplomatic approaches. Setting the notion of strategic culture aside, the key issue raised is how to operationalize the dependent variable, strategic choice or response.The typological approach ties different strategy types primarily to how the threat is defined. It seeks to expand the conceptualization of the threat beyond zero-sum-variable

sum dichotomy so that we do not lose the richness of grand strategy content. See Alastair Iain Johnston, 'Thinking About Strategic Culture', *International Security* 19/4 (Spring 1995) pp.46–9.

87. George Bush, *The National Security Strategy of the United States* (Washington DC: The White House 1990) p.7.
88. Fred C. Bergsten, 'The Primacy of Economics', in Eugene R. Witkopf (ed.) *The Future of American Foreign Policy* (NY: St Martin's Press 1994) p.96.
89. Paul Kennedy, 'American Grand Strategy, Today and Tomorrow: Learning from the European Experience', in Kennedy, *Grand Strategies in War and Peace* (note 25) p.184.

4

Technology's Knowledge Burden, the RMA and the IDF: Organizing the Hypertext Organization for Future 'Wars of Disruption'?

CHRIS C. DEMCHAK

a collection of data is not information
a collection of information is not knowledge
a collection of knowledge is not wisdom
a collection of wisdom is not truth[1]

Today we can compensate
for the lack [of strategic resources]
by projecting ...not troops but
by projecting effects...[2]

I. CHANGING TOWARDS NETWORKS AND THE US-DEFINED RMA MODEL

The 'Revolution in Military Affairs' (RMA) has become synonymous with the highly networked use of advanced information technologies (IT), the associated emerging doctrine of information warfare (IW), and the more basic use of networks in information operations (IO). In dealing with complex technologies, however, one cannot separate the technology from the organization using it. The two form a socio-technical system such that, the more integrated the technical applications across an organization, the more the technology's own design, use, maintenance and vulnerability characteristics drive human organizational responses.[3]

For an implementation of the RMA model to succeed, it must adequately acknowledge the dynamic interactions among the elements of this never-before implemented design for organized activity. The key elements include not just the hardware ('artifacts'), and software and associated use rules ('technique'), but also organizations (people and associated processes, rules and distribution of latitude), the relevant cultural social constructions (meanings and values), and the crystallizing futures conceptions (leaders' expectations, policy preferences and visions). This mix is dynamic and difficult to predict in advance, save in general trends. The system under construction is complex and such systems are strongly dependent on initial conditions. A fixation with the capabilities of hardware platforms and associated networks encourages surprise outcomes in its neglect of the other elements such as human processes, social constructions, and expectations.

The RMA debate in the United States has increasingly defined a model of a modern information-enabled military that is heavily focused on the hardware and software elements. In particular, it is a highly integrated but small professional force in which all the elements of the technology are highly synchronized in their actions by an overlain 'system of systems'.[4] This combination of large-scale intricately networked powerful computer grids, highly accurate real-time standoff weapons, and professionalized highly skilled people trades away expensive conventional force structure for promise of information operations that assure 'battlespace dominance'.[5]

The great lure of the RMA model is that it comprehensively integrates new technologies to provide critical knowledge in unprecedented abundance and at an expected cost considered low by historical standards and offers small standing forces, quick resolution of any hostilities and very low expected casualty rates. Much of what we consider characteristic of militaries, such as drill and redundancy, are evolved responses to a likely lack of accurate knowledge in time to act successfully.[6] Anything that seems to reliably provide this much sought information at an affordable cost induces strong pressures for change in the foundations of modern militaries. In particular, today's westernized democracies increasingly include any loss of friendly life as unacceptable.[7] A large selling point of the RMA-associated technologies is that their long-range reach endangers dramatically fewer friendly soldiers or 'innocent' casualties on both sides.[8]

While skeptical in language and in pronouncements, Israel's military leaders have found it difficult to resist the RMA's promises for Israel – a small nation where knowledge in advance and acquired at a distance is exceptionally critical to compensate for extremely limited strategic depth and many potentially hostile neighbors acquiring ballistic missiles.[9] The

RMA military's vast information networks transmitting by satellite also promise real-time knowledge during battle, something the Israelis have rarely had historically.[10]

Furthermore, during crises and hostilities, the Clausewitzian fog of war can be viewed as really a lack of timely, accurate knowledge. The RMA promises Israel's defenders a possible edge in crisis management given the possibility of manipulating transparency misperceptions during snowballing events. Since the 1991 Gulf War was portrayed as the new age in electronic warfare,[11] a rudimentary RMA model has become so attractive that it is increasing being accepted globally as the defining model of what is possible and even expected of militaries in the future.

For Israel, the US and others, however, the difficulty is that complex technical networks impose a sticky expensive 'knowledge burden' on using organizations. That is, the requirement to have the precisely correct knowledge at exactly the right place and time when needed, or surprises will send ripples through the highly integrated processes of the large-scale system. While this knowledge can come in many forms from humans to software to hotlinked manuals, it has to be there when the initiating surprises occur. That level of precision – so valuable when it works well – is the Achilles heel of complex large-scale systems, and imposes the major elements of risk and cost over the lifetime of these systems.

Furthermore, due to the need to fully construct the system before one can see its operations clearly, one cannot adequately test for these surprises in advance of implementation. Such implementation is not inexpensive and there is much we do not know about linking and using all these systems. The risk of 'artifactual success but system failure' is not insignificant.[12, 13]

A similar challenge is found in the corporate business world's turn from the 1980s focusing on evolutionary change promoted by the Japanese examples such as 'total quality management' (TQM) to the more dramatic 1990s reorganization that both streamlines and integrates all functions simultaneously. This often-traumatic sea change is called 'business process reengineering' (BPR) and it usually involves what are called 'enterprise-wide' information system applications that control all the other subordinate systems. More recently, companies with a very ambitious survival and expansion plan turn to a complete integration of their activities by engaging in 'enterprise resource planning' (ERP), using a BPR to produce an enterprise-wide system.

Other than semantic differences, the IT-enabled BPR and the associated ERP are integral to the RMA military being pursued by the US defense establishment and for much the same reasons: cheaper, faster, more productive (in marketplace or battle) and more control throughout the system. Like the RMA model, the ERP process engages in knowledge management (KM) intensely. It closely couples all processes, often using such processes as 'just-in-time' (JIT) logistics to keep inventory costs to a minimum. Unfortunately for the RMA designers, the record of business experience is not encouraging. While there are some remarkably successful BPRs that integrated large corporate structures effectively, some 80 per cent of BPRs fail.[14] While there may be many reasons for the failure of the RMA-equivalent in the business world,[15] a good portion of these have been due to a failure to understand the firm's initial conditions across all the elements of this socio-technical system right from the outset, especially the knowledge burden.[16]

A further complication is that these failures occurred in organizations able to operate daily in their core competencies; they were most likely to have tested all their functions frequently. Most militaries rarely actually use all of their systems because battles are simply infrequent. Hence, a direct translation of the enterprise-wide system from the commercial world to the IT-enabled modernized military is highly problematical but it is at the heart of the RMA image being promoted by the US.

This contribution builds on this understanding of the knowledge burdens inherent in constructing and operating large-scale technical systems such as the one embedded in the RMA and on the experiences already demonstrated by the corporate and computer business world to explore the implications of an RMA implementation in the Israeli Defense Forces (IDF).[17] Calling this transition a 'revolution in security affairs', Cohen, Eisenstadt and Bacevich argue that the IDF will not fully copy the US RMA model but, rather, muddle through into something very Israeli as both internal effectiveness and external political pressures channel the organization's future paths. Furthermore, they argue that Israel is handicapped in that it must maintain four types of military that overlap somewhat but pose conflicting demands on future paths.[18] This work uses a knowledge-centric approach to address the knowledge requirements of a full implementation of an RMA 'BPR' in Israel first and then its implications for conventional deterrence, surprise, stability, and IDF structural options.

While echoing many of the observations of the observations of Cohen, Eisenstadt and Bacevich, I suggest that there does exist a less socially traumatic version of a modern networked military that may resolve the need for four different kind of forces as identified by Cohen *et al.* while not dangerously mimicking the US-defined RMA's elements. With an explicit recognition of the role of information in the design of the new forces, I propose a militarized variation of the 'hypertext organization' proposed by Nonaka and Takeuchi.[19] The military version integrates information databases as an organizational player called the 'Atrium' – both a real and virtual space that acts through, and with, the members of the organization. This socio-technical design is not only possible with today's data mining techniques but it is also organizationally better suited to Israeli conditions than the US's RMA model.

II. DEFINITIONS: IW, RMA, AND A GLOBALLY DIFFUSING MODEL OF MODERN MILITARY AS WEB-BASED SOCIO-TECHNICAL SYSTEM

The major premise of this work is that a successful IW-enabled, RMA-oriented, or fully modernized military will be a deliberately designed socio-technical system that is necessarily web-browser based, graphically client-server indifferent, and critically dependent on novel understandings of knowledge-management. Not all organizations can be equally receptive to the socio-technical demands of IW. It is therefore necessary to understand how these demands are refracted in requirements for knowledge management, networks, and web technologies in Israel.

A. RMA and its Close Associate – Information Warfare

The dominant model for a 'modern' military is emerging through the United States military's 'Revolution in Military Affairs' (RMA) continuing debate and enactment in the US force structure.[20] The 'revolution' is ill defined, but is emerging as a rough social consensus on what constitutes a modern military. The US Department of Defense's Office of Net Assessments defines RMA as 'a major change in the nature of warfare brought about by the innovative application of technologies which, combined with dramatic changes in military doctrine and operational concepts, fundamentally alters the character and conduct of operations'.[21] In 1996 and in 1997, the United States Joint Chiefs of Staff published two documents capturing their consensual image of information warfare and what kind of organizational functions will be available with the move to this new kind of warfare: 'Joint Vision 2010'[22] and 'Concept for Future Joint Operations'.[23] Together these capture the imagery of the future structure, capabilities, operations, and potentials for success that the senior leaders want to guide the evolution of the current force into an information era military.[24]

Over the years since the 1991 Gulf War, this RMA has increasingly become more defined in its attributes. The US militaries' stated goal is to modernize into rapidly deployable forces using advanced IT, becoming smaller, more highly skilled, faster, more flexible, and putatively much more lethal.[25] A major assumption underlying the American pursuit of information warfare technology is the following: once the ability to acquire, move around, and store information in great volumes and speed exists, then a military will at all levels be able to effectively sift that information and convert it to knowledge. RMA militaries in principle collect, manipulate and use digitized information so effectively that what they are able to conduct 'information war' (IW) or, more recently, 'information operations' (IO).[26, 27]

It depends on information far beyond knowledge – the right information with the right amount of precision in the right modality with the right amount of time to apply the correct electronic or other response. 'The RMA transforms time and space... Such forces can scan the battlespace looking for targets, sift through large amounts of data looking for high priority battlespace knowledge and strike whichever enemy poses the most urgent threats ... To achieve this, the RMA exploits communications to link all echelons, computers both powerful and proliferated, big but accessible data banks, fast displays, highly sophisticated and integrated sensors, and software that yields an intuitive grasp of the battlefield.'[28]

Second, it is further presumed that the necessary knowledge will be available, given the right choice of sensor technology, and with fast communications, it can be expected to arrive in advance of its need and therefore enable the military to act equally rapidly. A corollary to the first two assumptions is that unnecessary functions, forces, supplies and activities can be identified and efficiently purged from the operations and perhaps the entire force, cutting 'waste' and becoming 'lean and mean'. These advantages are further predicated on enhanced control over resources, and the accurate, rapid way in which these resources can then be managed. This ability to command more quickly and accurately and to control more precisely will, it is presumed, automatically provide dominant advantages over any foe.[29]

Key to this image of future operations are the rapidity and near instantaneous character of deployment actions, the lack of need for force structure called 'mass', and pinpoint accuracy of information, targeting, and delivery of lethal power.

> *Information superiority and advances in technology* will enable us to achieve the desired effects through the tailored application of joint combat power. Higher lethality weapons will allow us to *conduct attacks concurrently that formerly required massed assets*, applied in

a sequential manner. With precision targeting and longer-range systems, commanders can achieve the necessary destruction or suppression of enemy forces with fewer systems, thereby reducing the need for time-consuming and risky massing of people and equipment. …Providing *improved targeting information directly to the most effective weapon system* will potentially reduce the traditional force requirements at the point of main effort.[30]

This image is consistent through several years of iteration. In 1994, then US Army Chief of Staff General Gordon Sullivan stated,

digitalization of the battlefield – the electronic linking of every weapon system in the Battlespace – [which] will allow the commander to synchronize all the elements of combat power … [to] simultaneously prepare, execute and recover from operations very, very quickly … [and instead of] huge stockpiles, … to anticipate and respond just in time to sustainment requirements. …Battle command will be based on …a near-perfect appreciation of the real situation.[31]

The Joint Vision 2010 document reinforced this assumption of near-perfect level of knowledge acquisition and use across all military elements, stating that the desired level of 'command and control, [will be] based on fused, all-source, real-time intelligence [which] will reduce the need to assemble maneuver formations days and hours in advance of attacks'.[32] Across the various documents and time, then, is the enduring presumption that information technologies will provide real-time organization-wide distribution of accurate and appropriate knowledge. Whatever else IT may or may not do, that constitutes a fundamental element of this new military: the rapid, accurate, widespread dispersion of knowledge.

These presumptions about information technologies (IT) have changed the battlefield to 'battlespace' in the symbolic language of modernizing military organizations as well. Called IW or 'information warfare' in US defense circles, the globally integrated networks bouncing off satellites and moving vast volumes of data are often heralded as a great compensator for the unknowns of military operations. An early US Army planning document stated bluntly, 'the future battle enabled by IW innovations will be multidimensional, simultaneous, non-linear, distributed, precise, and integrated, and will be undertaken by fighting organizations variously described as small, task-force oriented, and highly networked for maximum speed and efficiency'.[33]

In the promotional literature, IW is presented extremely broadly, largely as armies of military personnel using computers, linking to an extraordinarily powerful computerized network, performing real time data transfers, perhaps breaking into another computer system with the aim of disrupting files or operations, and protecting against unauthorized users in their own systems, as well as collecting information from vastly different sources and applying the results to real time, extremely lethal, accurately targeted destructive sorties. The general focus in the literature is on the product – using information to distress an opponent and avoid similar disruptions. One writer long associated with the topic has gone so far as to publicly declare information warfare in progress, stating 'the United States is at war...a prelude to global information warfare'.[34]

The difficulty here is that IW needs more precise organizational definitions. It is more than merely extremely fast data transfers and protection against hackers.[35] In 1994, a senior US Army officer stated: 'As was the case in Desert Storm, victory will be determined in many cases by which side has the best electronics.'[36] But the 1991 Gulf War was not a particularly electronic war, except on the side of the Allies who needed electronics to run their own complex systems.[37] Gross, brutal, effective war can still be waged with little information, not much knowledge, and piss-poor targeting, if the weapon is sufficiently large and the desire to destroy sufficiently indiscriminate. IW is also less than everything computerized. IW cannot not be present merely if anyone in the military uses a computer or is linked to an email network.[38] Nor is it largely the act of hacking into another computer system to disrupt files or widespread social threats to all computer systems.[39] It is more and less than 'an electronic conflict in which information is a strategic asset worthy of conquest or destruction'.[40]

For the purposes of this work, I define information warfare organizationally and confine it to defense-related organizations. At the end of the day, organizations fight wars, not generals, artifacts, or small cohorts of people. Only organizations can proceed successfully through increasingly complexifying spectrum of war from rest or *preparing* to fight, through *peacekeeping* to *peacemaking* to, finally, *prevailing* destructively in a nation-state conflict. Furthermore, information warfare plays a decisive but not exclusive role in John Boyd's now famous OODA loop which is today commonly called the 'decision cycle'.[41] One may argue that the first three elements of the loop – Observe, Orient, Decide – are more strongly dependent on information than the fourth – Act – which is what organized humans just past the point of decision actually do with knowledge.

Thus, information warfare is more usefully defined as a strategic, operational or tactical option available commensurately with the organization's capability to covertly or overtly disable, divert or destroy another organization's ability to process and disperse information into timely and accurate knowledge or to accommodate the surprises of complex large-scale systems, while successfully protecting its own set of these abilities. In particular, successful IW relies on the accurate socio-technical organization of knowledge – that is, the right information with the right amount of precision in the right modality or format for absorption with the right amount of time to apply the correct electronic or other response. In short, IW like the effective application of all other advanced technologies depends as much on the organization of the people around the artifacts than on the quality of the artifacts themselves.[42] Not all organizations can be equally receptive to the socio-technical demands of IW. It is therefore necessary to understand how these demands are refracted in requirements for knowledge management, networks, and web technologies in Israel.

B. Model Diffusion among Global Militaries, Israel Included

The importance of such commonly held images of the 'modern military' via the IW and RMA discussions and promotion for the future composition of the global military community cannot be overstated. In large organizations, published statements do more than merely meet the need of legislative reporting requirements; they are an essential mechanism of communications from the institutional level of the organization to guide the overall directions of the decisions taken among dispersed organizational managers.

Furthermore, these images are guiding the expectations and proposals of the multitude of external actors dependent on organizational actions such as defense contractors, neighboring and allied militaries, and other organizations needing to coordinate their actions with the general directions of the US military services.[43] Hence, inevitably such statements ripple through the interconnected defense community to alter its evolutionary vector in some measure. Promoting globally by the unique transparency of the model of the modern military promulgated by the US Army, this emergent 'model' of a new military has become an evolving international image of an all-purpose, highly scalable, fully informed, tightly networked human machine of unprecedented range, accuracy, speed, and lethality – forces that are 'rapidly tailorable, rapidly expansible, strategically deployable and effectively employable… in all operational environments'.[44]

As a result, such statements are defining the basis of an emergent international social construction of a modern military and the consequent increasing structuration of the global military community. A 1996 General Audit Office report asserted that over 100 nations were planning modernization of their militaries.[45] In September 1996 using more stringent coding than GAO, I identified 50 modernizing states. In 1997, this number had increased by 36 per cent to 68 nations, or a third of the world's military community.[46]

While militaries have always copied each other, it is unprecedented to have countries as disparate on a similar and relatively simultaneous evolutionary path, especially with a focus on having small and nonconscript forces.[47] A process has accelerated among the world's militaries especially over the past five years, redefining the taken-for-granted minimum in military capabilities to mean intensive use of IT and precision munitions. As a result, military leaders are not seeking these capabilities to meet objective or potential security threats,[48] but rather because they view such an IT-intensive, small, professional military to be the norm for the twenty-first century. Barring another measure of preparedness for all eventualities, the level of modernization becomes the major measure of potential effectiveness against possible foes and prestige among key referent groups.[49]

This diffusion is not based on organizational capabilities or experience. It is spreading unlike traditional relation-based theories of diffusion in a global pattern that appears similar to what Strang and Meyer have labeled 'diffusion by theorizing' actions and then actors.[50] Because of the US worldwide promotion of these new 'systems of systems', smaller countries have begun to 'theorize' about how modern war is conducted ('actions') and how modern military actors may have capabilities equivalent to much larger countries.[51] Hence, one may argue that this model of a modern military appears to offer leveling opportunities that are said to be cheaper than larger traditional forces while equally effective. This social construction presents a great incentive to seek modernization wherever one can and in whatever measure without regard to actual organizational requirements of that modernization.

First, this model has some particular characteristics based on the US experience. Highly integrated battlefield platforms and battle management systems are characteristic of this model. Second, conscription is viewed automatically as 'nonmodern' at best and an asset-draining legacy at worst. Third, military formations in the reserves are viewed as largely a necessary but expensive, nonmodern conventional backup system. Professionalism in smaller more readily deployable units is a hallmark of this mode, along with centralized visibility of all operational events. Hence, even nations that do not need such forces by relatively objective assessments of their strategic situation but want to be seen as 'modern' in their national security apparatus have begun to dismantle traditional elements such as conscription, a large reserve system and nonintegrated weapons platforms.

C. The Knowledge Burden of the RMA's Large-Scale Technical System (LTS)

The RMA has, at its core, a technology driven transformation of military organizations into large-scale highly synchronized systems using intricately and far ranging networked computer technologies.[52] In the United States, this has become captured by the term 'system of systems' indicating a massively integrated overarching network of computer networks that are equally facile in acquiring, providing, and processing real-time information for nearly instantaneous long-range actions.[53] It is an overwhelming venture.

With a smaller force lacking the redundancy of large standing forces, an RMA requires a profound and unprecedented transformation in militaries, if it is to be accomplished successfully.[54] The complexity of the networked technologies force new organizational designs that emphasize 'synchrony', that is, the elements moving in tightly coupled closely coordinated, extremely rapid operations. While this vision of an invincible human machine has been dreamt of and even attempted by countless military commanders, only now with massive computerization and the 'death of distance' through networks can it seem to be possible to know enough to make the vision real.[55]

1. NETWORK – WEB TECHNOLOGIES KEY TO NEW MODEL

Achieving an all-purpose, highly scalable, fully informed, tightly networked human machine of unprecedented range, accuracy, speed, and lethality requires extraordinary geographical reach, rapid absorptive capacity, and surprise-mitigation in a social system. To get information reliably across distances requires electronic (or future equivalent) networks. To present the information for rapid and accurate find, access and absorb operations across a multitude of different terminal and human filtering characteristics requires quickly interpreted iconography and client-server independent graphical mechanisms. Humans with different linguistic and psychological filters interpret and absorb graphical information more rapidly and accurate than text data. Finally to make this exchange as timely for the local situation as needed requires a continuously and simultaneously available many-to-many format with the organizational emphasis on real-time updating, refreshing and refining of material.

Web technologies are integral to this modernization in the model and its implementation. They are also a medium for supporting the diffusion. The world wide web offers the description of how such a military should be constructed as found on the US military's 1,500–2,000 websites. Surprisingly, however, it also offers a window on how ready the recipient military is to implement this model. Military services, even the most secretive such as the Israeli Defense Forces, are coming up on the web and, in the process, also revealing how receptive they are internally to implement a nontraditional web-oriented organization necessary for the emergent model of a modern military.

The new model clearly involves widely shared knowledge and, by implication, the new approach to knowledge management. In complex systems, effective systems fit depends on knowledge both reliably accurate, extremely rapidly and widely disseminated and, importantly, requires that the people at the nodes are able to acquire and know how, when and when to use the knowledge pumped through these networks. In the American image, this volume of information is constant, seamless and intensely active, linking sources from overhead unmanned aerial and satellite sensors to the infrared night vision device of the individual solder, from the massive data maps in the Pentagon to the full color near real-time battle map display of the rugged laptop of the tank commander, to the deployed US streamlined IW forces which will operate quickly, accurately, lethally. These forces will be protected against enemy jamming, logic bombs, sniffer programs, herf guns (variation of jamming) or computer worms while able to impose the same and much, much more in direct explosive material on opposing forces.[56]

The new military model intrinsically requires the attributes of web technologies – geographically networked, graphically interfaced, and terminal independent, and continuously available to multiple simultaneous accessors, as well as a new approach to knowledge management. Organizations will need to be widely familiar with these technologies – and routinely adapted to them – in order to operationally achieve effectiveness in becoming a 'modern' military on this model.[57] Not understanding these organizational requirements while modernizing into this model risks dangerous mismatches between operational orders and actual organizational capabilities. In particular, these networks need to be established, effectively used and maintained for real-time accessibility even before hostilities begin, not retained and energized just when hostilities are imminent as traditional militaries operate.

2. PROBLEMATICAL NETWORKS AND LARGE-SCALE TECHNICAL SYSTEMS

Just as knowledge is the savior, however, it is also a burden to ensure its availability. The artifacts and technique of advanced information systems cannot effectively perform without the critical knowledge at the right time in the right organization to provide that knowledge.[58] The difficulties for the global military community in this sea change search for modern capabilities lie in what is clear from the promotional literature – that the new model of a military is an incredibly rapid, accurate, lethal, and small set of networked systems that are crucial. What is implicit or omitted from the discussion is that these systems are complex and dependent on web-based technologies in which the more integrated the system, the greater the surprise potential simply from the intricacies of the systems themselves. This section addresses how introduction of networked technologies into military functions will affect their effectiveness across the full spectrum of operations using the RMA's IW options.

For most of the past 200 years of western development, technology was presumed to be a net benefit for the using organization and, as Marx once argued, historically inevitable.[59] A network is a system characterized by a set of nodes linked by a set of relationships of a specified type and these networks are built on loci of human-oriented activity to provide the substrata of all complex socio-technical systems.[60] However, yet undeveloped is a robust theory stating the rules by which a network emerges and continues to exist.[61] Only in recent years has it become clear that large interdependent social systems tied increasingly by technical artifacts in large, generally computer-networked systems have been emerging. The difficulty is that a network is not like an organization in that it does not have to have a discernible boundary, defined rules for membership, or some expression of purpose to exist[63] and the scholarly study of the relationship between technology and organizational structures, risks, and survival is still developing.[62] For lack of a better term, these emergent compilations of human-machine networks have been labeled 'large-scale technical systems' (LTS).[64]

What is known is that a technology's 'material aspects' have an immediate effect on the 'nonrelational' work of an organization and, over time, these effects are mediated by the roles and social networks of the organization.[65] Over time, these mediated effects alter the structure of the organization as shared daily practices become taken for granted and eventually formalized.[66] Seminal network research on technology in civilian organizations suggests close attention to the initial conditions when introducing technologies, especially the social relations physically and cognitively experienced in the transition.[67] Recognizing that such large systems can manifest 'artifactual success combined with system failure',[68] scholars in this new field focus on the conditions under which these systems impose risks on unwitting organizations and their societies.

Large-scale technical systems (LTS) share several characteristics with the US-defined RMA model. Formerly independent technologies are combined to form an even larger technological system with relatively high levels of interdependence, differentiation and components and, often, relatively high requirements for precision in system interactions. Usually there is a central controlling entity but its reach may or may not be equally strong throughout the LTS. The components do not have to be in a formal hierarchical relation with each other, only a functional need for each other that spills over into ever more tightly coupled relations. As scholars have noted over time, the LTS is more organic than mechanistic in its development. That is to say, the LTS organizations seem to acquire life-like attributes, growing, changing their environments directly or indirectly, and, occasionally dying. The larger the system, the more it appears to be self-organizing as would any complex system and often self-developing.[69]

In the civilian world, these enlarged systems tend to become essential artifacts of their associated human makers, operators and beneficiaries, and begin to pose operational risks seen and unseen. As complex systems, their structural connectivity assures rogue outcomes and surprises periodically. The more critical their full functioning to the wider system, the more likely undampened deviations or rogue outcomes can have far-reaching disruptive consequences. For example, several years ago, a switching failure due to new software in the ATT telephone system shut down wide regions of the Midwest telephone communications for hours. In the worst conceivable cases, as disparate elements form an LTS, their rapid mutually dependent operations become so automatic and complex that nonobvious internally derived rules drive events out of individual human or external policy control. Under these circumstances, small-probability-large-consequences events can unpredictably cascade into major disasters such as the one at Bhopal or massive disruptions such as catastrophic electrical outages across large distances. Under these circumstances, accommodating such events needs to be a major focus of organizational design.

Studies of networks as well as complexity, therefore, reinforce the adage that, what militaries do in peacetime, they will necessarily revert to in wartime when surprised and stressed. Using information warfare then as an organizational design goal and as an operational option depends critically on how it is practiced in the lowest levels of operations as well as the highest.

3. COMPLEXITY, SURPRISE, LARGE-SCALE SYSTEMS AND KNOWLEDGE
   MANAGEMENT

Given the preceding discussion, what militaries are doing in peacetime can differ from what their leaders think the organizations are capable of doing. It is not merely that the RMA's level of synchronization might impose surprise, but that the level of complexity insures this development. What matters is the extent to which an understanding of this inevitability guides the initial design of the organization. In essence, a full implementation of the RMA 'system of systems' imposes an extensive knowledge burden for the using organization. This section reviews the essential terms behind this understanding.

Complex machines embody knowledge[70] and organizations need to be explicitly orchestrated with this knowledge burden in mind. Sophisticated or complex machines are not inherently pernicious to organization. When the surprises inherent in complex systems are accommodated through the explicit inclusion of slack – usually as redundancy, complexity is unlikely to have widely rippling deleterious organizational effects. If the information embedded in the machine is scarce in the wider society, the machine or network will be more expensive initially, as will its diagnosis, repair, training, parts and operating skills. These scarcities are a large part of the knowledge burden of the machine. A 'knowledge burden' is the amount of information that is needed to assure that critical outcomes of the system are not surprises.[71]

'Complexity' as an analytical term represents the complex relations within a system.[72] At some point unpredictable in form and/or frequency, the mass of varying relationships in a complex system[73] undermines even the most careful programming of every component. For humans in or dependent on the system, this outcome invokes feelings of being surprised, of being unprepared for the event(s). The importance of complexity and its inherent surprises is relative to the critical knowledge available about the system, that is, the difficulty knowing what will come of multiplying internal relations. The greater the complexity of the system, the greater the knowledge burden involved, namely, the more knowledge needed to run, support or replace it. The more complex the system, the greater the amount of information needed, especially when surprising outcomes occur.

There is no absolute threshold separating the simple from the complex. The level of complexity in any system is suggested by comparison with other organizations or itself in the past. The more complex the system, the larger the values are for its parameters, that is, greater numbers, differentiation and interdependence in the system – the more networked the system, the more likely the nodes and links are increasing the objective complexity of a given set of machines. In any system, some outcomes will always remain unknown ('knowable unknowns') and the rest because they are simply not knowable in advance ('unknowable unknowns'). In a complex system, the number of these unknowable unknown outcomes will be higher than known outcomes than in a more simple system. They are also more likely to be disruptive because the complex system is more tightly coupled internally.[74]

The greater the number of essential relations among a large number of components, the greater the likelihood of improbable events – 'deviant amplitudes' – rippling through the system and producing an unpredictable outcome (or 'dynamic instabilities').[75] The more tightly coupled the system,[76] the effect cascades as minor variations sum unpredictably into an unforeseen outcome that is as likely to be undesirable as desirable. This point in the evolution of the system has been called the 'threshold point' in the general systems literature or the 'edge of chaos' in the chaos literature.[77]

This set of undesirable unknowns, called here the 'rogue' set, produces unpleasant surprises for users of complex equipment.[78] Both machines and organizations are systems with rogue sets. The rogue set can be reduced by research that reveals the form and frequency of previously unknown outcomes. However, something must be done to avoid or mitigate these unpleasant outcomes before the rogue set can be truly reduced or, 'accommodated'. Extensive sensor sets inside a network or on a battlefield perimeter are conceptually similar efforts to acquire knowledge to reduce the rogue set.

If the tight coupling is reinforced in the design of the organization, only greater knowledge lessens the effects of rogue outcomes, either by revealing the form or frequency of some previously unknown outcome or by guiding the systems' responses accurately. Whether an uncertainty concerns the specific form or the actual frequency of an occurrence will have an effect on the nature of the accommodation required. For example, if the undesirable outcome is destruction of grain in a warehouse, if the rogue outcome is either marauding rats or deer that will only come at foreseeable intervals, then obstacles or deterrents that work at least once against each and can be replaced easily are necessary. If, however, it is certainly rats but they could arrive unexpectedly, then the obstacles or deterrents will have to be tailored to rats and reinforced for multiple, unforeseeable attacks. It is, of course, most difficult to accommodate undesirable outcomes when both form and frequency are unknown. If the form is known, then redundancy in the inventory of knowledge relevant to those outcomes is preferred. If only the frequency of disruptions is likely, then slack – which entails loosening the coupling among elements and may include redundancy – is preferred as an initial accommodation mechanism.[79]

Both slack and redundancy, however, are expensive. Constrained by operational, resource, and theoretical limits, an organization in a turbulent environment is likely to be unable to acquire all the knowledge it needs to maintain complex machine systems at peak operating synchronization. As a response, managers will increase the internal controls in compensation. Those efforts plus spontaneous informal adaptations will produce a more complex organizational network. The increase in organizational complexity means the organization itself now has a larger set of possible rogue outcomes. Especially damaged is the speed with which it can accurately respond to unpredictable crises in a highly uncertain environment. In responding to the rogue sets of complex machines, a constrained organization inadvertently increases its own rogue set. It becomes itself more complex and more prone to disruptive surprises. In short, the situation is one of a positive feedback cycle, initiated by the expensive unknowns of the complex network of organizational systems. Hence, knowledge structures and their implications need to be explicitly incorporated into the design of organizations from the outset to have robust and successful operations, not those plagued by rippling surprises due to unforeseen needs for knowledge.

Organizational design that is robust for surprises in a knowledge-intensive system incorporates slack in time or precision in processes or redundancy in elements that provide critical knowledge.[80] Militaries have traditionally chosen redundancy as the easiest way to accommodate surprise. In our work, that means a duplication of equivalent knowledge modalities at the time of need. For example, the US Army since World War II considered 100 per cent staffing of a unit to actually be 125 per cent because 25 per cent casualties were expected in any conflict.[81] Slack forces discontinuities in the organization's tight coupling that avert, reroute, mitigate, or ameliorate the deviant surprise event, dampening or stopping its ripple effects. In traditional systems, just as people are often the source of surprise events, they also form dampening agents for ripple effects by interrupting the automaticity of networked processes.

Key to knowing the amount of either redundancy or slack (which amounts to reduced automaticity) that will accommodate likely and unlikely surprises is trial and error in the organization under fully stressed conditions. For all their differences in approach,[82] the overlapping lessons of complexity theory and chaos theory are that both indirectly argue for trial and error learning in large systems, however expensive this form of accommodation.[83] In short, time occupied with trial and error learning is essential for mitigating surprise, especially rogue outcomes. In military terms, then, if the peacetime preparation operations do not enable trial and error of the operations intended for any other level of activity, then the organization is unlikely to be able to mitigate rogue outcomes when they emerge in these other activities. If the organization is not doing the activity in peacetime – and the more complex the activity, the more routinely performed it must be – then the organization is unlikely to be able to do it effectively under any other circumstances.

Complexity matters critically in this US RMA model because its initial approach to knowledge management given the likely burden is to limit slack and redundancy to speed up processes and reduce costs.[84] Effectiveness in these systems then is measured by the appropriate mesh of organizational knowledge, precision requirements and accommodation of surprise.[85] Since militaries cannot carry everywhere an extra set of everything, fully integrated and ready to be turned on, having mirrored all files, then slack must be built into the RMA military design. All complex systems, including organizations, are extremely dependent on initial conditions.[86]

In the US's RMA and its emergent notions of IW, there are three general issues particularly concerning information-technology (IT)-enabled militaries which touch directly on issues studied in complexity research.[87] These are (a) the physically and cognitively complex organizational interactions in a dynamic large-scale system, (b) the varying time requirements of pattern discernment and reconstruction in the successful military use of these systems, and (c) the differences between data, information, knowledge, and wisdom in accommodating surprise.[88] Put more baldly, the military uses of a fully implemented RMA stress the preciseness of the system's network flows, the smaller slack in transaction times, and accuracy in filtering for the right knowledge at the right place.

Unless redundancy and slack are deliberately designed into the human-machine mesh of the highly-synchronized RMA organizational design, the system will be highly brittle. Surprise is therefore encouraged in a system where the orchestration of elements form a whole which has a knowledge burden that the organization is unlikely to be able to accommodate.[89]

4. KNOWLEDGE BURDEN AND THE TRANSFORMATION INTO AN RMA MILITARY

Transformation of a military service into the US-defined RMA vision in particular, as stated by the Joint Chiefs, will be problematic both in operating and in the transition to operations. Trading information for mass force structure is more difficult than merely speeding up transfers of data. Surprise needs to be explicitly accommodated in complex systems and that understanding has not been adequately demonstrated in either the US's documents about the RMA nor in the publicly discussed Israeli moves towards adopting its key elements.

To be fair, there is a nascent appreciation of these information systems' peculiar conundrums in the US at the joint level and among several of the services. The Concept for Future Joint Operations (CFJO) begins with an assertion about operating in a holistic manner and ends with a second call for holistic integration. 'While technological innovation affords many advantages, it also increases our vulnerability if not advanced in a systematic, holistic manner.'[90] A list of vulnerabilities that follows this call for synthesis suggests that some of the authors knew of the difficulties of complex systems.[91]

However, the dominant metaphor remains mechanistic and oriented on combat applications of force at both the joint and service levels. The dominant attributes sought continue to be speed and accuracy as overarching values. The thinking is resolutely linear as well. 'Information superiority and the new concepts could greatly affect how the JFC [Joint Force Commander] arranges operations to achieve objectives. For example, a conflict that today might require committing US forces in distinct defensive and offensive phases might require only a single "decisive operations" phase in 2010...'.[92]

Furthermore, the US RMA model remains focused on the execution of operations, often in machine terms, to the exclusion of transition or pre/post crisis uses of these systems. Even the vulnerabilities listed do not address the possible peacetime uses of information technologies or critical transitional issues that the aperiodic cobbling of diverse systems will present. Innovative uses of information technology with peacetime potential are depicted solely in combat images such as attack rather than, say, manipulate or incentivize enemy organizational decisions.[93] Even the most explicit discussion of transition issues deals with the termination of hostilities, not the extraordinary task of melding these disparate services into such operations.

Even the metaphor 'plug and play' for blending forces en route to operation misses the difficulties of combining complex systems involving humans, expectations, and processes. For example, the key to integrating multinational forces is presented as having common electronic components in the networks. 'The 2010 JFC will be able to assimilate a wide variety of capabilities from across the joint community, including the RC, into the JTF [Joint Task Force] and employ them more quickly than today, much as emerging 'plug-and-play'[94] technology assimilates computer components for immediate use. These same benefits will also enhance the JFC's ability to operate within coalitions and actually integrate multinational forces into the JTF- common, relevant picture of the situation at any time.'[95] Finally, while much is said of common battle images and awareness, in depicting information superiority and its components, there is a consistent emphasis on the mechanisms or artifacts of information exchange, so-called 'pipeline over content'.

This consistent failing in the RMA model follows logically from a ubiquitous misunderstanding of the difference in complex systems between data, information, knowledge, and wisdom.[96] The CFJO acknowledges the first three types: data, information, and intelligence, but even the descriptions of these are themselves are phrased in mechanistic production language.[97] Complex systems are not easily captured in data streams meeting the specific needs of the user at the point of deployment or after. Data is merely numbers, information is numbers organized in groups, knowledge is information at the right time and place but wisdom is the ability to use knowledge prospectively despite dynamic and complex variables. The joint image focuses on such things as direct 'sensor-to-shooter' data streams. The difficulty with sensors is that they are mere pictures of actions, and cannot assess intentions or robustness of targets. Automaticity in real-time data can be misleading, even if taking from all conceivable aspects and resolutions at that moment. The RMA model neglects the fact that it is relatively easy to devise a scenario in which all the sensor pictures point in one direction but the actual intention of an enemy lies in another direction that only longer term study of the organization would have revealed. Predicting outcomes even roughly in complex systems involves the final level of knowledge development, wisdom. The current RMA model is unable to incorporate that developmental process in its emphasis on physical operations and pipeline automaticity in transferring data.[98] The likely knowledge burdens and surprise potential when such presumptions are embedded in the initial design of an implemented RMA will be daunting indeed.

III. IDF TRANSITION TO RMA – LUMPY, POLITICAL, TOSSED, AD HOC

The Israel Defense Forces' (IDF) leaders have now been iterating in its future visions towards embracing key elements of the US-derived RMA for more than a decade. The transformation of external national security conditions over the past 20 years in the MidEast have presented new threats to Israel, diminished others, and prompted this search for a new doctrine, organization, and overall strategy of defense. The internal societal changes have altered the premises on which the IDF can rely in its institutional mandate. In the midst of all these changes, the benefits implied in embracing the RMA military technologies are so profound that even cautious scholars are willing to consider giving up ground won and hallowed by Israeli blood – the Golan – in view of the presumed capabilities.[99]

A. Incorporating Key US RMA Elements into the IDF

In particular, three planned changes in the IDF indicate a transition to an RMA-like military along the American model.

The first is, of course, acquisition of the equipment as well as public statements by senior leaders attesting to a plan to 'modernize' with technical capabilities. The key arguments are the rise of standoff threats in the form of missiles held by potentially hostile states and, of course, the putative reduced costs of an RMA military.[100]

The second planned change is the move away from conscription. For a military seeking the US model, the arguments against total conscription mirror those of the US in its transition to an all-volunteer army, namely conscripts do not serve long enough to adequately train on highly technical equipment and hence are economically inefficient.

The third change is the development of an organizational structure that is no longer merely a peacetime cadre unable to act without the mobilization of reserves. This is coupled with a heavier reliance on technical sensors as a way to compensate for moving large reserve units to a second line of defense. After its near defeat in 1973, the IDF nearly doubled its size and redoubled its focus on technological warning systems and longer-range attack platforms.[101] As the IDF grew into a relatively large-scale organization, it began to take more and more of its cues from the only other successful large-scale force, that of the US. The subtle Americanization of the IDF's perspective underlies this transition to an RMA military.

1. ACQUIRING THE NETWORKS OF SYSTEMS

Since the mid-1980s, the IDF senior leadership has promised a leaner, less clumsy military organization that maintains its technological edge over its enemies. The IDF Chief of Staff in the late 1980s General Dan Shomron is credited with stating an intention to make the IDF 'smaller and smarter'.[102] The dragging war in Lebanon not only undermined the automatic support given the IDF by the wider society; it demonstrated serious shortcomings in the militia system itself for the defense of a modern Israel.[103] By the beginning of his tenure as Chief of Staff, General Ehud Barak (1992–94) stated an intention to have a more professional force.[104] Furthermore, by 1998, Israeli security scholars were declaring the superiority of the RMA technologies to have been demonstrated by the 1991 Gulf War.[105] By early 1999 in addition to advanced platforms such as Apache helicopters, American-like organizational structures were planned to be implemented in the IDF. These include a separation of the ground forces (GFA) from the air and naval forces and making the new GFA responsible for force development, not battle command, much like the US unified command structure. Also planned were the development of a light division with advanced battle management systems, and the elevation of the Operations Branch as a first among equals in the headquarters, all elements of the US RMA model.[106]

2. CLOSING THE 'SCHOOL OF THE NATION' TO TRAIN REGULARS

The commentaries and actions of senior IDF leaders portray conscripts as less and less desirable. The IDF increasingly accepts a multitude of reasons for non-service, especially from women. In an interview in 1992, a senior officer said his colleagues would get rid of all the young women if they could because the new IDF does not have jobs for all of them and they do not stay long enough to train for anything else but file clerks and coffee servers.[107] Indeed, since the early 1990s, desirable military specialties like military intelligence increasingly require training before actual conscription during the high school years if the conscript would like to have a choice of something interesting to do. By 1995, career personnel already constituted 40 per cent of the IDF. Not only were more of the available slots being targeted for professionals, officers were staying in longer and receiving more benefits to keep the uniform on for the long term.[108] By 1999, conscripts were explicitly being directed to less skilled and/or combat roles in order to free up slots for professionals.[109]

3. MINIMIZING THE 'PEOPLE'S MILITIA' AND CADRE FORCES FOR STANDING PROFESSIONAL UNITS

The average annual reserve duty has declined from a post 1973 high of roughly 45 days a year to considerably less than even the minimum two weeks required by the US military. By 1997, only 30 per cent of reservists were called to serve and many served only one day. The age at which combat reservists are eligible to be called to serve has been dropped to 45 years from the previous 53 and, in 1996, reserves constituted only 20 per cent of the active component, a considerably drop from the previous decades.

Furthermore, there has been a commensurate rise in the use and prestige of the special elite units whose officers have begun to dominate the thinking of the IDF. These units are made of conscript and professional volunteers and, spread across the services, they are used for special missions. Recently, these units have also seen a marked rise in the religious affiliations of these units in marked contrast to the majority secular population who would constitute the bulk of a reserve-based militia military.[110]

Increasingly then, while the language of senior officers supports a continuation of the conscript and reserve system, the reality of their actions says otherwise. Key elements of the US RMA – artifacts and networks, volunteers, and less reliance on nonprofessionals such as reserves – are being made hallmarks of the IDF's transformation into a more modernized military.

B. Israeli Context Advantages and Disadvantages for RMA Knowledge Burden

A successful fit of an organizational model, under these premises, begins with the inspection of the likely distribution of technological knowledge both outside and inside the organization.[111] The knowledge-conditions faced by the IDF may or may not support a full scale RMA design. For reasons other than the analysis presented here, IDF leaders seem to know fully copying the US model is not likely to be successful but neither can they demonstrate a consensus on an alternative suitable for their circumstances. Hence, whether implementing a full RMA or muddling through incrementally adopting parts of it, Israel is performing an organizational beta test. The likelihood of success depends heavily on the wider technological conditions that favor or hinder the provision of knowledge as required in a tightly coupled organization. This success is even more important given the intention of military leaders to construct an IDF that can, in the words of a senior commander, 'extract from the enemy such a severe price that they can't attack again'.[112] Another senior defense researcher and former military officer identified the promise of the RMA as the following: 'In the past in order to create that basic strategic resource that we lacked we had to project troops into enemy territory...Today we can compensate for this lack by projecting ... not troops but by projecting effects.'[113, 114]

But restructuring a militia force into a tightly coupled highly skilled real-time responsive force is, at the very least, challenging.[115] The following sections discuss the technical and other knowledge conditions favoring and hindering the successful transformation of the IDF into an RMA, given the society around it.

1. REQUIREMENTS FOR '24/7' KNOWLEDGE COLLECTION AND MANAGEMENT

Nations start wars but organizations fight them. More than ever since the industrial revolution, networked information systems profoundly embed large military organizations in the surrounding society 24 hours a day, seven days a week ('24/7') in peace as well as in war.[116] There is no real possibility of having a military institution of any reasonable size 'confined to barracks' in the emerging information era. Codified in the nascent notions of an RMA military, the knowledge requirements of the systems providing 'battlespace dominance' require use of the networks long before hostilities, though the offensive nature of these systems may be kept offline. Hence, although battle is infrequent, the monitoring of complex networks cannot be let go during times of peace, thereby pushing the operational boundaries between peace and war in electronic operations. The smaller size of the RMA military is a tradeoff for knowledge presumed to be instantly available. While not all the components of the systems of systems organization can be used during times of peace, their nodes and linkages must nonetheless be monitored internally for instantaneous use at all times. And so must those of potential enemies.

The kinds of comprehensive knowledge that must be collected in advance are daunting for any nation. In a nonlinear world of 'Information Dominance', key organizational attributes to track in addition to the traditional force structure capabilities include (a) operational trends in mission experiences, (b) normal error tendencies, (c) proactivity preferences, (c) essential gateways, and (d) the availability of substitutes.[117]

Operational trends are the historical trends of flexible use of information operations within recent institutional memory: under what conditions used and, among other questions, what percentage of the organization did what with information technologies.

Second, normal error[118] tendencies are the target organization's frequency of equivalent practice events (and their fidelity to real use) versus the likely ripple effects of errors in that organization's use of (including scale) information technologies.

Third, proactivity preferences are demonstrated in the level of the autonomous decisionmaking allowed subordinates and the likelihood of being proactive in response to individually perceived problems emerging from IT sources.

Fourth, essential gateways are the bottlenecks in the targeted organization's decisions (people, key sections or referent groups) and in the throughput of information assets to those who can alter the stream or social construction of information by direct access or by their response. Finally, the availability of substitutes captures how viable and rapid are the possible workarounds for the targeted organization in response to an overt or detected covert information-facilitated attack.[119]

The accuracy requirements of the RMA model's real-time responses tend to blur the operational distinctions between operating and not operating. For the purposes of avoiding failure (allowing the enemy forces to get far out of the barracks, for example), such organizations must logically try acquiring critical knowledge long before anything is deployed and in the format acceptable to the highly digitized elements of this force. Furthermore this level of collection is also necessary on the friendly organization as well as the likely targets, lest surprise from the sheer complexity of the networks either provide opportunities to enemies or simply disrupt friendly readiness catastrophically. The IDF has always collected information on its threats between any active hostilities but this level of continuous monitoring is unprecedented for the entire force.

2. KNOWLEDGE CONDITIONS WHICH FAVOR A SUCCESSFUL 24/7 INTEGRATION IN RMA IDF

When knowledge is scarce in a society, it is more likely to be expensive to purchase. As a result, highly budget-constrained organizations such as public agencies generally purchase only minimal amounts. The greater the availability of critical knowledge in the wider society, the more likely it will be affordable and then made available inside the organization. Under those circumstances, it is less likely that normal surprises will ripple as far through organizational processes.[120]

(a) Computer Knowledge Diffusing Rapidly throughout Israeli Society: Israel is one of the more internetted nations in the world. The per capita ownership of computers is extraordinarily high; in 1997 alone over 250,000 computers were sold in Israel, surpassing a number of European countries.[121] In just under four years, from 1996 to 2000, the number of domain sites in Israel has increased from 3,600 to nearly 27,000, an over sevenfold rise across the nation in the basic elements of networked computer use.[122] Domain names are themselves used by a multitude of subordinate users, making exact numbers of users difficult to determine. However, surveys taken in 1997 and again in early 1999 suggest that computer use in Israel rose from four per cent of the population to about 11 per cent.[123] There is every reason to assume that percentage has at least doubled again by the writing of this work.

In contrast, aside from the United Arab Emirates (about 9 per cent mid-1999), none of Israel's potential regional competitors are above five per cent of the population in terms of computer use.[124] Israel's general familiarity in early 1999 exceeded two-thirds of greater Europe's 24 nations and of East Asia's 16 (those with known Internet use), as well as all of the Latin American nations.[125]

While general familiarity with computers is rising across the society, so is the diffusion of more technical knowledge. The graduation rate of computer engineers per capita is also impressive and has been impressive for more than a decade. In 1988, about 11 per cent of the labor force were first degree engineering graduates, surpassed only by Japan with 12 per cent and well above the US's 7 per cent.[126] By 1998, 26 per cent of university graduates were studying science related degrees including computer science while, in 1994–95, 28 per cent of university students graduated in nonmedical fields of study involving computers.

Finally, even in high schools, the percentage of students matriculating in science fields is high. In 1998, 83 per cent of Jewish graduating high school students included in their fields the matriculating certificate in electronic systems, a percentage higher than that of less technical fields such as history and literature –77 and 75 per cent, respectively.[127]

Furthermore, while service across the traditional military specializations – including the infantry – is losing popularity among the younger generation of Israelis facing their conscription period, positions involving training with computers are highly prized and much sought.[128] Military training on information systems is strongly associated with success in the commercial world. Adding to the attraction, several prosperous individuals in the Israeli IT industry point to their military computer training as seminal events in their personal development that aided their future success.[129]

In short, the knowledge essential to holding down surprises in a large technical computerized system is becoming less scarce in the wider society's knowledge base, on which future careers are founded. Recently an Israeli company announced the local development of a compact Internet access technology usable with cellular phones.[130] That level of commercially available sophisticated technology suggests network computerizing will be less expensive in principle. By drawing off this population pool, the IDF should find it easier to keep its complexly interrelated systems functioning and to be able to purchase greater redundancy in knowledge sources throughout the force.

(b) Widespread Acceptance of Civilian Behavioral Constraints for National Security: Israeli citizens grow up under behavioral constraints associated with continuous war in order to be prepared to act immediately. A small society with nearly no strategic depth, Israel's military response to

threats has required this level of constant tension in order to be both credible and effective. Israeli socialization towards making sacrifices for national defense while in civilian life is well established. From the two–three years in conscription to the 45 days a year spent in annual reserve duty that was standard 15 years ago to the ultimate sacrifice paid in battle by the reserve units of a cadre army, national service has been portrayed for years as an essential element to survival of the Jewish state.[131]

For an RMA army heavily invested in IW technologies, this situation is advantageous because the peace-war boundaries are blurred when information is one's first line of defense. It cannot be collected at the last moment and, for the kind of continuous monitoring and evaluating necessary to be effective in IW, this wider societal predilection is extremely valuable. There is less need to socially construct a positive image to constantly collecting information on enemy societies as well as organizations, even in minute details.

Furthermore, these activities are themselves less likely to be discussed. What is less well known outside of Israel is the equally almost automatic censorship of published work by Israeli military censors. Even the most adamant of opposition groups submit their work for review by military censors; the most progressive and left wing of newspapers will submit their copy for daily review and publish what is not crossed off by the censor.[132] This acceptance of such control on public debate in a democracy provides the emergent RMA socio-technical system with a greater capacity for imposing surprise on opponents electronically as well as tactically in hostilities.

Finally, the general acceptance of reserve duty creates a pool of skills not normally affordable to most militaries without paying contractor fees. For example, the IDF's own website was constructed initially by a reservist and continues to be maintained by a team of civilian computer specialists for whom this was also *pro bono publico* reserve duty. The general reduction in the use of the reserves since the onset of publicly displayed military budgets in the mid-1980s and comparable pay rules has forced a greater selectivity on the part of the IDF to use its reserve pay dollars more effectively. This has included negotiating for computer skills with reservists by positing interesting projects that normally would be unaffordable in military budgets.[133] It is the vast reserve system with its assumption of a long-term relationship that predisposes the reservist to be open to this negotiation and enables the visibility of such skills to the IDF negotiators.

This social construction of service to the military as a positive item helps the implementation of an RMA by making it commensurately more likely –

in principle – that the new RMA system will have the knowledge it needs where and where required.

(c) History of Innovation with Government Support and Direction: Israel's defense establishment is well known for its emphasis on innovation. This historically impoverished and demographically outnumbered state had to constantly seek a surprising technological edge to deter and, if necessary, defeat a numerically superior enemy. Early military leaders strongly wanted advanced weapon systems but were stymied by the pariah status of the nation and the Arab boycott. After the first large groups of Soviet advanced technologies began arriving in the region in the 1960s, this desire for a technological advantage accelerated and has continued through the succeeding years.[134] As a result, the early organizational focus was on increasing the inventory of well-known, often surplus equipment and piecing together, replacing or upgrading otherwise obsolete equipment in any way possible and affordable to increase and improve the quality of the inventory. All militaries recover enemy equipment from the battlefield if possible. The IDF turned this normal behavior into a fine art considered essential for survival.[135]

Furthermore, early national survival often directly depended on much trial-and-error learning, scraping together any workable alternative irrespective of the costs. Pre-independence underground factories of the 1930s and 1940s constructed mortars and artillery bit by bit in kitchens and sheds under intense British surveillance. This resulting culture of making-do has been transmitted to the government-owned military manufacturers who are generally the direct organizational descendants of these underground factories.[136] The post-independence factories specialized in finding innovative ways to upgrade obsolete foreign military systems or devising low cost alternatives.

Another acquisition innovation was the effort to remove and standardize subsystems across larger pieces of equipment such as tanks as a way to substitute for the lack of new equipment. Again, this modularity strategy was taken to a high level. Over time, while the inventory may have ballooned into 17 different types of tanks, many of these would have, for example, the same sighting subsystem.[137, 138] In the post-Cold War period, until the recent surge in information-enabled systems, Israeli manufacturers specialized in weapon system component design and construction and the incremental upgrading of systems, even those of Israeli origin.[139]

This early trial and error method allowed for considerable slack in integrating not only within nodes but also along linkages of the wider IDF systems. The modern IDF implementation of this trial and error learning is found in the tradition of testing new ideas in smaller isolated tests that do not leave the entire force unable to respond conventionally as needed. For example, the tendency is to try out new organizational ideas in small units that may or may not ever be integrated with overall force. This inclination towards innovation encourages the development of less expensive forms of knowledge needed especially at nodes within the wider system. To the extent that full synchronization of an RMA military can be interspersed with the traditional forms of IDF slack and component redundancy, then the IDF has a natural advantage in having the knowledge available to contain surprises to specific types of nodes or links.

3. KNOWLEDGE CONDITIONS WORKING AGAINST EFFECTIVE 24/7 KNOWLEDGE
    MANAGEMENT IN AN RMA IDF

The IDF cannot escape its cultural milieu in its organization, social constructions, and futures expectations. For all its vibrancy and innovativeness, Israeli culture is not inherently systematic. Research in international management confirms what scholars of public organization and of culture have observed. Israelis demonstrate both high levels of individualism and low power distance but also strong uncertainty avoidance.[140] When these individual tendencies to act without consulting others and to generally discount the judgments of those in authority positions are combined with a strong need for security, much activity is initiated suddenly and with small regard for overall plans and goals. Ad hoc responses as a management style are common throughout the wider society as a function of the circumstances of struggle for independence and then survival.[141] One senior officer noted that the planning arrangements of the 1970s and 1980s were 'casual'.[142] The chief scientist of a major Israeli satellite company recently commented that 'Israel doesn't know what process is.'[143]

In a military that is intimately intermingled with its social milieu then, such responses become commensurately taken for granted. If the widespread presumption is that some kind of attack is always imminent in unpredictable ways, then improvisation as a cultural norm is also consistent with a widespread military need to provide novel responses unpredictable in advance. These responses, however, pose exceptional difficulties for the full synchrony of an RMA military regardless of the knowledge available in the wider society.[144] Several elements are particularly problematical: the need for internal monitoring of the IDF itself as a complex system, privatization and its commodification of essential RMA knowledge, and the centralization tendencies of these enterprise-wide systems.

(a) Monitoring Comprehensively, Friends as well as Enemies: The RMA highly synchronized system requires constant monitoring of its elements for not only enemy induced problems but also for inherent surprises occurring naturally in large-scale complex systems. This is especially true if the force has been streamlined to a smaller professionalized organization with limited slack. For the IDF, the level of monitoring implied by the system of systems of the RMA military is extremely difficult to achieve across the entire force, even if it is considerably smaller than it is today.

First, the small community of scholars of Israeli administration who publish in English demonstrate a common assessment of Israeli administration as one that is highly personalistic, sets unrealistic but politically charged goals and implements them poorly, and is widely intermingled in all aspects of the society in this former socialist state.[145] Rosenbloom argues that divergent operating norms, values, and operating styles are typical for public administration in Israel and that a weak or missing ethic of public service is linked to a high degree of personalization and a low degree of formalization of roles and obligations.[146]

This situation is historically long-lived according to Caiden who characterized Israel's administrative culture as 'opportunistic dogmatism'.[147] Sharkansky argues that Israel's polity failed over 40 years of development to establish strong norms of neutral professionalism in its administration.[148] Sharkansky and Wrightson characterize the Israeli public administrative state (including the military) as 'overloaded'. Powerful, turf-protecting bureaucracies have poorly managed its extensive public enterprises and social services, politicized public sector employment, and produced a host of centrally-issued rules which are routinely evaded at the local level to produce ad hoc responses to emergent situations.[149]

Israel's military administration reflects these wider operating norms: improvisation, casual planning, inconsistent implementation, and extensive presumption of local autonomy. A retired senior Israeli general noted in an interview that Israelis were innovators, not maintainers, because of a general impatience with the kind of careful routine tasks involved.[150] For a highly synchronized RMA organization, these attributes are highly problematical. Inaccuracy in information collection or failure to note inconsistencies can be exceptionally costly if the entire force is transformed into a highly synchronized RMA military.

As peace arrangements are concluded with near neighbors, the likelihood of a large-scale conventional attack drops dramatically. Two other sources of disruptions, however, do not necessarily drop in possible consequence: sudden hostile actions by far neighbors and local dissenters, whether Arab or settlers. Because both sources are less likely to announce their arrival as would conventional forces, continuous and accurate monitoring of the IDF areas of concern becomes essential in order to trigger the nearly instantaneous response to either kinds of threat.

Because the general complexity of interpretations from enemy indicators changes with RMA, the monitors will also have to be highly skilled. A plethora of electronic indicators are not necessarily as unambiguous as those designed for conventional forces. It is one thing to have smooth sand borders that show footsteps and to know where to start tracking intruders, and quite another to have less obvious sensor indicators such as thermal heat indicators.[151] Cows as well as humans give off heat, for example. Under sophisticated attack or multiple source failures, computers themselves may often give only transient and easily overlooked indicators of the surprise to come. A bored computer scientist discovered a major intrusion in the late 1980s by happening to notice unexpected changes in the checksums of a network on which he worked.[152] Today, over 60 per cent of businesses report hacker attempts and some successful attacks. These statistics suggest there are real threats buried in the general inattentiveness of many business organizations.[153]

The refinement of these kinds of information into knowledge will require highly skilled individuals doing generally lower skilled and tedious monitoring of indicators continuously. Unfortunately, experience in the nuclear power industry in the US has shown that such people become bored easily and then do not monitor closely enough.[154] This has proven to be a grave challenge for the nuclear power industry and will prove an even graver one for the IDF. Monitoring is deadly dull in general, unless outside indicators suggest a reason that the monitoring will prove useful in the near term. A good example of how this may be experienced in the implementation of an RMA is the Israeli experience with the Chernobyl virus in April 1999. Although both the attack day and the antidote were widely available on the web long before the attack day, in Israel somehow the basic attentiveness waned in several major actors. Thousands of computer systems, a senior financial institution, an intelligence service, and a major Internet service provider nonetheless lost their computer systems.[155]

Furthermore, integrating all the information available through effective monitoring will prove daunting for this organization. Other than the operations of the Israeli Air Force (IAF) in combat missions and the individually unique operations of special forces units, there is little historical evidence of a wider IDF ability to integrate broad swathes of knowledge effectively across organizational, nodal, and modal boundaries in truly combined large-scale operations. IDF is already tightly coupled to the use of GPS – a system of satellites that provide the person on the ground with precise information on their location. The GPS links to a multitude of dependent systems – including precision-guided weapons and unmanned aerial sensors – anything that needs to know its own location, ranging from artillery to navigating in all environments.[156] It is simpler, however, to determine the reliability and availability of a satellite system's downlinks than it is to be sure of the reliable operation of a complex system integrating humans and complex nodes and links. The former involves only the first two elements of this system: the hardware (artifact) and software (technique), not the other three. Ensuring the reliability of the entire synchronized military system requires a level of sophisticated, comprehensive and continuous monitoring that is extraordinary for any nation, but especially so for such a young impatient culture.

Second, this monitoring must be imposed on family as well as enemies – tough again for a society in which strong clan attachments are deliberately fostered among the Jewish elements of the society.[157] Monitoring the enemy, no matter how boring, has inherent interest value, but the synchronicity of the RMA means internal surprises caused by IDF members themselves can be as damaging as some enemy action. The knowledge burden of monitoring is not limited to the enemy's actions and must include monitoring the friendly organization in peacetime. For Israelis who did not grow up under the heterogeneous distrust institutionalized in, say, the US, this comes close to a violation of the homogeneous socialization emphasized since the beginning of the state. More than anything, this activity is much like that kind of monitoring that is pursued by nuclear power plants seeking that seemingly insignificant event that triggers a low probability but high consequence event. The difference is that, in the Israeli case, this kind of monitoring will feel distasteful when spread across the total force. It is not that Israel security services have never observed, questioned, or tried to silence dissident Israelis; rather, it is the necessity of monitoring an entire RMA-designed IDF. In the mid-1980s, Israelis trusted the IDF more than they trusted God for their defense, hence, the social construction of this necessary activity will be very difficult in this nation.[158]

(b) Commodification of RMA Knowledge: Israel is coming of age among the western nations from the rise in its democratic struggles and loss of automatic consensus of a nation under siege to its younger generation's increasingly skeptical attitudes towards the service and corporate responsibility maxims of their elders.[159] This decline in consensus opens up the possibility of greater tendency to share technical information outside of

military circles, especially if there is financial gain to be achieved. This is the commodification of RMA knowledge as a side effect both of privatization in Israeli military industries and of the general surge in computer startups in the nation.

First, privatization enhances the street value of knowledge about IDF RMA acquisitions plans and experiences. In 1998, Tel Aviv alone hosted about 1,000 computer startups, most of who were subsidized by generous government income tax waivers.[160] The privatization of military industries has been ongoing for at least a decade. Until the recent sea change in computer knowledge and needs, however, the material produced was not particularly commercially valuable save in derivative forms, often a long way from the original technology. In addition, particularly attractive technologies could always be sold in a modified version that obscured the actual capabilities of the Israeli systems. Now a highly electronically integrated military poses a much lucrative target for both contracts with the government but also for the development of crossover skills and information valuable in commercial venues. For example, Microsoft is negotiating to buy an Israeli satellite company whose skills could have only been developed in the military context in Israel.[161] Whether the IDF or the security services like it or not, knowledge about their activities is being purchased in this booming market. This makes it less likely a highly synchronized RMA IDF will be able to curtail knowledge about its capabilities and, importantly, vulnerabilities.

Furthermore, a smaller force concentrates the internal options of the IDF, making the street value of particular information even higher. Special knowledge of what exactly is possible within smaller RMA-type IDF would make it nearly irresistible for some military members or contractors to make focused contracts with wealthy outsiders using knowledge gained from the now fewer contracts to IDF. Keeping secrets becomes difficult with 'dual use' technologies and these privatized firms will be engaged exactly in that kind of product.[162] Forced to privatize in recent years, for example, the more successful Israeli defense-related firms have turned to selling sophisticated component upgrade services to foreign governments.[163] It is a step well known in the United States in the transition from upgrading electro-mechanical components to upgrading network and application components if the appropriate knowledge and skills can be bought in the commercial market. In this process of commercializing military skills, technology transfers more rapidly than it otherwise would.[164] The RMA's ability to impose surprise is likely to be compromised unless many other elements of an internal security system more like that of the US are instituted.

Second, myriads of government-sponsored computer startups are competing for military-educated computer skills. Due to national service, a large proportion of young people who have the talent but not the funds to attend computer science courses are being introduced to computers in their military service. Many delay service for a few years to get some computer science education and then do longer service in compensation. Furthermore, officers are increasing sent off to highly technical schools as a lure to keep them in the service, an expensive but increasingly necessary benefit offered professionals. As a result, most of the entrepreneurs creating the computing boom in Israel were educated in the military.[165] While this is good news now, a smaller more professional RMA IDF will not be pumping this kind of training into the wider society. And it will face what the US services already face – the braindrain as commercial firms competing for skills essentially buy the expensively trained professionals out of the military. In short, dispensing with the large automatic inflow of young talent in transforming to an RMA military, the IDF begins to cut off its traditional sources of inexpensive skills as well as possible innovation.[166]

(c) RMA Precision versus IDF Tactical Decentralization: Precision is dicey but it is the key element in an integrated system whose requirements must be observed. Precision is not the same as accuracy; a broken analog clock is accurate only twice a day but precise at all times. The level of intolerance for deviation in inputs in processes (precision) bind the strategic and tactical decisions of an RMA military in ways never before achieved by a military organization. This level of integration will be particularly difficult in a military historically adapted to independence among subordinate units and designed as a cadre organization heavily dependent on conscripts and reservists who also embrace a culture of highly localized autonomy.

First, precision encourages centralization in processes in order to achieve control over expensive deviations and to quickly impose enterprise-wide upgrades.[167] This phenomenon is strongly at variance with Israeli historical experience in which traditional IDF ground force operations are doctrinally decentralized and individually preemptive. Wide latitude is given to aggressive, fiercely independent subordinates.[168] Highly automated networked systems (necessary for very fast reactions) present challenges differently from the less automated, more dampened, slower human-interspersed systems used effectively by the IDF in the past. During interviews conducted in the early 1990s, one IDF military interviewee noted that Israelis were good at tinkering and intensely training individuals to be able to improvise but poor at planning. Another officer said until recently acquisition largely consisted of building something and relying on working out the 'bugs' as they went. A civilian defense analyst (also a reserve officer) noted that the Israeli way is to define the military goal and let 'the other follow'. These predilections make the IDF less able to conduct highly precise operations save on an exception basis.[169]

Furthermore, the bulk of the warfighting organization has historically consisted of temporary soldiers in the reserves or conscripts less than 21 years old. The constant rotation of conscripts and reservists in and out of the organization has reinforced the decentralized cultural characteristics found in the wider society. As a result, peacetime administrative functions are similarly loosely coupled. Discipline is generally lax. It is a point of pride among IDF officers that a more knowledgeable subordinate can feel free to disagree with a commander's proposals. The autonomy is also hallowed in the peer-based, physical endurance-oriented psychological selection process choosing officers from second year conscripts.[170] These predilections, however, can discourage the kind of consistent interpretation and predictable response necessary for system-wide precision in constant monitoring of process outcomes.

Success in a knowledge-intensive highly synchronized environment also requires as much trial and error in high fidelity practice as possible. Research on high reliability organizations suggests that this kind of practice must also occur under the actual conditions of use and are necessary for the successful transition during a crisis. The more integrated and complex that US Navy aircraft carriers have become, the longer and longer it has taken to prepare a new crew for sea service. In highly integrated systems that are prohibited from failing, such as air traffic control, three levels of nested hierarchies become involved when the crisis is surprising. The three levels are, respectively, the lowest or routine level of military hierarchy, the intermediate matrix level based on expertise that only emerges when an intermediate level crisis occurs, and the final planned formal hierarchy to which the group reverts when no one is perceived to have any more expertise than any other. It is the intermediate, informal level that has to be developed over time through high fidelity practice and that level is responsible for innovative responses. Survival depends on the consistency of the members in recognizing which hierarchy needs to function at any given moment and so the learning burden of a consistent interpretation takes longer with an increasing knowledge burden.[171] Israelis have successfully produced the intense practice in operations necessary to, for example, save the hostages aboard an airplane in Entebbe. Those circumstances were, in effect, less intricate than the knowledge conditions faced today.

Furthermore, reliance on young largely male conscripts in an ever reducing force structure and infrequent use of reservists will pose a management challenge for a highly precise force. Even if the wider culture did not have a tendency for impatience, young males decidedly demonstrate poorer impulse control and the ability to sit for long periods assuring the precise operation of systems.[172] Although generally conscripts one year ahead of their subordinates, sergeants of the Israeli army and a much smaller pool of junior officers perform all the duties separately given to senior NCOs and to junior officers in the larger western armies such as those of the US and Britain. Officers higher than captain are normally career officers, not conscripts, and are traditionally an even smaller population.[173] As a result of this deliberate concentration of youth, IDF battalions have had to include a military psychologist on hand to intervene in, and guide, the aggressive exuberance of the young leaders.[174]

Even the computer industry has had to deal with youthful exuberance. While the burgeoning computer industry is rapidly being dominated by young males, over the same period a growing chorus of exposés of the industry's shortcomings is emerging in the United States. In particular, they are critical of increasingly rampant instances of poor documentation, sloppy programming, and general lack of attentiveness to details in design and maintenance of complex applications. Systematically knowing enough to recognize and then accurately respond to a covert IW attack anywhere along a highly integrated system requires a more routinely consistent response than such a young impulsive population can produce.[175]

Similarly, the selected use of reservists endangers precision inputs. If called up infrequently, they rapidly lose their specialized skills for particular military systems. However, given the argument about needing stable, comprehensive and consistent interpretations, reservists are preferred for the standoff force given their greater emotional maturity.

4. BALANCING KNOWLEDGE CONDITIONS IN INITIAL DESIGNS FOR KNOWLEDGE
    MANAGEMENT

In sum, the conditions favoring success in redesigning of the whole institution towards an RMA military do not clearly outweigh the conditions working against such success. If the current trends proceed, then the widespread integration of IDF elements has no extant equivalent. Not even the US has implemented its own model. The IDF's leaders will in effect produce an 'organizational beta test' (OBT). This process of using users to test an application began in the computer industry as the complexity of computer applications grew and so did the need for tests of their capabilities under a variety of circumstances. It was too expensive to employ internal staff to just push an application to its limits under many different environments but such levels of complexity in integrated systems cannot be tested to any great level of reliability in advance of implementation either. The name itself comes from the programming community in which the 'alpha' or initial test of the new program is done inside the firm developing the program while the second test, the beta test, was pushed outside to these users. Since the next step is to get someone else, preferably a potential user, to spend time pushing the program's limits, that process became the 'beta' test.[176]

Inadvertently many organizations have performed their own 'organizational' beta test (OBT).[177] By contracting for in-house programs tailored specifically for their situation or preemptively reorganizing organizational components in order to facilitate computerization, senior leaders have often unwittingly used their organization as a 'beta' test of the new program, the new arrangements, or both. As such, the entire organization has to work out the bugs in the process of operating, enduring, and adapting to the inevitable shortfalls between performance and the projections of reality of the program designers or the reorganizers.

According to the amount of organizational slack left in the organization when the network-computerization was implemented, an organizational beta test can be positive, neutral, or deleterious to the organization's future. Unfortunately for the IDF and any other organization implementing the US-defined RMA military, trading standing forces away to pay the costs of highly synchronized networked computer systems entails slim organizational designs. These structures have little of the slack needed to make the organizational beta test an effective – if expensive – learning experience. When wholesale conversions to new systems are attempted and slack allowing trial and error of the entire future system – humans and their informal operations included – is constrained, the ripple effects of surprises across tightly coupled systems are likely to be the most costly.[178] It is a misunderstanding of the dynamic interplay of processes, humans, and artifacts in maintaining essential knowledge slack that has doomed many business process-reengineering efforts. It is a mechanistic focus on artifacts and software that has made enterprise-wide systems prohibitively expensive to implement, maintain and operate successfully without external consultants.[179]

IV. OUT OF THE BOX: ORGANIZING FOR THE DETERRENCE,
STABILITY AND THE SHAPE OF THE IDF IN LIKELY
FUTURE OPERATIONS

For Israel, the presently growing peace in the region is not necessarily stable over the long run, given the mismatch between economic and population growth rates of neighboring states. Unlike the US, Israel is not a large wealthy nation that is normally expeditionary in its security responses and can afford the risk of getting it wrong in its implementation of a highly integrated new large-scale technical system. There is considerable distance between the US and potential enemies, even with ballistic missiles, and its leaders can afford to implement new organizational plans while retaining elements of the old. For the US, innovation does not involve placing high stakes on one path to the future. The US Army, for example, could afford in the late 1950s to reorganize completely for ground operations in a nuclear war and then two years later decide it was a mistake, reorganizing yet again to a standard box division format.[180]

Small nations with limited resources like Israel, however, cannot afford to commit to such a fully integrated system in their main military forces and then find they cannot sustain it properly or that it does not provide adequate security. For such countries, the national resources involved in implementing an RMA-modeled military are huge. The risks of a failed transition for conventional deterrence, stability, and acceptable survival conditions are also large. The new electronically enabled, highly networked environment changes fundamentally the designs and processes of organizations most likely to succeed. This final section reviews these risks if current RMA trends in the IDF are pursued doggedly, and it offers an alternative view of most likely operational challenges and a possible organizational future path that is more congruent with traditional Israeli conditions.

A. Israel's Conventional Deterrence and the Role of Surprise

Geostrategic changes have forced a change in Israel's conventional deterrence strategy from taking the battle to the enemy's military backbone massively and/or by surprise to enacting such severe retaliation for hostile actions that the fear of such retaliation serves as deterrence.[181] If the world's militaries sign up for the US's model of an RMA and all its promises, the IDF should have an easier task in deterrence by publicly modernizing along this model as well. If the RMA's 'standoff' war with few friendly casualties can be conducted effectively, then having the world believe Israel has fully implemented an RMA, naturally with a few typical Israeli surprises, is eminently desirable.[182] To the extent that deterrence is essentially image manipulation, by adopting the most modern image, Israel's deterrence standing should benefit from the positive social construction developing across the global military community.

However, if the argument about complex systems and the US image of an RMA is correct, actually implementing this model will involve the IDF in eliminating its traditional sources of innovative and surprising knowledge sources (government R&D, bright conscripts, active reserves). Making the US RMA an IDF reality would be tantamount to constructing a surprise-prone organization waiting for the first major application under unexpected and stressful conditions in which to fail. A small professional force dedicated to the RMA defined systems will have little slack to test its operations under high fidelity conditions for a variety of budgetary and image constraints until it is time to actually use the force. It was known but not acknowledged by the US Army during the 1980s that it continued to have trouble accurately diagnosing its M1 Abrams tanks. As a result of similar shortcomings in knowledge provision for complex systems and high fidelity tests of systems, the US military putatively able to conduct two full-scale wars simultaneously had to double and sometimes triple its planned support forces in only one medium-sized theater during the 1991 Gulf War.[183]

Even if the image of the IDF's success in implementing RMA is perfectly established and taken for granted abroad, hostile external actors will endeavor to disrupt normal operations and probe for weak areas in ongoing malicious operations. The combined weight of externally imposed surprise and internally generated rogue sets can likely to prove dangerously disruptive when the force actually is used in short-term, high-intensity comprehensive operations.

B. Crisis Stability and Future 'Wars of Disruption'

Crises are naturally or socially constructed, the former being physically unambiguous and the latter being interpreted by all parties using internal lenses. Unless the enemy is about to come across the border physically in some way, all national security crises are socially constructed on various information frameworks. In the 1991 Gulf War, US aircraft killed British solders in a friendly fire mishap. The event, however, was not socially constructed into a crisis but as an accident between allies. Complex systems challenge all users and offer a variety of possible refractions of information. A certain suppleness of mind is needed to correctly assess the fragments of patterns that are being presented. Wisdom, not merely the movement of data quickly, is a more appropriate tool for defusing socially constructed crises in complex systems.

The RMA model is focused on battlefields, not peacetime operations and thus misses key ongoing value-added aspects of military information technologies for militaries. This work presumes that the wider global community has hostile elements that will, for a variety of reasons, attempt ongoing 'wars of disruption' against disliked societies, irrespective of the level of modernization of the military organization. Sometimes these efforts will result in socially-constructed national security crises, sometimes they will succeed in hostilities expressed physically. In any event, military organizations throughout the world will eventually be drawn into protecting national assets from the cross border attacks. Moving beyond the RMA focus, military information systems aimed at obtaining wisdom for leaders can be of great value in both reactively dampening escalating misinterpretations but also in proactively channeling data and knowledge interpretations in opposing military organizations and political leaders before crises begin. They can also respond to these mini 'wars' through the knowledge-based application of IW systems long before any deployment to, perhaps, disrupt the coordination of opposing parties to a dispute.

This broader view of information operations allows for a wider range of options in international system management than foreseen in the RMA model, including if needed such activities as predeployment and even precrisis disruption. Playing to its strengths in knowledge development, then, an IW force in peacetime should be focused on collecting organizational data on a large field of possible opposition organizations and then formulating the means to disrupt these critical nodes if necessary. Rather than waiting for the deployment signal and then worrying about sensors data at that moment as predicted by the RMA discussion, the innovative IW force will have already been able to disrupt the hostile organization from the moment the force is authorized to act.

For Israel, only with the reach of internetted and international communications has this more subtle option emerged but it is the revolutionary aspect of information operations, not merely the focus on speed and smaller footprints. Under these circumstances, a modernized state such as Israel can push the development of military capabilities much further than usually considered wise in terms of international intentions and nonobviously be more militarily intrusive to preempt coordination of hostile activities than previously assumed without risking full-scale war. While preparation for war does not ensure peace, neither does it ensure war if intentions can be made plain before deployments.[184]

Also, the vigorous development of knowledge about potential enemies is more likely to make actual deployment a last option that, if forced, will be undertaken against other organizations whose essential coordination elements have already been studied and diagnosed for disruption targets comprehensively, continuously, and consistently. This approach is the no-nonsense end of what has been called a 'knowledge strategy'.[185] An organization-oriented IW force that is also robust offers the possibility of management of the international system before that last resort deployment. This policy option is purely speculative and will be explored more fully in future discussions.

As it stands, however, the current image embedded in the RMA model of future warfare is still linear and too strongly mechanistic to achieve this wider set of policy options. If the IDF were to continue in its current path adopting key elements of this model, it would be trading mass for information as if the real challenge is merely to fit the pieces together more compactly. This US-derived model is unlikely to produce the suppleness of pattern recognition and organizational reaction necessary to suddenly act when key indicators emerge. Whatever the future IDF's shape, its adoption of information technologies must extract slack in time and knowledge in order to accommodate surprises in dynamic complex situations that the remaining superpower does not have to contemplate.

Structuring automaticity with a view to knowledge management in the face of surprise should be the critical factor, not the attractiveness of networks. Muddling through with key elements of the US system will produce, at best, an operating system that will function like a network of allies, although Israel has not historically done well in combined arms operations. At worst it will be a transient large-scale technical system (LTS) with all the risks involved with a regular LTS but no way to know in advance of the emergence of the system just how it is going to work dynamically. In the latter case, accommodating surprises will be extremely difficult unless, quite literally, the widespread redundancy such as was available for all of Israel's previous wars is serendipitously reintroduced into the force structure.

C. An Alternate Transformation of the IDF – the 'Atrium' Hypertext Organization

The challenge therefore is to modernize the IDF keeping its traditional knowledge-development advantages and still have the benefits of a networked integrated system. For that goal, the US-model of an RMA is not sufficiently knowledge-centric and adapted to Israeli conditions.

The current IDF modernization by muddling through is an approach certain to doom successful integration across systems.

First, the organizational strategy has been to acquire pockets of networks and skills in elite units and to minimize the expenditure in training other non-technically competent individuals. This is a focus on knowledge needed now, not knowledge creation or accumulation.

Second, the strategy is to copy the US in reducing overall costs of personnel training by decreasing conscript numbers, moving to essentially a de facto selective service.[186] This move expresses an underlying premise that no knowledge can be acquired or adequately inculcated in two or three years of a young person that can be of further use to the organization. An even stronger focus on the present circumstances in a conventional military where young minds are generally an accumulation of fingers to point lethal things at enemies, not full players in development of the surrounding internal and external knowledge environment.

Third, reservists are less and less used because they are too expensive for the training support, they need, today. But it is the surrounding community that provides the knowledge context and makes new knowledge more or less scarce and expensive to acquire. The misplaced emphasis on reservists as simply older fingers to pull triggers is producing this path away from deepening knowledge development.[187]

According to Cohen, Eisenstadt, and Bacevich, this strategy is emerging because the IDF is torn by the need to construct four different types of forces that can only uneasily coexist in a small nation. These are elite units for current limited war problems, force-on-force large conventional units to repel unlikely but possible massive assaults by neighbors' forces, longer reach forces for outer ring nations, and highly airmobile intermediate forces to stop assaults from neighbors whose political instabilities allow the resumption of hostile regimes with surprise attacks in mind.[188] Furthermore, wider societal changes in public willingness to serve and desire to legally control conditions of service have forced the IDF to move away from its traditions of being as heavily integrated with the nation's civilian activities to become a more distinct institution as found in other more established democracies.

The three key elements of the IDF's modernization strategy, however, are only likely to work if (a) essential knowledge is an automatic byproduct of any activity at all and (b) creativity from lower skilled newcomers is simply irrelevant to successful operations. The difficulty is that the modern military technologies across both machine and human systems are based on information sharing, not hoarding, as a way to be both act quickly and to counter surprises. Knowledge is not an automatic byproduct unless the system deliberating seeks to capture that knowledge. Shutting down the links to society not seen as directly useful is an older social construction of information and its ubiquitousness. Ironically, this kind of military and social distinction is more sensible in an expeditionary service like the US than in the IDF. In the US, one can envision sending a complete system out to operation, one with a long tail back home to be sure, but nonetheless a system that has distinct boundaries and an internal structure that can operate differently than the wider society. The IDF cannot do this and, in any case, should not want to since those boundaries will make the knowledge development much more expensive in the long run.

Organizations are knowledge-producing entities and the more distinct they are from a supporting and surrounding knowledge base, the more expensive the internal development of knowledge.[189] Complex systems are also path-dependent on initial conditions. The more the initial organizational design facilitates absorbing and accumulating knowledge from the outset, including more slack, redundancy and trial and error, the more likely the design will be robust and successful in the face of surprise.

Therefore, the uncertainties of the Israeli circumstances require a different kind of modernization of the military organization – one that recognizes a new social construction of the role of knowledge as *a player in organizational operations and deliberately seeks and fosters this development*. With a different approach, the IDF could both modernize and accommodate its own social history as well as its needs. In particular, the IDF could retain its technological edge, its traditional role as school of the nation, and its close ties to the burgeoning knowledge development of the surrounding society through its reserves.

To meet these aims, I propose a variant of the 'hypertext' organization described by Nonaka and Takeuchi.[190] This refinement, which I labeled the 'Atrium' form of information based organization, is a design that treats knowledge as a third and equal partner in the organization. In the original model and in my refinement, the knowledge base is not merely an overlain tool or connecting pipelines. Rather, the knowledge base of the organization is actively nurtured both in the humans and in the digitized institutional integrated structure. At its base in the commercial world is the attempt by Nonaka and Tageuchi to reconcile the competing demands and benefits of both matrix and hierarchical organizational forms. They propose a 'hypertext' organization in which there are three intermingling structures: a matrix structure in smaller task forces specifically focused on problems at hand and answering to senior managers, a second hierarchical structure that both supports the general operational systems but also contributes and then reabsorbs the members of task forces, and finally a large knowledge base that is intricately interwoven through the activities of both matrix and hierarchical units.[191]

The knowledge base is more than a library or a database on a server; it is a structure in and of itself integrating applications and data. It reaches into the task forces who use it for data mining while also sustaining the general operations, sharing information broadly. But it is also socially constructed as a key player in the organization such that task force members are required to download their experiences in a task force into the knowledge base before they are permitted to return to their positions in the hierarchical portion of the organization. Similarly, operations in the general hierarchy are required to interact through the knowledge base systems so that patterns in operations and actions are automatically captured for analysis.[192]

The major contribution here is that the knowledge base is not a separate addition to the organization and irrelevant to the architecture of the human-machine processes. Rather, it is integral to the success of processes and the survival of the institution. Nonaka and Tageuchi have identified several Japanese corporations that seem to operate along these lines productively and one is struck by an interesting distinction – implicit knowledge developed by human interactions related to the job is not only viewed as a source of value by the corporation but also as key to long term survival. It is this view of knowledge that distinguishes these corporations and makes them more prepared for surprise in the marketplace.

In adapting this design and social construction to a military setting, I have given this concept of a knowledge base a name, the 'Atrium'.[193] The term captures the sense of being a place to which a member of the organization can go, virtually or otherwise, to contribute and acquire essential knowledge, and that it is also a place of refuge to think out solutions. The mental image is that it is overarching, not beneath the human actors, but something that protects as well as demands inputs. Entering into and interacting with the Atrium is essentially acting with a major player in the institution. Such a conception rationalizes the efforts to ensure implicit knowledge is integrated into the long term analyses of the organization, such as the time spent in downloads of experiences and information from the task force members before they return to a more hierarchical stem.

The 'atrium' form requires an explicit embrace of what has been called the 'new knowledge management'.[194] In particular, the new knowledge management means using network/web technologies to move from controlling information inventories as human relationship-based 'controlled hoards' to web-based 'trusted source' structures.[195] This approach faces considerable resistance because socially reconstructing knowledge from something to be hoarded for power within an organization to something to be shared to obtain and sustain capabilities is a significant transformation of expectations.[196] To make this transformation, a first step is to view of organizations as large-scale systems prone to rippling effects when relevant knowledge is not present. That is particularly true for societies under stress and militaries in active operations. A fully organizationally transparent, interactive, maintained and easily accessed web community with data warehousing and mining on call can become a 'trusted source' that is consulted when surprising rumors, shortfalls in knowledge, or routine information needs are encountered. It also allows the controller of the content of that site enormous leverage, albeit not face-to-face, over what is widely believed to be true.[197]

Applying this proposal to the circumstances of the IDF permits the following.

First, the IDF's traditional knowledge development sources (government R&D, conscripts, reservists) need not be abandoned for a borrowed streamlined expeditionary model.

Second, the four types of forces identified by Cohen, Eisenstadt, and Bacevich are no longer not incompatible, or all necessary as distinct forces.

Third, the diffusion of the RMA model globally and its associated technologies blurs the distinctions between peace and war capabilities. With networks, everything is dual use and sufficient technical familiarity can be found in foreign ministries as well as in basements inhabited by teenage geeks with a sociopathic attitude. Knowledge development will inevitably come through surprises that are encountered all along the spectrum of formal declaration of operations, from peace-building, through peace-making, peacekeeping, posturing, and prevailing in actual hostilities.

For Israel, the design of a modern knowledge-centric military must, in effect, accept 24/7 operations with all the ethical, legal, budgetary, socio-economic, and geostrategic constraints implied.

First, reservists and conscripts are not drains on the military if valued and directed properly in knowledge-development processes. Nor are very selective government R&D and procurement activities that build off the surrounding vibrancy of IT developments.

Second, each of the four forces identified by Cohen, Eisenstadt, and Bacevich remain organizationally distinct and seem necessary precisely because there is limited cooperative knowledge across the forces.[198] Operations are individually constructed because they are variously seen as decisions about applications of force, not about puzzles to be solved (exceptionally quickly if surprising) whose resolution may or may not be the direct application of force.

Third, as Israel has always known in its short existence, competition among neighbors is continuous and punctuated by wars, not resolved by them. Today security crises in a networked global community span modalities and spark options never before envisioned. The wider global community is less the wild anarchy of history and more like cities within large federated nations that compete madly, viciously, and continuously.[199] They do not individually go to war since that is socially constructed out of the realm of consideration. However, cities are increasingly acquiring dual use technologies with the means to improve services but also to try to disrupt the competitive advantage of another city. Nothing but the social construction of what is acceptable stands in the way until legal regimes define this competition more strictly. Hence, wars as the clash of tanks and missiles are becoming less frequent and less likely, but the task of national security before militaries has become extraordinarily less nicely contained in the peace-crisis-war triad.

Furthermore, it takes smaller losses of life to prompt a political declaration of military failure in most western nations. Since arbitrary death that is viewed as preventable has become someone's failure to act in most western nations, a terrorist killing 10 people today is viewed with horror and mass public activity to an extent that the loss of 160 people in a single building fire 80 years ago would not have engendered.[200] It is because Israel, unlike the US, has always known this level of uncertainty that a modern military design requiring this recognition can build on this widespread social consensus over the continuous need for knowledge.[201]

It is important whether the IDF muddles through or has a strategic design in mind in its modernization. Organizations evolve along a set of future paths predictable only in general terms but heavily dependent on initiating conditions. Transformation processes themselves alter future paths – the more radical the new design, the higher knowledge burden for the system during the transformation and less likely success – as envisioned initially – will emerge. Hence, the transformation is eased to the extent that existing features of the organization are congruent with the intended new design of processes. Moving the IDF into an Atrium hypertext organization will not be a traumatic as it might seem because, rather than eliminating and replacing several key knowledge-developing elements of the current IDF, these can be incorporated with new social constructions into the modernized structure. The goal is to move these elements towards the new understanding of knowledge without having to destroy them.

In this proposed transformation, the overall structure of the IDF would be recategorized into, as initial conditions, three main elements with several sub-elements: the small matrix-structured task forces built on the existing special forces structures, the hierarchically and functionally structured core which is largely the current main structure of humans subdivided into the three main services (air, ground, sea) and cross-leveling support agencies (such as the technology and logistics branch), and the digitized hypertextual knowledge base called the Atrium which evolves into an integrated system of robust knowledge grids with intelligent applications and information demands/services familiarized and readily available to all members of the services. The main organizational elements are both linked by the Atrium's ubiquitous nets but also interactively involved in evolving the inputs to, services from, and analysis by Atrium digital and human components.

1. THE 'ATRIUM' – COMPUTER AS COLLEAGUE AND MAIN KEEPER OF
    INSTITUTIONAL MEMORY

Key to this model is the stabilizing the locus of institutional memory and creativity in the human-Atrium processes. In principle, according to their rank, each member of the organization will have the chance to cycle in and out of task forces, core operations or Atrium maintenance and refinement. As they cycle into a new position, gear up, operate, and then cycle out, each player does a data dump, including frustrations about process or data and ideas, into the Atrium. Organizational members elsewhere can then apply data mining or other applications on this expanding pool of knowledge elements to guide their future processes. Organizational institutional knowledge thus becomes instinctively valued and actively retained and maintained for use in ongoing or future operations.

Naturally, critical to this process are both the current advancements in data warehousing and data mining, and the rising societal familiarity with human-digital skills. Middle school children today are fearless in their willingness to experiment with computers, in ways young people ten years their senior cannot conceive. These two trends – data manipulation advancements and the social changes – make this design possible, at least parametrically, and appropriate for Israel, a nation exhibiting these trends in particular.

2. THE CORE – MAIN OPERATIONAL KNOWLEDGE CREATION AND APPLICATION
    HIERARCHIES

With this new social construction of what one does with information in the military (one creates, stores, refines and nurtures it), the Core then embraces the new knowledge potential of conscripts and reservists by reinforcing the 'school of the nation' concept first promoted by Ben-Gurion in Israel's early days. That is, service in the IDF involving computers is not only promoted as a benefit of conscription but training in computers irrespective of the actual military function is also pursued. Knowledge about diagnostic workarounds in maintenance units is then socially constructed as something the maintainer will expect to find in a foray into the Atrium, as well as being expected to give back to the system. That maintainer – a youngster of 19 years – will have been taught not just how to do that but how to manipulate digital applications in general, both to enhance the surprise-reducing potential of the organization but also to improve the soldiers' future marketability to the economy and their long term contribution to Atrium nurturing as a reservist. As a side benefit, the growing unwillingness to serve in anything but elite or intelligence forces among secular youth is mitigated when all conscripts and reservists receive what is considered valuable educations in networked technology.

Furthermore, the Core also embraces the potential of reservists, assigning tasks that can be done on weekends, most likely off military sites, and that furthers the knowledge development of the Atrium. Reservists can then still serve physically in uniform in the Core when called up but that period can be limited and infrequent since it is not expected the reservist will do much active humping of basic infantry loads. Rather the reservist will be able to draw upon reserve years of solving puzzles or petting data to keep their skills at usable levels. Naturally, all the current advantages of the reserve system – such as reservists thinking of innovations that the IDF then adopts – will be retained. So also will be the close connection between the wider society and the reservists without having the constant and resented disruption of an assigned time whether or not a task was required. As described, the Atrium will not lack for tasks, both in initial creation of applications, elements, processes, and uses but also in the coordinating and integration of these evolutions.

These more mature and experienced individuals will also provide an essential dampener on the tendency of all managers to automate and overcontrol processes that can result in tighter and tighter coupling of grids. In this constant intellectual recharge available from the reservist community, the Atrium will be able to avoid iterating into a brittle bureaucratic equilibrium. By having the problem-solving of the task forces as well as the intense attention of young conscripts for the period of their service, the Atrium will be an intelligent agent rather than a mindless amalgamation of individual databases onto which a rigidifying lattice of rationalizing controls has been imposed. In short, the vibrancy of the Atrium in providing knowledge to accommodate surprise is due not to the professionalism of the small permanent Core party but to the newness of perspective and rising familiarity of the conscripts and then reservists.

This injection of possible ingenuity is a genuine Israeli strength. With the exception of the Lebanon war, every Israeli war has been won by the courage and improvisation of mostly part-time or new independent-minded young soldiers.[202]

It is also important to note that, under this construction, the intelligence of half the population, for example, females, is not abandoned after their conscription period. There is no reason why females cannot be required to serve as reservists in equal status, or, for that matter, other currently waived minorities such as the religious, especially since there are long term wider socio-economic benefits to this kind of continuing education aside from the service to the IDF.

At this point in the discussion, the major differences between the current IDF and this model are only the construction of the Atrium's artifacts, software, processes and social construction, along with change in educational and tasking approach to conscripts and reservists. The Core does not differ much from the current structure of the IDF in general. However, this organization will be surrounded by complex systems as well as being a complex system itself.

Problems beyond the normal Core operations and Atrium knowledge analysis will emerge constantly. Some of these will be physically dangerous and immediate, such as eliminating a cache of standoff weapons rumored to be amassing somewhere in and around an Israeli civilian population. Some will be prospective, such as determining why certain neighboring political leaders have allocated budget amounts to shadowy organizations putatively also establishing political parties as cover for terrorist cells, again in and around Israel's region. Some will be long term, such as rechanneling the design goals of key data chunk allocations within the Atrium or retargeting some of its uses in the light of wider global trends. For these kinds of problems, a matrix organization is much preferred and hence we come to the final element, the task forces.

3. THE TASK FORCES – SPECIAL RESPONSES IN KNOWLEDGE CREATION/ APPLICATION

Israel already has the structural elements for task forces in its five varieties of special forces units spread across the IDF services. Ranging from the US Ranger-like 'sayerot' to the more shadowy anti-guerrilla units, these are considered elite fighting forces. Conscripts compete vigorously to have one of the few but prestigious slots.[203] The operations have been, as publicly known, largely physically dangerous missions to eliminate 'current security' threats.[204] The difficulty is that these units are fiercely independent and secretive. Although the training is admirably rigorous and the members dedicated, it is not clear from public evidence that all these units are needed for the amount of physically demanding tasks essential for national security.

In knowledge development terms, the secrecy of these units ensures that they are not sufficiently contributing to the wide development of the organization's institutional wisdom. Leaving secrecy aside, when each service has its own units, the sharing of information between special forces units is even less effective than it is normally among and within service arms.[205]

Furthermore, assignment to such units becomes a military identifier for the rest of the conscript's association with the IDF since unit members do not rotate unless they become career officers. That singular experience strongly affects the intensely secretive perspective towards military knowledge found in the predilections of senior military officers, including the recent prime minister, Ehud Barak.[206]

Many of these existing units can be altered to function as task force structures answering to the senior military officers in a knowledge-centric organization.

First, to capture the implicit information currently lost or buried, members of elite units will rotate in from the night fighting operations to download implicit knowledge, update their understanding of the Atrium's holdings and possible insights, and contribute to the Core.

Second, some of the elite units will be retargeted along different modalities of knowledge acquisition and use, away from being solely focused on stopping, interrogating and recording information on suspects in control zones, such data in knowledge mining combined with other information presented in the Atrium.

Some units will be left with the more physically challenging missions but their members will also be rotated in and out on longer cycles, perhaps a year, to accommodate exceptional physical requirements. Other units will be gradually altered to problem analysis units – moving from simply gathering data on all suspicious activity in Ramallah to meta-analyses of such activities over time and locations with an eye to proactively disrupting the initiating efforts rather than sending squads after the Hamas cell when it is well established. For this, the members will have to be digitally creative as much as physically hardy.[207]

Furthermore, elite units will be temporary structures housed beyond individual services and directed at problems by the Chief of the General Staff. Since rotating organization members among the three – task forces, Core and the Atrium – is a basic tenet, even senior leaders must rotate. For example, senior leaders could spend most of their time leading each of the geographic commands (Northern, Southern, etc) but they must rotate in for Atrium service, as well as heading task forces occasionally. While on rotation, the senior leader must be free completely from leadership duties, thus attention must be paid to a functioning deputy leader culture. Finally, the explicit assumption is that each task force is solving a problem or exploring an opportunity but also developing important nonobvious information that must also be inputted into the Atrium's processes. Senior leaders just like lowly conscripts have implicit knowledge to contribute to, and skills to refine in extracting and manipulating data from, the Atrium resources.

Altering this segment of the IDF is essential for modernization but will have to be conducted with close attention to the normally elevated resistance of elite units to change, especially if it appears to lower their prestige allocations in an organization. Not all of the existing units will change in their mission. The ones that retain the more physically dangerous missions will alter only in that their members will rotate out of Core positions for a position in the elite force and then back through an Atrium tour before returning to the Core. The time spent in the elite force will be dictated by the problem that the task force is assigned.

For the other units that are explicitly channeled into analytical units given nonroutine problems, the prestige concern is more likely to be critical for a relatively smooth transition. Fortunately, the value placed on computer skills and a civilian career to follow military experience offers a way to socially construct this change for easier acceptance. Also, placing them directly beneath the senior leaders also mollifies grievances over a loss of prestige. Personnel rotating in and out of these units are assured not only of interesting current problems for six months to a year but also greater visibility at senior levels. The units will benefit from the strong advantages of a matrix structure in creativity and will produce more innovative problem solutions than can be produced today.

4.   ADVANTAGES FOR VARYING FORCE REQUIREMENTS AND KNOWLEDGE
      CONDITIONS

This design has other advantages in integrating the Israeli need for four different kinds of forces – current security, conventional defense, strategic early warning, and response, and deployed conventional preemption.[208] The biggest threat is surprise by the opponents but in this model, critical slack to mitigate unknowns is provided by extensive and redundant knowledge buffers in and through the Atrium processes. As a result, while Israel still needs conventional forces, it does not need as many of them on constant alert. While Israel still needs strategic forces and standoff weapons, the knowledge development during noncrisis periods, especially the focus on knowledge acquisition, refinement and dissemination across all organizational players, permits other electronic options to emerge such as targeted disruption efforts that may overtly or covertly derail threatening postures by missile owning states.

Finally, current security inside Israel cannot be fully digitized but the information acquired in the basic infantry operations can be stored and used to make the next set of operations more effectively targeted. It is possible to conceive of a situation in which creative data mining on information provided by a multitude of Israeli sources – data that is unrelated at first blush – can provide more information of value about future operations than the intensive interrogation of one Palestinian suspect over many months. In any event, the effective combination of the two is inevitably advancing.

Finally, this proposal also mitigates the more problematical elements of the Israeli knowledge-context such as the need for internal monitoring of the IDF itself as a complex system, the likely privatization and its commodification of essential RMA knowledge, and the centralization tendencies of these enterprise-wide systems. First, the need for continuous tedious monitoring for small, possibly complex indicators is eased by the retention of knowledgeable reservists, many of whom could conceivably work online at some distance. This load is therefore shared across more individuals, providing more organizational slack and opportunities for training and refinement of other solutions among the full-time professionals or conscripts. Furthermore, integration of a wide variety of information is more possible when human organizations become digitized. Mindless accumulation of data is also possible but neither it nor wisdom-enhancing integration is feasible over this size of organization and within its time requirements without this digitization.

As for more monitoring the organization internally, while the task may still be obnoxious, it is easier and less intrusive to scan across employee actions when work is digitized. A person who walks out with a copied stack of papers is more vulnerable only when copying and walking; a person doing the same digitally is vulnerable to discovery as long as the backup tapes of the main servers are intact, a potential lifetime of vulnerability.

Second, privatization and its attendant commodification of formerly secret stores of knowledge are inevitable but a greater threat when the organization is crucially dependent on that information for survival. The street value is highest if few people know the data and they will pay a great deal to either hide it or have it secretly integrated into some capabilities. When conscripts and reservists are rotating in and out of all functions and their implicit knowledge is also being accumulated in the Atrium, then individual elements of knowledge are potentially spread all over the society, much like it is today in the current IDF. The data most valuable is, in effect, in plain view but obscured by the variety of sources and possible interpretations. With so many knowing in general the overall structure and uses of the Atrium and the IDF's capabilities, the competition is less for secret information which automatically provides some kind of leverage over the IDF in acquisition but for positive social assessments by chief acquisition officers in the IDF. Hence, knowledge that must be kept secret – as decided by senior level officials – can be buried in the noise and are less likely to be manipulated for lucrative contracts.

This approach is nontraditional but consistent with a world of information overload where data is not valuable if hoarded, only if trusted and creatively formatted in relevant and effective tools. In the US, commodification of defense knowledge has been constrained by the sheer volume available in an open society. Israeli society is moving to being at least as open as the United States and the intense secrecy of the IDF is likely to be unsustainable in the end. A small RMA IDF with the traditional preference to hoard information will be an exceptionally attractive target for both entrepreneurs and spies and, of course, more vulnerable due to its lack of slack in processes and organizational resources. Furthermore, the US's continuing problem with the brain drain of highly skilled individuals being bought out of service into civilian jobs and then sold back as contractors is less of an organizational contingency when that individual is due back as a reservist anyway. The expensive contract may be less necessary.

Third, centralization is a function of managerial need for control, which increases with the lack of slack in the organization's resources or time. The RMA model explicitly promotes synchronicity of battlefield operations, encouraging the move towards centralization across networks. The 'Atrium' concept, however, builds on shared knowledge and wisdom but does not dictate the kind of operations. There is nothing in this model to require the level of automaticity necessary for the RMA.

First, this proposal does not assume wisdom comes automatically with 100 per cent visibility of any battlefield. On the contrary, this 'Atrium' organizational model presumes that the 24/7 accumulation of information, much of which implicit and never before digitized, will use data mining techniques and a constant inflow of new pairs of eyes to construct new visions of operations. A new information warfare or peace-ensuring mission could, conceivably, be deliberately asynchronous with another in order to achieve a long-term, slow-roll deception goal that diverts potential hostile actors from other more dangerous choices.

Second, forced centralized accommodation among a myriad of elements is the fastest and most effective mechanism of response only if, during the operation, no surprises emerge. The 'Atrium' concept presumes surprises and a sudden lack of knowledge. It presumes partial answers to that lack are available before the fact by creatively combining and recombining patterns in existing explicit and implicit knowledge. Even more, it presumes that surprise during operations is normal and only slack built through knowledge mechanisms can really accommodate or mitigate or dampen the effects on a large-scale organization.

Finally, this model is based on an understanding of complexity across large-scale systems. If only trends can be seen in advance, not explicit outcomes, then the best preparation is to have the knowledge-base and the skills in creative combinations ready and waiting for the elements of the trend to take concrete shape. Having socialized into unit members some key central themes in operations is as close as the Atrium endorses centralization. Furthermore, centralization cannot only get the answer wrong, the fixation on central decision-making and synchronized actions can encourage devastating ripple effects in an organization.

In contrast, the 'Atrium' model encourages a dampening of rippling rogue outcomes by the rotation of members and inclusion of reservists. Particularly in Israel, there are naturally more likely to be sprinkled across any operation some humans distrustful of standard interpretations and willing to stop to investigate the origins, whether or not centrally instructed to do this research. Given the relative frequency of Atrium rotations, there is likely also to be others who are recently returned from negotiating the knowledge base explicitly and who can skillfully conduct this digital investigation on the spot. Hence, the Atrium concept builds on the Israeli cultural preference for independent thinking while permitting widespread coordination and integration across the organization, time, and operations.

D. Future Research and Issues

Aside from refining this concept, subsequent research will be needed to address tough issues.

First, the great stepchild of all new organizational forms must be directly addressed to keep the general future path on track: the transition, its form, timeframe, and strategies.

Second are the budget strategies most likely to encourage success in this kind of modernization, including issues such as the tradeoffs between funding the (computer) school of the nation and the myriad of small computer startups, and the role of government-owned computer research with defense implications.

Third, domestic and international marketing of this modernization needs to be conducted as a campaign in itself in order to ensure relatively crisis-free transitions. In particular, since this organization does explicitly accumulate information all year round, considerable efforts to allay the concerns of less technologically advanced neighbors will be necessary. However, the good news is that the IDF will look externally much as it does today, making these transition, budgetary and perception issues less traumatic than those associated with the RMA model's implementation.

Ultimately, this is an initial design aiming the IDF on a future evolutionary path intended to both meet Israel's geostrategic conundrums and its internal trends. This proposal obviously needs more elaboration but its presentation is designed to offer an alternative to adopting in an ad hoc fashion the short-term budget-reducing attractive elements of the US-defined RMA such as the costs of so many conscripts. Furthermore, Israel's history in innovation suggests that, set upon the path of designing a functioning knowledge-centric and creative military organization along the lines of the Atrium, the IDF is probably one of the few militaries in the world likely to succeed. The RMA model defined by the United States remains a socio-technical arrangement most appropriate for an expeditionary army of a relatively isolated and wealthy society where time, distance, and money provide slack in case of misjudgments. Israel must do something more advanced in ensuring slack through knowledge and more tailored to its own strengths.

NOTES

1. See Neil Fleming, 'Coping with a Revolution: Will the Internet Change Learning?', Canterbury, New Zealand: Lincoln University (http://www 1990s) http://www.lincoln.az.nz/educ/learning, downloaded 10 Feb. 2000.
2. Shimon Naveh, head of Israel's National Defense College, March 1998 quoted in Arieh O'Sullivan, 'Facing Reality: The IDF Embarks on a Restructuring Program', *Armed Forces Journal International* (April 1999) pp.17–18.
3. Some prominent scholars have gone so far as to use the term 'technology', to mean all the technical equipment and applications combined with the organization as a whole. For a

seminal work on this theme, see Todd R. LaPorte (ed.) *Organized Social Complexity* (Princeton UP 1975).

4. See JV2010, Joint Chiefs of Staff, Department of Defense, United States Government, *Joint Vision 2010* (Washington DC: US Government Printing Office 1996).

5. This overarching goal is also called 'full spectrum dominance', and considered 'the key characteristic we seek for our Armed Forces'. See CFJO, Joint Chiefs of Staff, Department of Defense, United States Government, *Concept for Future Joint Operations* (Washington DC: US Government Printing Office 1997) p.2.

6. This is the 'fog of war', discussed by Clausewitz and made famous in the Western militaries when his works were finally translated after World War II. For a good translation, see Michael Howard and Peter Paret (eds. and translators) *Carl von Clausewitz* (Princeton UP 1976).

7. See James Adams, *The Next World War: Computers are the Weapons and the Front Line is Everywhere* (NY: Simon & Schuster 1998).

8. Innocence in war is very tough to define but an emerging disinclination for arbitrary death among westernized nations is defining innocence as the nonparticipant in a military force or military action, increasingly including the enemy's civilian populations. This has profound effects on military doctrine. Here the televised media's pictures of victims on both sides encourages the distaste for any kind of killing. These make anything other than extremely accurate killing – i.e., only the 'guilty', – increasingly unacceptable in western societies. Unless it can be 'sanitary', with few deaths, war as a legitimate institution is itself undermined.The RMA with its emphasis on IW offers such sanitization, at least in principle. See Robert L. O'Connell, *Ride of the Second Horseman: Birth and Death of War* (NY: Oxford UP 1995); Adams (note 7); and Michael Howard, George J. Andreopoulos and Mark R. Shulman (eds.) *The Laws of War: Constraints on Warfare in the Western World* (New Haven, CT: Yale UP 1994).

9. For relatively in-depth discussions of these points, see Eliot A. Cohen, Michael J. Eisenstadt, and Andrew J. Bacevich, *Knives, Tanks and Missiles: Israel's Security Revolution* (Washington DC: The Washington Institute for Near East Policy 1998); Hirsh Goodman and W. Seth Carus *The Future Battlefield and the Arab-Israeli Conflict* (New Brunswick, NJ: CT Transaction 1990); Chris C. Demchak, 'Numbers or networks: Organizational and modernization dilemmas in the Israeli Defense Forces', *Armed Forces and Society* 23/2 (Winter 1996a) pp.179–208; and the volume by Shai Feldman (ed.) *Technology and Strategy: Future Trends (conference summary, Tel Aviv University 1987)* (Tel Aviv Jaffee Institute for Strategic Studies 1989).

10. Israel's military successes are often due to extraordinary sacrifice on the part of tactical commanders. It is a history of tactical innovation and personal sacrifice but not one of exceptionally efficient cross-leveling use of organizational resources. In particular, the IDF's ability to perform combined arms operations has never been great, especially in wartime. For both the military and political problems of the Israeli wars, see Trevor N. Dupuy, *Elusive Victory: The Arab–Israeli Wars, 1947–1974* (NY: Harper & Row 1978); and Samuel Sager, *The Parliamentary System of Israel* (Syracuse UP 1985). See also Richard A. Gabriel, *Operation Peace for Galilee: The Israeli-PLO War in Lebanon* (NY: Hill and Wang 1984); and Yoram Peri, *Between Battles and Ballots: Israeli Military in Politics* (Cambridge, UK: CUP 1983).

11. This vision of the 1991 Gulf War has been repeatedly undermined in analytical publications but the imagery produced by television is much stronger than the reality. For one such early critique, see Gene I. Rochlin and Chris C. Demchak, 'The Gulf War: Technological and Organizational Implications', *Survival* 33 (March 1991) pp.260–73. For a later analysis, see George Friedman and Meredith Friedman, *The Future of War: Power, Technology and American World Dominance in the Twenty-First Century* (NY: St Martin's Griffin Press 1996).

12. See Gene I. Rochlin, 'Broken Plowshare: System Failure and the Nuclear Power Industry', in Jane Summerton (ed.) *Changing Large Technical Systems* (Boulder, CO: Westview Press 1994) pp.231–61.

13. Faced with mind-boggling complexity across millions of lines of code and the addition of

the deviant human into the process, the computer industry began sending its not-quite-finished programs out for volunteers to play with to see what went wrong. This was called the 'beta test', after the initial functioning or 'alpha', test occurred inside the firm.the highly integrated RMA military's system of systems shares many of the characteristics of these early programs, including the difficulty of testing in advance of completing the program. There are real limitations to organizational simulations and, as of now, the actual use of a highly integrated organization cannot reliably be simulated in advance. Not only scale matters but humans are remarkably deviant in their activities, posing exceptional difficulties for the simulation community in struggling to model organizational behavior. See Richard W. Pew and Anne S. Mavor (eds.) *Modeling Human and Organizational Behavior: Application to Military Simulations* (Washington DC National Research Council: National Academy Press 1998). All RMA-associated future paths are, at this point, completely opaque because no nation has yet performed this 'beta test', for anyone else's benefit. Hence, any nation implementing a highly integrated RMA military will be, in effect, performing an 'organizational beta test', (OBT), facing the surprises and knowledge burden across all the elements of the socio-technical system on its own.

14. See Efraim Turban, Ephraim McLean, and James Wetherbe, *Information Technology for Management: Making Strategic Connections for Strategic Advantage*, 2nd ed. (NY: John Wiley 1999). See also Thomas J. Buckholtz, *Information Proficiency* (NY: Van Nostrand Reinhold 1995).

15. This kind of integration in one major business firm cost $200 million and involved thousands of consultants to install the system and keep it operating effectively. This firm purchased the most successful of these huge integration applications, the one by SAP of Germany. The firm employs 10,000 maintenance consultants who oversea the installation and maintenance of the 70 odd module program. The selection of these programs is usually the outcome of 'enterprise resources planning', (ERP) by a firm, a process that is a highly rationalized, comprehensive effort to get every single process in the organization operating in perfect synchronization with every business goal and opportunity. For a discussion of this case and of the managerial challenges of what are called enterprise-wide applications, see Turban *et al.* (note 14) Chs.7–9.

16. The business press does not use this language but the stories of failure clearly indicate the knowledge burden to be a shortcoming. See Joseph L. Badaracco, *The Knowledge Link: How Firms Compete Through Strategic Alliances* (Boston: Harvard Business School Press 1991). See also Turban *et al.* (note 14) for illustrative cases throughout the text.

17. In 1996 I published a piece on the modernization of the ground forces of the IDF and will draw upon that work in some parts of this discussion, especially the historical material. See Demchak (note 9) pp.179–89.

18. See Cohen *et al.* (note 9) p.104.

19. See Ikujiro Nonaka and Hirotaka Takeuchi, 'A New Organizational Structure', HyperText Organization, in Laurence Prusak (ed.) *Knowledge in Organizations* (Boston: Butterworth-Heinemann 1997) pp.99–133.

20. There is a continuing debate on whether this is or is not a 'revolution'. See Earl H. Tilford, 'The Revolution in Military Affairs: Prospects and Cautions', *US Army War College Published Papers* (Carlisle, PA: May 1995) p.1; Andrew R. Krepinevich, 'Cavalry to computer: The pattern of military revolutions', *The National Interest* 37 (Fall 1994) pp.30–42 and the edited volume, Robert L. Pfaltzgraff, Jr and Richard H. Shultz Jr (eds.) *War in the Information Age: New Challenges for US Security Policy* (Washington DC: Brassey's 1997).

    Others argue this is merely the next step in incremental technological changes. See Stephen Biddle, 'Assessing Theories of Future War', paper presented at American Political Science Association annual conference (Washington DC, Sept. 1997).The debate is not relevant to this discussion.

21. See Tilford (note 20) p.1; and Krepinevich (note 20) pp.30–42.

22. See JV2010 (note 4).

23. See CFJO (note 5) p.2.

24. For the use of another frequently-used term – the 'Military Technology Revolution', see

James R. Fitzsimonds and Jan M. van Tol, 'Revolutions in Military Affairs', *Joint Force Quarterly* (Spring 1994) pp.24–31; Dan Goure, 'Is There a Military Technical Revolution in America's Future?', *The Washington Quarterly* 16/4 (1993) pp.175–92; and Kenneth F. McKenzie Jr, 'Beyond Luddites and magicians: Examining the MTR', *Parameters* (Summer 1995) pp.15–21. The label 'RMA', however, has come to encompass a military that successfully employs networked computerized innovations in military technologies and operations, and so will be solely used here.

Other terms such as the 'Revolution in Security Affairs', (RSA) are too specialized for a general publication but are hereby noted. See Cohen *et al.* (note 9).

Information warfare (IW) is widely used, although at this time there is no real consensus on what exactly is involved other than offensive-defensive use of computer networks by someone. For an introduction to IW, see JDW, 'Jane's Special Report – Information Warfare 1997', *Janes Defense Weekly online* (Oct. 1996) downloaded 14 July 1999. See also John Arquilla and David Ronfeldt (eds.) *In Athena's Camp: Preparing for Conflict in the Information Age* (Santa Monica, CA: RAND 1996); and Chris C. Demchak, 'High reliability Organizational Dilemmas in the Information Age', *Journal of Contingency and Crisis Management* 42 (June 1996b) pp.93–103. For a broad view, see as well Martin C Libicki, *Defending Cyberspace and Other Metaphors* (Washington DC: National Defense University Press 1995a); and idem, *What is Information Warfare?* (Washington DC: National Defense University Press 1995b).

Another term gaining in usage among military analysts is 'Network Centric Warfare', but this has yet to be widely employed for IW. See David S. Alberts, John J. Garstka, and Frederick P. Stein, 'Network Centric Warfare: Developing and Leveraging Information Superiority', *Department of Defense C4ISR Cooperative Research Program* (Washington DC: DoDCCRP Publications 1999).

Finally, information operations is increasingly used as a generic term for all activities using the information associated with computerization, whether or not these operations are ever directly employed in battle.This term is so easily integrated into the common military lexicon that I could find no seminal article defining the term, while there are many using the term without any definition. For an excellent critique of this linguistic morass, see James F. Dunnigan, *Digital Soldiers* (NY: St Martin's Press 1996).

25. The central coordinating statement of these visions is the Joint Chiefs' of Staff 1996 statement, 'Vision 2010', and their May 1997 follow-on elaboration, 'Concept for Future Joint Operations (CFJO)'. I also draw upon the equivalent vision statements of the subordinate services.These documents express how these senior leaders expect implementation of the advanced information technologies will change their future military activities, costs, and successes in both the actual execution of an operation and in power projection en route.
26. See JV2010 (note 4).
27. It is important to note that 'information war', can be attempted by any organization. It is more properly the full range of applications of information across all spectra of operations. The RMA organization differs in that it is in principle optimized to use information operations most effectively. See Defense Science Board (DSB), Department of Defense, US Government, *Report of Defense Science Board Task Force on Information Warfare – Defense (IW-D)* (Washington DC: US Government Printing Office Nov. 1996) URL: http://cryptomeorg/iwdmain.
28. See David C. Gompert, Richard L. Kugler and Martin C. Libicki, *Mind the Gap: Promoting a Transatlantic Revolution in Military Affairs* (Washington DC: National Defense UP 1999) pp.33–4.
29. See JV2010 (note 4).
30. See ibid. p.17.
31. See Gen. Gordon Sullivan, US Army Chief of Staff, 'America's Army – Focusing on the Future', in Association of the United States Army (AUSA), *Army Greenbook* (Washington DC: AUSA Press 1994) pp.19–29 (20). The doctrine of the US Army is largely driving the organizational notions of the RMA.Early in the 1990s, the US Army had begun to specify the outcomes the RMA would achieve once implemented. For example, the Army's

doctrine developers in TRADOC had defined the so-called Force XXI by five characteristics: 'doctrinal *flexibility*, strategic *mobility*, *tailorability* and modularity, joint and multinational *connectivity*, and the versatility to function in War and OOTW (Operations Other Than War)', [emphasis mine]. See US Army Training and Doctrine Command (TRADOC), Department of the Army, *Dimensional Operations for the Strategic Army of the Early Twenty-First Century, Pam 525-5* (Washington DC: US Government Printing Office 1994) p.3-1 and US Army Training and Doctrine Command (TRADOC), Department of the Army, *The Airland Battle and Corps: Operational Concepts series* (Washington DC: US Government Printing Office 1995).

These attributes are themselves developing with the organizational changes emergent in the process of translating the information warfare (IW) visions of senior US defense leaders into military organizational structures. See National Research Council (NRC), National Academy of Science, *Star 21: Strategic Technologies for the Army of the Twenty-First Century* (Washington DC: National Academic Press 1992). Later joint documents demonstrate the influence of these early expressions of what future militaries will contain by the use of language such as connectivity, modularity, real-time and synchronized operations. For examples of this commonality, see JV2010 (note 4) and the subordinate service documents.

32. See JV2010 (note 4) p.17.
33. See TRADOC 1994 (note 31).
34. See Winn Schwartau, 'An Introduction to Information Warfare', in Pfaltzgraff and Shultz (note 19) pp.47–60.
35. See Manuel De Landa, *War in the Age of Intelligent Machines* (NY: Zone Books 1991).
36. See Leon E. Salomon, 'At AMC, the Future Begins Today', in Association of the United States Army (AUSA), *Army Greenbook* (Washington DC: AUSA Press 1994) pp.69–76 (70).
37. See Rochlin and Demchak (note 11); Williamson Murray, *Air War in the Persian Gulf* (Baltimore, MD: Nautical and Aviation 1995); and Bruce W. Watson and Peter G. Tsouras (eds.) *Military Lessons of the Gulf War* (Novato, CA: Presidio Press 1993).
38. See Alvin Toeffler and Heidi Toeffler, *War and Anti-War* (Boston, MA: Little, Brown 1993).
39. See Schwartau (note 34) as well as Winn Schwartau, *Information Warfare* (NY: Thunder's Mouth Press 1994).
40. See Schwartau (note 34) p.49.
41. See Franklin C. Spinney, *Defense Facts of Life: The Plans/Reality Mismatch* (Boulder, CO: Westview Press 1985); and Ian McDonald, 'Exploiting Battlespace Transparency: Operating Inside an Opponent's Decision Cycle', in Pfaltzgraff and Shultz (note 19) pp.143–68.
42. See James Q. Wilson, *Bureaucracy: What Government Agencies Do and Why They Do It* (NY: Basic Books 1989) and Peter F. Drucker, *Technology Management and Society* (San Francisco, CA: Harper & Row 1959).
43. These concepts are dutifully, if not exactly, echoed in the vision statements of the subordinate services and, in future work, I will explore the implications of the inexactitude in these subordinate service echoes.
44. See TRADOC 1994 (note 31) p.3-1.
45. See Rick Maze, 'The War That will Never be Won', *Army Times* (5 Aug. 1996) p.26.
46. See Chris C. Demchak, 'Creating the Enemy: Worldwide Diffusion of an Electronic Military', in Emily Goldman and Leslie C. Eliason (eds.) *The Diffusion of Military Knowledge from the Napoleonic Era to the Information Age* (Edited volume under review by university publisher, forthcoming).
47. See Robert L. O'Connell, *Of Arms and Men: A History of War, Weapons and Aggression* (NY: OUP 1989); and Martin van Creveld, *Technology in War* (NY: Free Press 1989).
48. This model is spreading in the absence of any local or, often, strategic need. By some accounts, peace appears to be breaking out all over in the arenas of military competition between states. See John Mueller, *Retreat from Doomsday: the Obsolescence of Major War* (NY: Basic Books 1989); and John Lewis Gaddis, 'International Relations Theory and the

End of the Cold War', *International Security* 17/3 (Winter 1992) pp.5–58. For a longer range historical view, see also Lynn White Jr, *Medieval Technology and Social Change* (Oxford: OUP 1978). As the international system regroups following the demise of the Cold War, potential enemies have become less well defined and declared wars are becoming fewer and more deadly. Even while military budgets around the world are being reduced in response to an apparent relative reduction in imminent threats, military leaders around the globe are declaring their intention to modernize their organizations using information technologies (IT) and precision weapons in smaller, more professional force structures. It is possible that nations simply no longer declare their hostilities as war and, hence, while large wars are infrequent, lethal conflicts are more likely. Nonetheless, this explanation for diffusion does not adequately explain the geographic spread of modernization.

49. The taken-for-granted aspect of this structuration is best captured by the following statement by the Chief of the People's Army of Vietnam. Despite halving a 1.2 million strong armed forces since 1988, by 1993 Vietnam was planning on having 'regular and modern armed forces by the end of the century'. See Robert Karniol, 'PAVN strives to modernize in a climate of austerity', *Jane's Defence Weekly* 3 (3 April 1993) p.18. A long-time intelligence analyst specializing in East Asia dismissed regional competition as a factor in the modernization programs of East Asian countries, characterizing the process as 'keeping up with the neighbors', with no perception of hostile intent by neighboring countries. See JDW Interview, 'Hugh White, Deputy Secretary, Strategy and Intelligence, Australian DoD', *Jane's Defence Weekly* (24 July 1996) p.32.

    Finally, a curious case is Botswana, whose modernization tendency is clearly an anomaly for Sub-Saharan Africa. Its geographic location suggests no opponent aside from South Africa which could pose a sophisticated threat, and that one potential foe has recently experienced a peaceful transition to democracy. See Demchak forthcoming.

50. See David Strang and John W. Meyer, 'Institutional Conditions for Diffusion', *Theory and Society* 22 (1993) pp.487–511.

51. For a better rendition of this argument that the patterns of world wide military modernization are difficult to explain using traditional realist explanations, see Chris C. Demchak, 'Watersheds in Perception and Knowledge', *Contemporary Security Policy* 20/3 (Dec. 1999).

52. See Adams (note 7) as well as Friedman and Friedman (note 11).

53. See JV2010 (note 4).

54. More precisely, this system of systems links four large networks for complete battlefield overview by the commander.

    The first is a sensor grid providing long range (up 300 km) real-time and detailed information streams. The second is an engagement grid with graphical real-time depiction of all elements of the battle (and refined trend analyses on the spot presumably).

    The third is an enormous database grid providing query, drill down, summary, and push information in all directions of the command structure.

    The fourth is an offensive information operations network that enables the overt or covert destruction, disruption, diversion, intrusion, insertion, and inspection of the targeted organization's use of information technologies. For elaboration of these concepts, see JV2010 (note 4); Gompert *et al.* (note 28) p.34; and Allen and Demchak forthcoming 2000.

55. See Frances Cairncross, *The Death of Distance: How the Communications Revolution Will Change Our Lives* (Cambridge, MA: Harvard Business School Press 1996).

56. See Adams (note 7).

57. Likely effectiveness (F) of an organization is defined as the level of 'systems fit', between the precision requirements built into the system and the surprise potential inherent in the level of unknowable or knowable unknowns extant coordination of activities through knowledge exchange and the validity of the information exchanged for the situation at hand. For a discussion of 'systems fit', and effectiveness, see Michael Harrison, *Diagnosing Organizations: Methods, Models and Processes* (Beverly Hills, CA: Sage Publications 1987). For a discussion by a panel of organization scholars which placed effectiveness as one of the key components of productivity, see Douglas H. Harris (ed.) *Organizational Linkages: Understanding the Productivity Paradox* (Washington DC:

National Academy Press 1994) p.8. The definition of effectiveness is always under debate among both practitioners and scholars, especially in security studies and defense policy debates due to the material and human costs of mistakes.

58. See Wilson (note 42); Drucker (note 42); and Renate Mayntz and Thomas P. Hughes (eds.) *The Development of Large Technical Systems* (Boulder, CO: Westview Press 1988).

59. See Carl Mitcham, *Thinking Through Technology: The Path Between Engineering and Philosophy* (U. of Chicago Press 1994); and White (note 48).

60. See Nitin Nohria, 'Is a Network Perspective a Useful Way of Studying Organizations?', in idem and Robert G. Eccles (eds.) *Networks and Organizations: Structure, Form and Action* (Boston: Harvard Business School Press 1992) pp.1–22 (4).

61. See Gerald R. Salancik, 'Wanted: A Good Network Theory of Organization', *Administrative Science Quarterly* 40/2 (June 1995) pp.345–54.

62. As a side note for further research, it is possible that the basic form of an organization is neither a market nor hierarchy as suggested by Williamson nor any other bifurcated typology. See Oliver E. Williamson, *Markets and Hierarchies* (NY: Free Press 1975). Rather, Priore argues that markets may be at one end of a continuum with hierarchies at the other and the continuum may be composed of various kinds of networks. See Michael J. Priore, 'Fragments of a Cognitive Theory of Technological Change and Organizational Structure', in Nohria and Eccles, *Networks and Organizations* (note 60) pp.430–44.

63. See Theodore Caplow, *Principles of Organization* (NY: Harcourt, Brace 1964).

64. For an introduction to the field and to further references see Sheila Jasanoff, Gerald E. Markle, James C. Peterson, and Trevor Pinch, *Handbook of Science and Technology Studies* (Thousand Oaks, CA: Sage Publications 1995); Mitcham and Jane Summerton (ed.) *Changing Large Technical Systems* (Boulder, CO: Westview Press 1994). For discussions of technology in organizations across varying circumstances, see Urs Gattiker, *Technology Management in Organizations* (Newbury Park, CA: Sage Publications 1990); Luis R. Gomez-Mejia and Michael W. Lawless (eds.) *Organizational Issues in High Technology Management Monographs in Organizational Behavior and Industrial Relations*, Vol.11 (London: JAI Press 1990); and Jon Clark, Ian McLoughlin, Howard Rose, and Robert King, *The Process of Technological Change: New Technology and Social Choice in the Workplace* (Cambridge, UK: CUP 1990).

65. See Stephen R. Barley, 'The alignment of technology and structure through roles and networks', *Administrative Science Quarterly* 35/1 (Spring 1990) pp.61–103; and Marlene E. Burkhardt and Daniel J. Brass, 'Changing patterns or patterns of change: The effects of a change in technology on social network structure and power', *Administrative Science Quarterly* 35/1 (1990) pp.104–27.

66. See Philip Selznick, *TVA and the Grassroots: A Study in the Sociology of Formal Organizations* (Berkeley, CA: U. of California Press 1949); and Johannes M. Pennings and Peter Buitendam (eds.) *New Technology as Organizational Innovation: The Development and Diffusion of Microelectronics* (Cambridge, MA: Ballinger 1987).

67. See Shoshana Zuboff, *In the Age of the Smart Machine* (NY: Basic Books 1984).

68. See Rochlin (note 12) for a discussion of this kind of outcome in the nuclear power industries of Europe.

69. See Summerton (note 64) as well as Mayntz and Hughes (note 58).

70. This use of the term knowledge is unusual. If one perceives organizations as 'knowledge-producing', entities or as information processing systems, then knowledge is the lifeblood of operations. See Martin Landau and Russell Stout Jr, '"To Manage Is Not to Control: The Folly of Type II Errors"', *Public Administration Review* 39 (March–April 1979) pp.148–56. In my work, knowledge comes in any form that is critical to completing the mission at hand. Hence, the right spare part, manual or technical education in the repairer's head can all contain the same essential knowledge. In principle, they may be considered interchangeable if the knowledge is exactly replicated. In practice, all three are needed because each has unique types of knowledge. The part contains the ability to operate, the manual the information about how to connect and disconnect, and the repairer the knowledge to remember patterns in diagnosis and to pick up, select and turn things. In the abstract, however, any of the three can be perceived as bringing essential knowledge to the situation.

It is a much broader notion of knowledge than is normally used. It has a great deal in common with the recently emerging economic notions of Romer who has revolutionized economic thinking by adding 'K', for knowledge to the established Capital-Labor equation. See Chris C. Demchak, *Military Organizations, Complex Machines: Modernization in the U.S. Armed Services* (Ithaca, NY: Cornell UP 1991); Chris C. Demchak, 'Coping, Copying, and Concentrating: Organizational Learning and Modernization in Militaries (Case Studies of Israel, Germany and Britain)', *Journal of Public Administration Research and Theory* 5/3 (July 1995) pp.345–76; and Paul M. Romer, 'Beyond the Knowledge Worker', *World Link* Davos '95 (Jan./Feb. 1995). Correspondingly, the conception of slack is based on the notion that accurate knowledge at the time and place of deleterious surprises is the fundamental component of slack.

71. See Jay R. Galbraith, *Organizational Design* (Reading, MA: Addison-Wesley 1976). See also LaPorte (note 3) and Demchak (note 70).

72. The literature on complexity is incomplete; the work so far has focused on some aspects of complexity and neglected the power of the phenomenon as a whole. Examples of conceptual difficulties with complexity and surprise in their various guises exist even in some of the better works. One well-known author observes that size and wealth decrease internal and external uncertainty (for militaries) without much explanation as to how this intuitively problematical outcome can be true. See Barry R. Posen, 'Nationalism, the Mass Army and Military Power', *International Security* 18/2 (Fall 1993) pp.80–124 (49).

A second author suggests that a war without chaos can exist if it is solely between machines – no surprises or uncertainty. See Zvi Lanir, Baruch Fischoff, and Stephen Johnson, 'Military Risk-taking: C3I and the Cognitive Functions of Boldness in War', *Journal of Strategic Studies* 11/1 (March 1988) pp.96–114 (100).

Even Perrow, in an otherwise excellent book, seems to muddle the concept of complexity by linking it to loose coupling and, indirectly, to both greater and lesser redundancy. See Charles Perrow, *Normal Accidents: Living with High Risk Technologies* (NY: Basic Books 1984) p.280. The operational difficulties are obvious. Complex systems produce the unexpected with annoying regularity but the fragmented set of approaches has often produced inconclusive research and little broadly applicable guidance. For example, redundancy is either a cure for, or a cause of, complexity, depending on the author chosen. See Martin Landau, 'Redundancy, Rationality, and the Problem of Duplication and Overlap', *Public Administration Review* (July–Aug. 1969) pp.346–58.

The situation is exacerbated by the tendency of complexity to vary in its significance across systems. For recent works specifically on the development of a science of complexity, see M. Mitchell Waldrop, *Complexity: The Emerging Science at the Edge of Order and Chaos* (NY: Simon and Schuster 1992); and John Casti, *Complexification: Explaining A Paradoxical World through the Science of Surprise* (NY: HarperCollins 1994).

73. There is considerable disagreement about how one measures complexity. In my original work I drew upon LaPorte (note 3) in measuring it parametrically by the number of components (N), the differentiation among them (D) and their interdependence (I). In brief, increases in one attribute not accommodated by decreases in another constitute an increase in complexity. Space constraints forbid reproducing the necessarily lengthy defense of this measure but it has proven consistent with similar measures in both engineering and psychology. See Demchak (note 70) for an application of the measure. For other variations, see Casti (note 72) as well as Waldrop (note 72).

74. The actual origin of the term 'tightly coupled', is unclear but it appears Karl Weick first used the term to mean strong interdependence between elements whose operations are critical to the organization. It is a term with a good deal of evocative power, expressing the consequences of high levels of interdependence. See Karl E. Weick, *The Social Psychology of Organizing*, 2nd ed. (Reading, MA: Addison-Wesley 1979 <1969>).

75. See Lee Sproul and Sara Kiesler, *Connections: News Ways of Working in the Networked Organization* (Cambridge, MA: MIT Press 1991), and Casti (note 72).

76. See Weick (note 74) as well as Perrow (note 72) for this use of the term 'coupled'.

77. See Waldrop (note 72). Four newer literatures with rising conceptual power are directly

relevant to understanding the rising complexification of modern military structures, environments and missions.

The first is complexity theory led by the Santa Fe Institute scholars. See Waldrop (note 72); Horgan; and Ralph Gomory, 'The Known, the Unknown and the Unknowable', *Scientific American* 272/6 (June 1995) pp.120+. This approach is also distributed across disciplines as other scholars individually seek a way to handle largescale, dynamic, integrated systems. For various complementary approaches, see Demchak (note 70); C.F. Larry Heiman, 'Understanding the Challenger Disaster: Organizational Structure and the Design of Reliable Systems', *American Political Science Review* 87/2 (June 1993) pp.421–35; and Emery Roe, *Taking Complexity Seriously: Policy Analysis, Triangulation and Sustainable Development* (Boston: Kluwer Academic 1998). Increasingly, variations of this work are called 'surprise theory'. See the volume by Casti (note 72). This literature focuses on how qualitative rules operating through a complexifying system can produce unpredictable and path-dependent outcomes which can differ each time the system operates. The goal is to seek the minimal set of underlying rules that govern the surprising outcomes in complex systems and to be able to identify the broad outlines of likely outcomes – the 'trends', – in advance.

The second is the chaos theory or nonlinear dynamics literature. For basic introductions to these concepts, see James Gleick, , *Chaos: Making a New Science* (NY: Viking 1987); L. Douglas Kiel, *Managing Chaos and Complexity in Government: A New Paradigm for Managing Change, Innovation, and Organizational Renewal* (San Francisco, CA: Jossey-Bass 1994); and Margaret J. Wheatley, *Leadership and the New Science* (San Francisco, CA: Boerrett-Koehler 1992).

The third is the network literature which studies groups of elements which have formed into structures whose relations show important characteristics. See Priore (note 62); Nohria (note 60); and Salancik (note 61).

Finally the fourth is the literature on largescale technical systems (LTS) which focuses on identifying the constellations of socio-technical circumstances most likely to incur costly and/or catastrophic surprises for whole communities. See again Mayntz and Hughes (note 58); and Summerton (note 64).

78. See Casti (note 72) in particular.
79. See Demchak (note 70).
80. While fully aware of the oversimplification of the measure and that a healthy statistical literature on sensitivity analysis exists, I have nonetheless proposed a simple measure of possible changes in robustness as the multiplication of redundancy by slack. Intuitively appealing, the term rises or falls as the combination of redundancy and slack rises and falls. See Demchak (note 70). If system A has high slack and low redundancy and system B has low slack and high redundancy, then it is intuitively clear that both could have the same level of robustness. The processes resulting in robustness vary considerably, and more needs to be known about both systems and the slack or redundancy at their critical nodes. This measure is extremely rough but heuristically useful for focusing on the relationships between complexity and robustness via redundancy and slack.
81. See Demchak (note 70).
82. Chaos theorists start with an equation and watch the outcomes to discern the rule changes over time. Complexity theorists set up the rules for change and then watch the outcomes to see if any general unifying relation or equation is at work. See Gleick as well as Gomory.
83. See Gleick (note 77); Gomoryn (note 77); and John Horgan, 'From Complexity to Perplexity', *Scientific American* 272/6 (June 1995) pp.104–9.
84. See Roe (note 77) for a discussion of how taking complexity seriously has profound implications for social interactions.
85. See Turban *et al.* (note 14) p.530.
86. See again Casti (note 72); Waldrop (note 72); and Demchak (note 70).
87. For organizations using networked computers, effectiveness (F) can also be defined in web-related organizational terms as the least constrained systems fit between the coordination of activities through knowledge exchange and the validity of the information exchange. See Chris C. Demchak, Christian Friis and Todd M. La Porte, 'Webbing

Governance: National Differences in Constructing the Public Face', in G. David Garson, *Handbook of Public Information Systems* (NY: Marcel Dekker 2000). For more discussion of applying this approach see also the CyPRG web site (www.cyprg.arizona.edu).

88. Published statements of expected outcomes by senior leaders, given sufficient emphasis through a large organization, are powerful influences on the social constructions of reality emerging in the rest of the organization. For a useful introduction to this social construction approach, see Anne L. Schneider and Helen Ingram, 'How the Social Construction of Target Populations Contributes to Problems in Policy Design', *Policy Currents* 3/1 (Feb. 1993) pp.1+. For the emergent model, I draw primarily upon the expected characteristics of the new information technology military as stated by the US Joint Chiefs of Staff (JCS) and by the subordinate services.

89. For complementary discussions of this problem, see Weick (note 74); Demchak (note 70); and Galbraith (note 10).

90. See CFJO (note 5) pp.31–3.

91. Among the vulnerabilities are: 'may outpace our allies and coalition partners' ability to integrate[,]... data overload[,]... [competition with commercial uses,] assured military access to all required frequencies can not be taken for granted[,]... strategic and operational commanders [tempted] to take control of tactical actions[,]... [o]ver reliance on, or unrealistic expectations from, information systems could inhibit or lengthen decisions. ...Sophisticated information systems can fail... [need to]develop a new skill set of knowing how to correctly evaluate digitized information ... success results from technological advances and innovative ways of considering and combining them for warfighting ...'. See CFJO (note 5) pp.31–3.

92. See ibid. pp.67–71.

93. 'The JFC uses knowledge about the adversary and the battlespace to determine enemy centers of gravity – which may be forces or functions – and to identify vulnerabilities which render these centers of gravity susceptible to attack and destruction. Information superiority ways and means, particularly information manipulation, computer viruses, and other information intrusions, will increase the JFC's capability to asymmetrically attack a variety of enemy targets'. See CFJO (note 5) pp.67–71.

94. 'Information superiority will help the JFC determine when termination is appropriate or imminent and will help the joint force monitor termination actions. The JFC will rely on capabilities of the four new concepts to keep an adversary in check during this unstable period and to enforce termination conditions'. See CFJO (note 5) pp.67–71.

95. See ibid. pp.67.

96. For this insight about complexity, I thank Lt. Col. Dennis Lowrey (ret.) who worked for years to combine simulations and real forces in useful learning exercises.

97. '...data include both open sources and traditional intelligence, surveillance, and reconnaissance systems and architectures. Collected data becomes information when processed into usableforms such as reports or images. This information is transformed into intelligence by purposeful analysis, interpretation, and collation with related information and background to meet the specific needs of the user.' See CFJO (note 5) pp.46.

98. Much of this discussion was previously published in Chris C. Demchak, 'Information Warfare, Organizations, and the Power of Disruption', *L'Enjeu Atlantiques* (June 1996).

99. This is currently an extremely divisive political debate but credible analysts and scholars are declaring support for ceding the Golan in view of the new IO capabilities. See Uri Bar-Joseph, 'Israel's Northern Eyes and Shield: The Strategic Value of the Golan Heights Revisited', *Journal of Strategic Studies* 21/3 (Sept. 1998) pp.46–66. See also Cohen *et al.* (note 9).

100. See Reuven Pedatzur, 'Obstacles Towards a Regional Control Mechanism: Israel's View of Ballistic Missile Proliferation in the Peace Era', *Contemporary Security Policy* 16/2 (1995) p.163.

101. See B. O'Shea, 'Israel's Vietnam?', *Studies in Conflict and Terrorism* 21/3 (Sept. 1998) p.307.

102. See Stuart A. Cohen, 'Small States and Their Armies: Restructuring the Militia Framework of the Israel Defense Force', *Journal of Strategic Studies* 18/4 (Dec. 1995a) pp.78–93 (81).

103. See Gabriel (note 10); O'Shea as well as Scott Peterson, '"Grapes of Wrath" Blitz Still Bites Back at Israel', *Christian Science Monitor International Online* (15 Oct. 1997) http://www.csmonitor.com/durable/1997/10/15/intl/intl.1.html, downloaded 22 Oct. 1999.
104. See Cohen (note 102) p.89.
105. See Bar-Joseph (note 99).
106. See Arieh O'Sullivan, 'IDF targets 21 days the millennium bug could strike', *Jerusalem Post (online)* (17 Jan. 1999b) www.jpost.co.il, downloaded 21 Oct. 1999.
107. This material was obtained during interviews with senior IDF officers, active and retired, in 1990–93 and referred forthwith as 'interviews 1990–93'.
108. See Stuart Cohen, 'The Israeli Defense Forces from a "People's Army" to a "Professional military" – Causes and Implications', *Armed Forces and Society* 21/2 (Winter 1995b) pp.237–54 (241–3).
109. See O'Sullivan (note 106) pp.17–18.
110. See Stuart A. Cohen, 'From Integration to Segregation: the Role of Religion in the IDF', *Armed Forces and Society* 25/3 (Spring 1999) pp.387–406. The current uprising has changed Reservist service time right now but is not clear the new service lengths are permanent.
111. See Wiebe E. Bijker, Thomas P. Hughes and Trevor J. Pinch (eds.) *The Social Construction of Technological Systems: New Directions in the Sociology and History of Technology* (Cambridge, MA: MIT Press 1987) p.240.
112. See O'Sullivan (note 106).
113. This intention has been gaining momentum for some time, beginning in full force with the tenure of former Chief of General Staff Ehud Barak (1991–94) who strongly promoted the professionalization of the force and reduction in dependence on the reserves. See Cohen (notes 102 and 108) for a particularly informed discussion of these changes.
114. See Jonathan Marcus, 'Israel's Defense Policy at a Strategic Crossroads', *The Washington Quarterly* 22/1 (Winter 1998) pp.33–48.
115. See Cohen (note 102).
116. '24/7', as a short name for continuous operations has emerged with the rising popularity of ecommerce where website stores are 'open', all the time. For a basic discussion of this widening phenomenon, see Turban *et al.* (note 14) p.236.
117. See Pat Allen and Chris C. Demchak, 'An Information Operations (IO) Conceptual Model and Application Framework', paper presented and accepted for proceedings of Military Operations Research Society (MORS) Symposium, 20–22 June 2000, US Air Force Academy, Colorado Springs, CO.
118. A 'normal error', is simply the inherent surprise encased in large complex systems with limited sensor sets. All complex systems have this error in some fashion. See Perrow (note 72) for a full explanation of this term and concept.
119. These essential elements and their interrelation are discussed in greater detail in Pat Allen and Chris C. Demchak, 'The Need for, and Design of, an IO-ISR Federation of Models'. Paper presented to Simulation Interoperability Standards Organization's (SISO) conference, 26–31 March 2000, Orlando, Florida.
120. See La Porte (note 3); Demchak (note 70); Roe (note 77); and Sproul and Kiesler (note 75).
121. For comparison, Turkey with a population of 65 million bought just 300,000 in the same year. See Nisso Cohen, 'The Israel High-Tech Industry – Fifty Years of Excellence', *Ministry of Foreign Affairs website* (Government of Israel 1999) URL:www.israel-mfa.gov.il/mfa/goasp?MFAH01vu0, downloaded 17 Oct. 1999.
122. See iGuide, 'Israeli Internet Guide: Growth Data', *NetVision Corporation* (2000) www.iguide.co.il/stats, downloaded 20 Jan. 2000.
123. See NUA, 'Internet Users in the Middle East (estimated)', *NUA* (1999) www.nua.ie/surveys/how_many_online/m_east, downloaded 15 Jan. 2000.
124. See ibid.
125. See ibid.
126. See IIS, 'Science and Technology in Israel Ministry of Foreign Affairs Online', *Israel Information Service* (1999) gopher://israel-info gov.il/00/facts/science/, downloaded 17 Oct. 1999.

142   *Israel's National Security Towards the 21st Century*

127. See Israeli Central Bureau of Statistics (ICBS), *Statistical Abstract of Israel* (Tel Aviv: Government of Israel Press 1999) http://www.cbs.gov.il/, downloaded 15 Jan. 2000.
128. See Cohen (note 108).
129. See Barbara Tuck, 'Israel: A Remarkable Hotbed for Hi-Tech', *Electronic Systems Technology & Design: Computer Design* 36/7 (July 1996) pp.16–23. See also Barbara Kollmeyer, 'Israeli hightechs talk e-commerce', *CBS NewsWatch online* (27 Oct. 1999) www.cbs.marketwatch.com/archive/19991027/news/current/israel.htx, downloaded 27 Oct. 1999.
130. See Israel Line, 'Economic Briefs: Israeli company Go SMS has developed a technology enabling cellular handset owners to retrieve information from Internet sites', *Israel Line* (NY: Israeli Consulate Online, 6 Feb. 2000).
131. See Reuven Gal, *A Portrait of the Israeli Soldier* (NY: Greenwood Press 1986).
132. This is not something Israelis like to talk about but most of them see as necessary for their survival – that potential enemies know as little as possible about the Israeli national defense structure. This has led, for example, to the closure of an IDF English language publication by then Chief of Staff Ehud Barak who is supposed to have said that it only educated Israel's enemies. See interviews 1990–93.
133. Material obtained during interviews with senior webmasters across major government agencies in Israel as a part of National Science Foundation (NSF SDEST) grant no. 9602007 Hotlinked Governance (grant period 1996-1999).
134. The focus on science and technology is reinforced in the wider society. In the early 1950s, Prime Minister David Ben-Gurion, considered the founder of modern Israel, called for government policies to form a society based on advanced skills in science and technology. He argued this focus was needed because agriculture would not ultimately sustain a modernized Israel and the country had few other resources but their education and wits. Hence, the military drive for advanced technologies also had a strong economic basis. This scientification of Israel to replace agriculture as its main comparative advantage would directly help the defense industries who were until recently all owned by the government. See Michael Bar-Zohar, *Ben-Gurion* (NY: Adama Books 1978); Ze'ev Schiff, *A History of the Israeli Army* (NY: Macmillan 1985, orig. 1974); and, in particular, Howard M. Sachar, *A History of Israel*, Vol.II (NY: OUP 1987) p.218.
135. See Gunther E. Rothenberg, *The Anatomy of the Israeli Army* (London: Batsford 1979) pp.99–100.
136. See Shimon Engel, 'The Long Road from Molotov Cocktails to Missiles, Tanks and Lasers: A Technological History of the IDF', *IDF Journal* III (Summer 1988) pp.22–31; Gerald Steinberg, 'Recycled weapons', *Technology Review* 58 (April 1985) pp.28–38; and Benny Michelson, 'Born in battle: A history of the IDF through four decades', *IDF Journal* 15 (Summer 1988) pp.8–21.
137. See ibid. p.11.
138. It is interesting to note that these innovations were a work-around to an overall equipment shortage. See Engel (note 136). According to senior officers interviewed in a series of visits 1990–93, if the early acquisitions could have been entire systems of the first quality, the innovative piecemeal upgrading would not have been valued over acquiring intact new systems. The Israelis always would have preferred new equipment even if it posed severe maintenance challenges and were not interchangeable in any way with existing equipment. See also Stewart Reiser, *The Israeli Arms Industry* (NY: Holmes & Meier 1989).
139. See Aaron D. Rosenbaum, 'How Israeli Engineers Improve US Weaponry', *IEEE Spectrum* 25 (Nov. 1988) pp.38–9.
140. See Richard M. Hodgetts and Fred Luthans, *International Management: Culture, Strategy and Behavior* (NY: McGraw-Hill 2000) pp.118–23.
141. The small community of scholars of Israeli administration who publish in English demonstrate a common assessment of Israeli administration as highly personalistic. It sets unrealistic but politically charged goals and implements them poorly, and is widely intermingled in all aspects of the society in this former socialist state. Rosenbloom argues that divergent operating norms, values, and operating styles are typical for public administration in Israel and that a weak or missing ethic of public service is linked to a high degree of

personalization and a low degree of formalization of roles and obligations. See David H. Rosenbloom, 'Israel's Administrative Culture, Israeli Arabs, and Arab Subjects', *Syracuse Journal of International Law & Commerce* 13 (Spring 1987) pp.435–73. This situation is historically long-lived according to Caiden who characterized Israel's administrative culture as 'opportunistic dogmatism'. See Gerald E. Caiden, *Israel's Administrative Culture* (Berkeley: U. of California Institute of Governmental Studies monograph 1970) p.28.

142. See interviews 1990–93.
143. See Tuck (note 129).
144. In interviews, current and former officers noted the casual, unplanned nature of operations in peacetime, whether in acquisition, training, maintenance or command and control, which turned in war or crisis into frenzied self-sacrifice and intense, sometimes contradictory *ad hoc* efforts to find expedient solutions to organizational shortcomings ignored or endured in peace. During the 1982 Lebanon War the constant switching of commanders and commands in order to improvise a task organization around a situation is said to have 'created confusion and negated the much valued cohesion'. See Gabriel (note 10) p.185. In interviews, senior retired officers have argued that, since Israel's wars have been successes for the most part, there has been little incentive for the IDF organization to alter the widespread presumption that improvised operations will ultimately suffice. See interviews 1990–93.
145. See Demchak (note 9).
146. See Rosenbloom (note 141) pp.435–73.
147. See Caiden (note 141) p.28.
148. See Ira Sharkansky, *What Makes Israel Tick: How Domestic Policy-Makers Cope with Constraints* (Chicago, IL: Nelson-Hall 1985).
149. See Ira Sharkansky and Margaret Wrightson, 'The Overloaded State: Response to Ira Sharkansky', *Public Administration Review* 49 (March/April 1989) pp.201–5.
150. See interviews 1990–93.
151. See Israel Line, 'Assailants Fire on Israeli Bus Near Hebron', *Israel Line* (NY: Israeli Consulate Online, 3 Nov. 1999).
152. See Clifford Stoll, *The Cuckoo's Egg: Tracking a Spy Through the Maze of Computer Espionage* (NY: Doubleday 1989).
153. There is a vast literature on computer security today and the marketing of most of it promises 24/7 automatic protection. Nonetheless most of them required a skilled operator to keep ahead of the equally determined and skilled attacker. For a good basic primer on the issues, see William R. Cheswick and Steven M. Bellovin, *Firewalls and Internet Security* (NY: Addison-Wesley 1994).
154. See Perrow (note 72).
155. See Chris Nuttall, 'Chernobyl Virus Causes Asian Meltdown', *BBC Online News* (27 April 27 1999) URL:http://news2.thls.bbc.co.uk/hi/english/sci/tech/newsid_329000/329688, downloaded 10 May 1999.
156. See O'Sullivan (note 106).
157. In particular, the 1995 assassination of Prime Minister Rabin by a devout Yeminite Jew was extremely disturbing to the Israeli Jewish population because of their long held belief that 'Jews don't kill Jews', an extremely strong clan tenet. For a discussion of how the current divisions among Jews in Israel are affecting the IDF, see Cohen (note 110) pp.387–406.
158. See Gal (note 131).
159. There is a large literature acknowledging this change in Israel, much of it by Israelis themselves. For a brief introduction to these changes, see Jonathan Marcus, 'Israel Sharpens its Military Strategy', *BBC Online Special Report* (April 29 1998) http://news 2.thls.bbc.co.uk/hi/english/events/israel_at_50/israel_today/newsid_79000/79617, downloaded 17 Oct. 1999. For more depth, see works by Cohen (notes 102 and 108) and Efraim Inbar, 'Israeli National Security, 1973–1996', *Security and Policy Studies* 38 (Bar-Ilan University, Israel: BESA Center for Strategic Studies Publications Feb. 1998) p.76.
160. See Tuck (note 129).
161. See Israel Line, 3 Nov. 1999.
162. See Jacques S. Gansler, *Defense Conversion* (Cambridge, MA: MIT Press 1995) and Lauren Holland, *Weapons Under Fire* (London: Garland 1996).

163. See Rosenbaum (note 141) pp.38–9.
164. In the more technically advanced industries, it is increasingly assumed that a product on the market will be copied relatively rapidly. Hence, rather than trying to hoard technical secrets as the Apple Corporation did and ultimately losing them anyway, the current wisdom is that it is better to make something exceptionally complex (hard to reverse engineer) or exceptionally linked to derivative products that are too rapidly produced for a competitor to copy effectively. See Turban *et al.* (note 14) Ch.6.
165. See Tuck (note 129).
166. Cohen (notes 102 and 108) has noted that the IDF is iterating towards a de facto selective service by making it easy for the less competent conscripts to avoid military service. Unfortunately, the wider society's current support for conscription, based on a widespread belief that everyone serves, will be undermined over time if the IDF tries to only take the already computer literate middle and upper class conscripts.
167. See Turban *et al.* (note 14).
168. Doctrine is used here to mean the way in which operations are supposed to be conducted as accepted by the leaders of the organization. It is the 'way', not the purpose, of warfare. This definition differs from the former Soviet notion of doctrine adopted by much of the Third World. The latter includes the political purposes of conflict in the decisions concerning military strategy. The Israelis, like the British, have been reluctant to commit a standardized statement of 'doctrine', as defined here to paper. In general, aside from generally accepted tenets such as the necessity to be ready to improvise and subordinate autonomy, doctrine is defined locally in the training camps of the various corps such as Armor, Artillery, etc. In this situation, key generals define doctrine in their decisions and, until the next general with differing ideas comes along or all the implementing officers retire, this version prevails. It is for this reason that the memoirs of generals, routinely marginalized in countries like the US which publish doctrine, take on a greater importance in countries where only the retired will speak freely of the changes that occurred during their tenure. See Avraham Adan, *On the Banks of the Suez* (Novato, CA: Presidio Press 1980) and Shabtai Teveth, *The Tanks of Tammuz* (NY: Viking Press 1969) for examples of these post hoc revelations. One cautionary note: in such a small personalized society, it is not unusual to find that intra-organizational political battles continue in these memoirs.
169. See interviews 1990–93.
170. See Gal (note 131).
171. See Todd R. La Porte and Paula Consolini, 'Working in Practice but Not in Theory: Theoretical Challenges of "High Reliability", Organizations', *Journal of Public Administration Research and Theory* 1 (Jan. 1991) pp.19–48.
172. Gurian has noted that inhibitions and a wait-and-see attitudes decline dramatically as a young male's hormone levels are elevated. Late adolescent males have about 20 times the amount of aggression-fostering testoterone hormones as females who, conversely, have much higher levels of serotonin – the calming hormone. Males are better soldiers when the battle is overt, the tactical goals near term and clear, and the response largely physical. But females are more likely to perform better when the battle takes time or is covert, the tactical goals are longer term and require constant attention for subtle adjustments during implementation, and the response largely at a distance and psychological. Hence, the IDF's plan to grow smaller and reduce the employment of females is at variance with the kind of average skills associated with each gender group at this age. In a 1986, 60 minutes interview, the chief of the California Conservation Corps, a Vietnam vet, stated that he would prefer to have more females to send out to clear out forests. His experience is that the young males hurt themselves too often by impulsively trying to do something they could not physically do alone while the females always teamed up before attempting large jobs. For more information of the effects of these testoterone levels on impulsivity, see Jan Norman, 'The Evolutionary Theory of Sexual Attraction', *Web of Human Sexuality Site* (University of Missouri-Kansas City 1998) URL: http://www.umkc.edu/sites/hsw/other/evolution.html, downloaded 8 Jan. 2000. See also Michael Gurian, *The Good Son* (NY: Putnam 1999).
173. See Gal (note 131) p.34.

174. See interviews 1990–93.
175. If the age and gender cannot fully explain this phenomena, it is often telling that game software – long the strongest province of young males in the US – tends to be the most inefficient in terms of memory use, the least helpful in troubleshooting options, and the most nonrobust on computers with multiple applications open. For a discussion of the security consequences of loopholes left in sloppy programs, see John Vacca, *Internet Security Secrets* (Foster City, CA: IDG 1996).
176. This process has also resulted in an interesting public relations phenomenon in which the number of beta testers is highlighted in promotional literature announcing the imminent arrival of the new program in the stores. This kind of test involves more than computer program bugs; it also engages the interactive effects of computerization on knowledge bases, anticipatory behaviors and other organizational incentives which are often forgotten by the programmers. Many systems fail to meet the promises of their promoters because the humans in the system were presumed to be relatively inert components of the new computerized organization.This 'buggy' phenomenon has become so common that, for a while in the early years of massive applications, the number of beta testers was used by Microsoft in its advance advertising for the new Windows 95. Interesting enough, nothing was ever said about what these over 400 beta testers reported or what was done in response. Today, application bugs are assumed to exist and customers' complaints back to the firm are used in lieu of this small army of formal testers. Applications are no longer held up to such scrutiny before being issued. Instead, consultants and firm technical support, for which the client pays additionally, are rapidly becoming the alternative to beta tests by volunteers.
177. See Zuboff (note 67) as well as Perrow (note 72).
178. The page limits of this piece preclude a full discussion of where and how to insert this slack. See Demchak (note 72) for more details.
179. See Turban *et al.* (note 14); and Nonaka and Tageuchi (note 19) pp.99–133.
180. See Russell F. Weigley, *History of the United States Army*, 2nd ed. (Bloomington: Indiana UP 1984).
181. See Marcus (note 159) pp.33–48.
182. See Bar-Joseph (note 99).
183. See Rochlin and Demchak (note 11); and William G. Pagonis, *Moving Mountains: Lessons in Leadership* (Boston, MA: Harvard Business School Press 1992).
184. See Gaddis (note 48) pp.21–2.
185. See Toeffler(s) (note 38) p.139.
186. See as noted by Cohen *et al.* (note 9).
187. An important side note: the US RMA also embodies less and less use of reservists but the political realities of the costs of a large expeditionary force as of now do not allow this part of the model to be pursued. As IW becomes dominant, however, I fully expect this portion of the RMA model to be more implemented in the US.
188. See Cohen *et al.* (note 9) p.104.
189. See Martin Landau, 'On the Concept of a Self-Correcting Organization', *Public Administration Review* (Nov.–Dec. 1973) pp.533–42.
190. See Nonaka and Takeuchi (note 19) pp.99–133.
191. 'The goal is an organizational structure that views bureaucracy and the task force as complementary rather than mutually exclusive... Like an actual hypertext document, hypertext organization is made up of interconnected layers or contexts... Nonaka and Tageuchi (note 19) pp.106–7.
192. See ibid. pp.99–133.
193. In a manuscript under construction now 'The Atrium – Refining the HyperText Organizational Form', I more fully explain the mechanisms of integrating an Atrium into an organization.
194. See Margaret J. Wheatley, *Leadership and the New Science* (San Francisco: Boerrett-Koehler 1992) as well as Gleick (note 77) for a more modern use of this term.
195. The evolution of the Internet or the World Wide Web is in essence a social history of information sharing among individuals embedded in organizations. There are several

versions of the history of the Internet. See Michael Benedikt (ed.) *Cyberspace: First Steps* (Boston: MIT Press 1991) for one discussion. See also the Internet Society website.

196. In organizational terms, especially for public organization, a webbed approach to information directly challenges the long-established notions of the fundamentals of bureaucratic power. Weber's sociological argument about such power, translated in the 1940s, was further symbolically captured by the 1970s concept of an 'iron triangle', in which public agencies, Congressional committees and interested corporate entities controlled outcomes nearly absolutely by controlling the information anyone outside the organization could acquire. See H. Gerth and C. Wright Mills (eds.) *From Max Weber: Essays in Sociology* (NY: Oxford 1947); and E. Sam Overman and Don F. Simanton, 'Iron Triangles and Issue Networks of Information Policy', *Public Administration Review* (special issue on public management information issues 1986) pp.584–9.

197. See Thomas H. Davenport, *Information Ecology* (NY: OUP 1997); and Charles Savage, *The 5th Generation Management* (London: Butterworth-Heinemann 1996) for interesting variations on these notions of integrating the web into the organization's and society's critical operational information flows.

198. See Cohen *et al.* (note 9).

199. I would argue the global community is currently bifurcated into regions where this city-like competition among more westernized nations dominates (e.g., the western hemisphere, western Europe) and regions marked by the lingering violence-prone less stable societies more typical of the realist perception of state relations (e.g., the broken states of Africa, the FSU states. The interesting distinction is that both regions are acquiring the network capabilities to touch each other in ways unprecedented historically. This interaction is the basis for is the oft too casually used term 'asymmetric warfare'. The term is conceptually handy for what it sums up but analytically vague. All warfare is, at the end of the day, asymmetric. See also Arquilla and Ronfeldt (note 24).

200. See O'Connell (note 47).

201. See Inbar (note 159).

202. Gabriel notes that, although mobilization was limited in the Lebanon War, the bulk of the very few medals the IDF awarded were given to Reservists. See Gabriel (note 10) p.11.

203. See David Eshel, 'Night Fighters: Israeli Military Maintains Wide Array of Highly Trained Special Forces Units', *Armed Forces Journal International* (April 1998) p.50.

204. The Israelis call terrorists and other threats below the state level by the euphemism 'current security'. See Cohen *et al.* (note 9).

205. See Stuart A. Cohen, 'Mista'arvim – IDF Masqueraders: the Military Unit and the Public Debate', *Low Intensity Conflict and Law Enforcement* 2/2 (Autumn 1993).

206. See Cohen *et al.* (note 9).

207. It is expected these forces will be matrix organizations in their deliberative or problem solving functions, not hierarchically linked military units, but they could evolve into nested hierarchies of both such as those seen in the high reliability research conducted in the US during the 1980s. See LaPorte and Consolini (note 171) pp.19–48.

208. See Cohen *et al.* (note 9).

5

Non-Conventional Solutions for
Non-Conventional Dilemmas?

YIFTAH S. SHAPIR

Since the end of the 1991 Gulf War Israel perceived weapons of mass destruction (WMD) as the greatest threat to its security. This perception is evident in interviews for the media by Israeli leaders, as well as by Israeli budgetary allocations. Israeli leaders repeated over and over again their concern about this threat. This was accompanied by messages of slightly veiled threats, addressed mainly at Iran or Iraq.[1]

For the purpose of this study the actual severity of this threat is less important.[2] Rather, it tries to analyze the options Israel has to mitigate the perceived threat. There are several optional means to address such a threat, and many of the options Israel can choose from were tried before. Israel invests in defensive measures, such as shelters and protective gear, in weapon systems aimed at the ballistic missiles themselves, and finally, in offensive measures designed to attack the missile launchers at their bases, before the missiles are launched.

In addition to these means there is deterrence: dissuading the other side from attacking by threatening it with massive retaliation. Finally, there is the political option – coming to some terms with the other side and achieving an agreement to prevent, or at least to limit the use of ballistic missiles or other types of WMD.

In the following section I will present Israel's perception of the threat, and Israel's overall doctrine of layers of defense. Then I will discuss in detail each layer in Israel's defense doctrine: a short description of each layer will be followed by a discussion of its merits and shortcomings. Finally, I will discuss the implications of the close relations between Israel and the USA regarding defense against ballistic missiles.

Israeli Perception of the Threat

Israeli leaders usually portray their perception of the threat in terms of 'circles of threats'. In this portrayal, the inner circle is the threat of terrorism; the second circle is that of the countries surrounding Israel and the third circle is the outer circle of hostile countries that have no common border with Israel.

The inner circle, or the threat of terrorism, is usually another term for the threat posed to Israel by the long conflict with the Palestinians and the threat posed by the lasting, low intensity conflict in Southern Lebanon.[4]

The second circle is the traditional threat of the neighboring countries. This has been so ever since the creation of the state of Israel in 1948, when the armies of Egypt, Syria, Trans-Jordan, and Iraq invaded the newly formed state. Today, only Syria and Lebanon are still in conflict with Israel. Nevertheless, even Egypt and Jordan cannot be discounted altogether as potential military risk to Israel.

The third circle is that of hostile countries that have no common border with Israel. This circle of threats emerged in the late 1980s, and materialized during the 1991 Gulf War, when Iraq attacked Israel with ballistic missiles. A special element in Israel's threat perception is that of weapons of mass destruction: nuclear, chemical and biological. These weapons are usually associated with the threat of lomg-range delivery systems, mainly ballistic missiles. That is because ballistic missiles enable Israel's enemies to circumvent its strong air defense and deliver their payloads unhindered. Thus ballistic missiles enable countries of the third circle to pose a threat.

An indication of the severity of this threat, as perceived by the Israeli military, can be seen in exercises conducted by the Homefront command of the Israeli Defense Forces: a scenario played in one of these exercises viewed three ballistic missiles falling on an urban area, one of which carried chemical agent. The scenario viewed 1,000 casualties, 50 of them fatal. In addition, it viewed 150 victims of shock, and 250 cases of unnecessary injection of atropine (an injection that is part of the standard gear handed to the population).[5]

Although this threat is not new, the importance of the third circle increased after the Gulf War. Since 1998 the Israeli Ministry of Defense and the IDF General Staff have been rewriting the official Israeli military doctrine.[6] The change was needed to underline the relative severity of the different circles of threat. The new doctrine sees the threat of WMD as the most severe, that of terrorism comes second, and the threat from the neighboring countries is considered as the least severe.[7] Brigadier General

Amos Gilead, Head of the Assessment Division of the Military Intelligence ('Aman'), warned time and again that the worst threat to Israel comes from a nuclear Iran or Iraq. Aman does notice the Egyptian conventional buildup, but assesses that as long as President Mubarak wants to continue the peaceful relations with Israel, there is no danger of war with Egypt.[8]

Israel's Doctrine

The Arrow ('Hetz') system gained much publicity as Israel's shield against ballistic missile threat. But Israeli officials stress that the Arrow system is only one layer in a multi-layered defense doctrine. Israeli multi-layered doctrine is no secret, and Israeli leaders stress it often in the media. Former Minister of Defense, Yitzhak Mordechai, outlined this doctrine in a lecture given in October 1997[9]. Mordechai named five different layers of defense. The first layer was the political effort to prevent war by peace agreements; the second was the effort to build reliable deterrence; the third layer was the Arrow anti-ballistic missile system; the fourth was the effort to build a capability to attack the missiles and their launchers in their bases; and the fifth was the element of passive defense. General Mordechai did not mention another layer of defense, which lies between the third and the fourth – intercepting the missiles during their boost phase. In this contribution I shall discuss this possibility as another layer and not as another technical means for the interception of ballistic missile.

PASSIVE DEFENSE

Israel's Passive CBW Defense

Israeli doctrine has always paid some attention to civil defense, although this issue was never a top priority in the security agenda.[10] Nevertheless, there have always been civil defense forces, and bomb shelters have been built all over the country. The civil defense doctrine was established in the late 1940s and the early 1950s, during the early days of the State of Israel, and was made into law in 1951. The doctrine was based on the perceived threat of bombers, and on a 10 minutes alarm. Only in 1988 did the military intelligence ('Aman') assess that ballistic missile attack was a real threat. As a consequence, it was recommended that the construction of bomb shelters should be ceased.[11]

Shortly before the break of the Gulf War, in January 1991, the IDF decided to warn the population against chemical and biological threats, rather than the threat of high-explosive bombs or missiles. Protective gear was handed out to the civilian population. People were advised that in case of an alarm, they should remain in sealed rooms in their own apartments, rather than go into underground shelters. This was a highly controversial policy, especially since the chemical threat did not materialize, whereas the conventional one did.[12]

After the Gulf War, and in the wake of the public outcry against the government conduct during the war, the defense of the civilian population gained higher priority than ever before.[13] The Civil Defense Forces were made into the Homefront Command, headed by a major general. A decision was made to continue the same policy emphasizing the CW threat. Thus, in October 1992 the Homefront Command launched 'Operation Ra'am' (refreshment of protective gear). It planned to operate up to 105 distribution points, which would deliver 25,000 – 30,000 sets a day. The operation lasted until December 1993.[14] By then the Homefront Command handed over some 3.8 million sets of protective gear to the population, at a cost of some 700 million shekels (approximately $250 million). These included some 200,000 sets of 'Shmartaf' ('baby-sitter' a special gear for infants), 340,000 hoods for toddlers ('Bardas') and 850,000 special hoods for children.[15] In 1994 the command handed over special masks for bearded men.[16] In 1996 the Homefront Command launched another operation of refreshing the protective gear held by the population at a cost of 720 million shekels.[17] In July 1996 the government decided to terminate the distribution of protective gear, but the events of January–February 1998 crisis with Iraq caused the reversal of that decision.

Another step taken was the introduction of new construction standards. Today every new apartment built must have one protected room ('Mamad' – an abbreviation for the Hebrew term for 'apartmental protected volume'), which can be sealed against gas attacks. Similar standards apply to public building. According to data held by the Homefront Command, some 300,000 new apartments have been built with protected rooms by June 1997, since the new standard entered force in 1992.[18]

The Homefront Command and the Israeli defense establishment invest in other means of protection as well. There are stocks of antibiotic medicines against a possible biological attack; there is a system of chemical weapon detectors in some of the more populated areas in Israel; and there is a constant investment in research and development of better equipment and better construction methods for enhanced protection of the population.[19] Current expenditures on civil defense are high. The FY 2000 budget allocated 232,637,000 new shekels ($53,500,000) to the civil emergency budget, which covers these expenses.[20]

Problems in Implementing the Civil Defense Measures

Implementing the civil defense policy is a very expensive project, yet it can never achieve the goal of full protection. The military must have a comprehensive database on the entire population. Newly born babies should be supplied with special protective gear. When they reach the age of three they should be supplied with a hood, and when they reach the age of eight their gear should be replaced once again. Besides, there are new immigrants, and temporary residents (mainly foreign workers). Special equipment ('Bardas Refu'i') must be supplied to elderly people, to people who suffer from respiratory system problems as well as to bearded men (most of whom would refuse to shave off their beards even in an emergency because of their religious beliefs).[21]

The protective gear has limited shelf life, and should be replaced from time to time. The special equipment for babies, children and elderly people, requires special lithium batteries, which must be refreshed regularly.[22] Even so, there were allegations that the protective gear supplied to children does not give adequate protection.[23]

There are psychological problems as well. A considerable proportion of the population disobeys instructions by the military, and does not come to distribution centers, neither to take the protective gear nor to refresh older kits. The State Comptroller underlined that problem, when she stated in her report for 1993 that 3.8 million sets were distributed, but 5.28 million citizens were invited to get them. The situation was worse for people who needed special gear: only 15,000 people, out of 30,000 eligible for special kits, actually showed up to get them.[24] The situation did not improve since then, and by the end of 1998, Major General Dan Halutz (then the IDF chief of operations) admitted that 25 per cent of the population have no adequate protective gear.[25]

Signs of problems with the civil defense policy were evident in February 1998, during the crisis in Iraq. The news from Iraq, together with some threatening declarations by Israeli leaders aimed at Iraq, caused panic. Thousands of people stormed the distribution stations, trying to renew their protective gear. People also raided the markets, trying to buy sheets of polyethylene and adhesive tapes to seal their apartments. The public pressure caused a panic reaction by the government. It authorized a special budget of some 240 million new shekels for a hasty acquisition of extra gas masks, antidotes for chemical agents and detectors.[26]

The Homefront Command encountered the psychological problem long before these events. Both in 1992 and in 1996 it shelved plans to prepare TV programs on the threat of chemical weapons, to prevent panic. A poll conducted just after the February 1998 crisis showed that only 66 per cent of the population would obey orders by the authorities. The poll proved also that most of the public has no confidence in the protection policy.[27]

Principles of Implementing the Civil Defense Policy

Two questions of principle emerge when considering the implementation of the civil defense policy. The first is the question of equality. On one hand, the economical logic would require larger investments in areas of higher risk. The assumption is that the main target for the enemy's ballistic missiles are major cities, and major strategic installations. Thus, investment should concentrate on citizens of the major cities, and residents of communities close to major strategic installations. On the other hand, less should be invested in residents of low-risk areas, like rural communities, considered to be unattractive targets for the enemy. There is no point in spending money either on reinforcing and sealing buildings in these areas, or on protective gear for their residents.

This approach contradicts principles of equality among citizens. The issue was brought up in appeals before the Supreme Court of Israel. In two important cases citizens demanded, and won the right for equal protection, thus overruling decisions by the civil defense authorities.[28]

It should be mentioned that the logic that allocates different risk factors to different areas stands behind the idea of protection by evacuating the big cities. An opposite approach was evident in the reaction of the Mayor of Tel Aviv, Mr Shlomo Lahat, who condemned the residents of Tel Aviv who fled the city during the Iraqi Scud attacks in 1991 and called them 'traitors'. This type of approach is deeply ingrained in the Israeli ethos.

A second problem is that of cost effectiveness. An economic approach sees a certain monetary value in human life. This monetary value is evident, for example, in insurance policies, and in health care budgets.[29] When it comes to assessing the investment in civil defense, the question of the cost of saving life is critical. Technically, it is very difficult to assess how many lives would have been saved by a certain level of investment. An analysis must be based on scenarios deemed to be reasonable in case of war, but rarely were the actual conditions of war foreseen before it. In each scenario analyzed there are many variables, which must be taken into consideration. By the end of the day, the problem always turns out to be a political one. On one hand one could always argue that money is spent in vain. This argument is particularly strong in retrospect, if no war occurred. On the other hand one could always argue that not enough sums are being spent, and the population is at risk, all according to one's political views.

The Israeli Anti-Tactical Ballistic Missile System

The Arrow ('Hetz') ballistic missile defense system is the flagship of the Israeli strategy against the ballistic missile threat. Its development began in 1986, when Israel responded to American requests to participate in its strategic defense initiative (SDI). The Arrow system was chosen for the joint program, and the Strategic Defense Initiative Organization (SDIO), and later the Ballistic Missile Defense Organization (BMDO) supported the program financially. The first phase of development was budgeted at $160 million, but Israel paid only 15 per cent of that sum.

In 1992 the project was authorized as an Israeli weapon development program, in the framework of a newly set up office – 'Homa' (Wall). The BMDO financed further development phases of the interceptor missile itself.[30] Thus $330 million were allocated for the project in 1992, 28 per cent of which were financed by Israel. Another sum of $200 million was authorized in 1994, and in 1998 $170 million were allocated for the acquisition of a third battery. Israel financed other elements of the program. These included the launchers, the acquisition radar, named 'Oren Yarok' (Green Pine), developed by Elta, and the command, control and battle management center 'Etrog Zahav' (Citron Tree) developed by Tadiran.[31]

The total cost of the system was estimated officially to be $1.6 billion, but in March 2000, it was admitted that the cost of the system was $2.2 billion.[32] Furthermore, it was revealed that an improvement program for the system would cost $1 billion.[33] Unofficial sources suspected as much long ago.[34]

The Arrow system succeeded in a series of tests, and Israel decided to acquire three batteries of the Arrow. The first elements were handed over for evaluation by the Israeli Air Force in late 1998, and were officially given to the Air Force in March 2000.[35]

Not many technical details have been published about the Arrow system.[36] The Citron Tree battle management system (produced by Tadiran) is manned by 7–10 operators. It can process data from the Green Pine acquisition radar, as well as from other sources: the American early warning satellites, US Navy Aegis ships or Patriot PAC-3 batteries. Each Citron Tree post is capable of controlling several Arrow interceptor batteries.

The Green Pine radar (produced by Elta) is a C-band (500–1000 MHz) phased-array radar, with a range of approximately 500 km. It is land mobile on trucks: the full system has an antenna vehicle, a power supply vehicle, a coolant vehicle and a communication vehicle.

The Arrow missile itself is a two-stage, solid-fuel missile. It is 6.95 m long, weighs 1,300 kg, and reaches a maximum speed of almost 3 km/sec. Its maximum intercept range is assessed to be 90 km and its maximum intercept ceiling is 50 km. The missile uses an infra-red seeker, and a proximity fuse. It has an explosive blast/fragmentation warhead designed to destroy several types of ballistic missile warheads, including cluster chemical or biological warheads, at a close miss.[37]

It should be mentioned here that the Arrow is not the only system Israel envisages for intercepting incoming ballistic missiles. During the Gulf War Israel deployed its newly acquired Patriot surface-to-air missile systems as well as US Army batteries deployed to Israel.[38] The Patriot system failed miserably in 1991, but it is being upgraded with the PAC-3 program. The most significant upgrade is the integration of a new interceptor – the ERINT, which is designed specifically to intercept ballistic missiles. It is quite conceivable that Israel would upgrade at least some of its Patriot batteries to the PAC-3 level[39]

A different effort is made by Israel, with the cooperation of the US Army, to use laser technology to intercept short-range rockets and artillery pieces. This program, code named 'Nautilus', recently entered its live tests phase. Although the USA is developing laser technology for intercepting ballistic missiles, the Nautilus is a tactical system, and therefore lies outside the scope of this analysis.

Problems Associated with the Arrow System

Intercepting an incoming ballistic missile is a difficult technical feat, often compared to hitting a gun bullet with another gun bullet. Yet, it has been proved in several tests that it is feasible. The problems associated with intercepting incoming ballistic missiles in general should be divided into technical problems, and problems associated with doctrine of defense.

TECHNICAL PROBLEMS
Of the many problems related to intercepting ballistic missiles, I shall try to highlight four points, which I consider to be the most important. First, when trying to intercept an incoming ballistic missile it is very important that its warhead is completely destroyed. Otherwise, the warhead might still cause damage on the ground, whether on its intended target or near it. This is most

important if the incoming ballistic missile is armed with a chemical warhead. A conventional warhead armed with high explosives might cause no harm if its detonation mechanism is damaged, but chemical or biological agents might still be lethal. Furthermore, the defender must be certain that by destroying the warhead its lethal content is completely eliminitaed. Intercepting the incoming ballistic missile at an altitude of 50 km, which is the Arrow's ceiling, should be enough to disperse any material not destroyed in the upper layers of the atmosphere. But intercepts will not necessarily take place at the maximum altitude. The Arrow system provides high probability of intercept by using at least two interceptors for each target; should the first interceptor miss its target, there would always be a second one. But the following encounters are necessarily both closer to the area to be protected and closer to ground level, and there is a danger of residual chemical agent hitting the ground.

The second point is the Arrow's method of destroying its targets. The Arrow employs a blast-fragmentation warhead, with a proximity fuse. This enhances the probability of hitting the target, which will be destroyed even at a close miss. But this method limits the energy used to destroy the target. The energy produced by the explosion of the interceptor's warhead is distributed in space, and only a fraction of it actually hits the incoming missile. The method used by the American interceptors is 'hit-to-kill': the kinetic energy of two bodies hitting each other at velocities of up to 5 km per second is enough to pulverize any warhead.[40]

The third point is the size of the protected area: how much ground does one battery protect. (This area is usually referred to as the battery's 'footprint'.) This is highly dependent on the time of alert available: does one rely on the battery's resources, or is there earlier warning, by satellites? It is also dependent on the geometry of the intercept. Is the incoming missile directed at the battery, or is it directed at a target that is located far from the battery? Israel decided to deploy three batteries. This is obviously a compromise between the will to defend and the cost of maximum defense. It means that some areas in Israel will not be covered.

The fourth point is the ability of the system to handle a finite number of targets simultaneously. There is a limit to the number of targets that the 'Citron Tree' and the 'Green Pine' can handle, and there is a smaller number of Arrow interceptors, which can be guided to targets simultaneously.[41] Thus an aggressor can try to over-saturate the system, by firing a large number of missiles simultaneously.

There is a very small probability that several countries would be able to coordinate a simultaneous attack, but Syria alone can fire up to 26 Scuds simultaneously. The problem of saturation will be aggravated if and when Israel should face the threat of missiles equipped with multiple decoys.

PROBLEMS ASSOCIATED WITH DOCTRINE OF DEFENSE

Taking into consideration the technical hurdles mentioned above, one can say that no defense system is capable of giving impenetrable defense. Thus an enemy can rely on its capability to deliver a certain fraction of its payload. This raises some questions of doctrine. First, is it cost effective? One must calculate the cost of potential damage to the defender and compare it to the cost of an intercept. In the case of Scud missiles armed with conventional explosives this damage proved to be relatively low, but the damage of a chemical warhead could be high. Of course, the question of the price tag for human life emerges once again.[42]

When the threat is nuclear, the equation is different. Obviously, since the potential damage is so high, the cost of one intercept becomes unimportant. But the defending system is required to give absolute protection. Otherwise, it is irrelevant. If an aggressor can deliver enough missiles to ascertain that at least one missile comes through, then the defending system does not fulfill its goal. In economic terms – every cent spent on it was a waste.

Supporters of the Arrow system point out that one of the most visible effects of the Scud attacks in 1991 was the panic that caused most of the inhabitants of Tel Aviv and Haifa to flee the cities, and move their families into rural areas, or even abroad. The missile attacks brought the Israeli economy to a standstill, for almost three weeks.[43] Israel cannot endure such a situation, and the deployment of the defense systems should reassure the population, and prevent such a panic. The counter argument is that the behavior of the population depends on its resilience and on its trust in its government. During the Gulf War there were several Patriot SAM batteries deployed, and officials promised that the Patriot was a viable defense system. Furthermore, during the attacks official reports claimed successful interception of incoming Scuds.[44] This did not change the population's reaction.[45] This is not likely to change in the future; even when the system deployed is technically superior to the Patriot. One or two incoming missiles that manage to penetrate and cause damage, should be enough to create panic, many successful intercepts notwithstanding.

One more argument raised by the opponents of the Arrow system is that it undermines Israel's deterrence.[46] When there are nuclear threats, no real defense is possible. In that case Israel should rely only on its deterrence. Deploying the Arrow would signal the enemy that Israel thinks of the possibility of being attacked. This posture, in itself, might encourage aggressors to try and attack. Therefore, deploying a defense system would destabilize the situation. The deterring message should be clear cut – being attacked is not an option.

SHOULD THE ARROW BE DEPLOYED?

I argue that the the important fact is that politically, deployment of the Arrow system is almost inevitable. It is true that the system is probably not cost effective. It might reduce the damage caused by conventional missile attacks, of the type that Israel suffered in 1991. Even so, this might be at a cost higher than the damage saved. But the real question decision-makers must take into consideration is a political one. Once the technical possibility of intercepting incoming ballistic missile is proved to be feasible, it is extremely difficult, almost impossible, to go ahead with a decision to shelve such a program. Any decision-maker must ask him/herself: 'What would have happened had I decided not to deploy, and then missiles were fired at Israel?' Could a politician convince the public that the defensive system would not have given the defense promised? The answer is most probably not. Therefore, once the decision was made in 1986, and since the system did not fail miserably in tests, all other issues become moot. The political and public outcry against the conduct of the military and the government, that shook Israel after the Gulf War, was an example that decision-makers should remember.

A second political reason for pursuing the Arrow system lies in its importance to the close strategic ties with the United States. The Arrow system began as a cooperation program between the USA and Israel, in the framework of President Reagan's SDI. Today, ballistic missile defense is still an important aspect of the American strategy. Thus the program serves as a channel for transferring funds from the Department of Defense (DoD) for research and development in Israel, and is an important item on the agenda of the close strategic ties between the two countries (see below).

A third argument in favor of the Arrow is its contribution to the Israeli defense industry. The Israeli defense industry is one of the most important elements in Israel's might. It stands on the cutting edge of modern technology; it gave Israel independence in many security-related equipment, and it was a driving force behind the whole Israeli hi-tech industry. This industry needs large level of investments to keep on going, and it needs a goal to strive to achieve: a very ambitious project that calls for the recruitment of all the assets, physical and intellectual. The Ofeq satellite was such a project, the Lavi combat aircraft was another such a project, and so is the Arrow.[47] The Arrow project means an investment of $2.2 billion dollars in the Israeli high-tech industry. Even if Israel could have done without it, or with an imported alternative like the Theater High Altitude Area Defense (THAAD) or the Patriot, there would have been good reasons to invest money in the Arrow system: to push the Israeli defense industry forward.

Today the Arrow is already offered as a product for overseas sales. Turkey showed interest, and recently the Israeli Air Industry began to search for American partners which would join the Arrow program – a prerequisite for possible sales, which require an approval of US authorities.[48]

BOOST PHASE INTERCEPT

Description

Ever since the first day of the anti-ballistic missile project, there was an appealing alternative to intercepting ballistic missiles on their way down. This was the option of intercepting them during the ascent phase of their trajectory. Techniques that implement this option are usually referred to as 'boost phase intercept' (BPI) methods. The idea is that during their boost phase, ballistic missiles are vulnerable. They are slow, they are easily detected due to the heat they produce, and above all, when intercepted they do not fall down on the the defender's territory. A variation of this method is called 'Ascent Phase Intercept' (API). This is an attempt to intercept ballistic missiles even after the boost phase of their flight, but before they reach the apogee of their trajectory. Today the US Air Force is developing an airborne laser (ABL) mounted on a heavy cargo plane (Boeing 747) that will intercept ascending ballistic missiles from as far as 400 km.

Israel launched a project called IBIS (Israel Boost-phase Intercept System),[49] which is based on a very rapid air to air missile, called 'Moab' carried by uninhabited airborne vehicles (UAV) with long endurance periods (over 48 hours), flying at high altitudes (over 60,000 feet) over the enemy's territory or close to it. The system is planned to act autonomously, to detect ballistic missiles shortly after their launch, and to automatically fire the interceptor missile. The idea was not unique to Israel. A similar project was proposed in the United States: the Talon/Raptor which was later canceled in favor of the airborne laser.[50]

There are no specific details available about the proposed system. Some sources believe that the Moab is going to be a kinetic energy kill vehicle, and that it will be carried on a proposed HA-10 UAV.[51] Other sources believe that the missile will be carried on F-15I manned aircraft (a method that would limit considerably the loiter time over the target area), or on Silver Arrow's Hermes-1500 UAV.[52]

The program had its ups and downs. When Israel considered US's offer to participate in the SDI, in 1985, Rafael (Israel Arms Development Authority) proposed an armed UAV. This proposal was rejected in favor of the Arrow.[53] Its development continued with very little funding, since the Israeli Ministry of Defense did not want to split its efforts on too many projects. The American side eschewed financing weapon systems that could be considered offensive and preferred to cooperate on purely defensive systems like the Arrow. It was also alleged that supporters of the Arrow within the Ministry of Defense blocked funding for the Moab, to prevent real competition to their favored system.[54]

There is little information about the price tag of such a system. The preliminary phases of the program received $34 million from 1994, 75 per cent of which came out of American sources, and the rest was financed by Israel.[55] Full scale development and integration is assessed at $1 billion over five to seven years.

In April 2000 it was published that the Moab program changed its course, and it is no longer a BPI system, but a BLPI – 'Before Launch Phase Intercept'. The idea is similar – UAV carrying missiles, but these missiles will be aimed at the launchers rather than at the missiles. According to this idea the system would include another UAV that will loiter in the area and gather information about the launcher's location.[56]

Technical Problems with BPI [57]

To understand the difficulty of intercepting ballistic missiles during their boost phase, let us consider the scenario for which the Moab is being designed: ballistic missiles fired at Israel from western Iraq, north-eastern Syria, or even from Iran. The area in which the launcher can be found might be as large as 200km x 200km – almost twice the size of Israel. Western Iraq or north-eastern Syria lie between 400 and 600 km from the center of Israel. An armed UAV would need between two to three hours to fly there, most of the way over hostile territory. The UAV should be stealthy, but it cannot be very small, and it will be very vulnerable during its flight. Needless to say, it will also be very vulnerable when loitering over its target zone. It cannot have much self-defense, and it would be a sitting duck for the opponent's air defense. If the threat comes from Iran the same problems would be aggravated due to the much longer distance.

While over the target zone, the UAV will have to detect a missile within a few seconds of its launch. Most intermediate range missiles of the Scud family use their engines for 60–100 seconds. During this time they rise from ground level to 30–50 km, and accelerate to 1,500–2,000 m/sec. The BPI system's sensors would have to acquire the target, usually within 15 seconds of the launch, and then be able to discriminate among many signals. Besides ballistic missiles, the area could be saturated with other signals: surface-to-air missiles could be fired against attacking aircraft (or the UAV itself). Other missiles might be fired from combat aircraft against ground targets or airborne targets. These could also distract the UAV's sensors.

Another problem is to have the UAV with its missiles within range of the ballistic missile. As mentioned above, the system would have no more than 100 seconds to identify a missile, acquire its target, fire its interceptor missile and shoot it down. The UAV might be as far as 50–100 km from the launch site, and the interceptor missile must be fast enough to cover this distance. The interceptor missile should also be capable of reaching the very high altitude, should the intercept occur at the end of the boost phase.[58] If the UAV was equipped with short-range interceptors, the target area will have to be covered, simultaneously, by a larger number of UAV.

Another problem is that unlike the Arrow, the whole system is unsuitable in case of surprise attacks. One would have to know in advance that a state of war exists, and that there is a fair probability that ballistic missiles would be fired from a known region.

Should the Israeli Boost-phase Intercept System (IBIS) be developed?

All technical problems notwithstanding, BPI systems have some very important advantages. The most important is that ballistic missiles intercepted would not fall down on Israeli territory. This is most crucial in case they carry chemical or biological warheads, which might cause damage, even if they are shot down. This feature could contribute much to the deterring effect of the system. Unlike other methods of defense, BPI has a real deterring effect. An aggressor could be deterred from launching ballistic missiles, or at the least, from launching chemical or biological warheads, if it fears the consequences of the missiles falling back on its territory.[59]

Another point is that parts of a BPI system could have other missions. An armed UAV designed to loiter over enemy territory could be adapted, for example, to suppress the enemy's air defense. It could also be adapted to carry air to ground munitions, and carry out other offensive missions. Thus investing in such a system could create other benefits in the future.

Finally, just as the Arrow project contributes to the Israeli defense industry, so does IBIS. It will need unique missiles, and unique sensors, and their development is a challenge to the industry. Furthermore, once developed, these items could be used in other development programs. The recent announcement of the BLPI concept is already a step in such a direction.

ATTACKING LAUNCHERS AND MISSILES

The Israeli doctrine sees the offensive option of attacking ballistic missiles in their bases as one of its layers of defense. This doctrine suits the old Israeli ethos of 'transferring the battle into the enemy's territory'. There is no information available on Israel's planned tactics for that mission, and we can only assess the difficulties in performing such a task and suggest possible solutions to overcome these difficulties. Lessons of the Gulf War indicate the difficulty of the task.[60]

Possible targets

FIXED SITES

Fighting ballistic missile forces involves several types of targets. The easiest targets are the fixed sites: meaning the garrisons, storage and logistic bases of the ballistic missile units. Since these are located in fixed sites, it is possible to plan an attack in detail in advance.

There are some technical problems though: for instance, some storage sites might be very large. Ammunition or fuel storage sites are usually composed of a large number of bunkers, widely spread, for safety or for security reasons, over a vast area. This means that in order to inflict an effective damage one must use a very large number of sorties, or use a large number of precision guided munitions (PGM). Another problem is that ballistic missiles might be stored in general ammunition storage installations, used for the storage of many types of ammunition. It might not be possible to distinguish between bunkers used for storing ballistic missiles and those used for storing other types of ammunition. This would require even larger number of sorties, to ensure the required damage to the ballistic missiles.

Some garrisons and storage facilities in Syria, Libya or Iran are found in deep tunnels, dug into mountainsides. These are protected by thick layers of rock, which is impenetrable by any conventional bomb.[61] In such places there is no point in trying to destroy the equipment stored in the tunnel. It is possible to attack peripheral targets around such an installation.

On a strategic level, there is the question of the purpose of destroying such installations. In wartime, the objective is to prevent further missile attacks on the rear. Unfortunately, it is impossible to prevent such attacks completely. Even if all the storage facilities were destroyed, the mobile missile units have their own stock – a number of missiles carried on the launchers themselves and on re-supply vehicles. Thus, the benefit of a successful attack on ballistic missile infrastructure is in limiting the number of missiles fired during a prolonged armed conflict, and as an element of cumulative deterrent for years to come.

FIGHTING MOBILE LAUNCHERS

In order to prevent or diminish a ballistic missile attack, the missile launchers themselves are the most important targets to destroy (usually they are referred to as TEL: transporter, erector, launcher). Unfortunately, they are very difficult targets indeed. This was clearly seen by the failure of the Coalition's effort to prevent the ballistic missile attacks on Israel and on Saudi Arabia during Operation 'Desert Storm' in January and February 1991. The Iraqis had 15–20 Scud (and Scud derivatives) TEL of several types.[62] During the conflict they fired more than 80 missiles. The Coalition dedicated 4,870 sorties to fight them, but no Scud launchers were destroyed.

The Iraqis fired from pre-surveyed launch positions, and moved constantly. Although preparing a Scud missile for launch is a long and complicated procedure, the Iraqis managed to accomplish this phase in hideouts, without being detected. The area from which the missiles were fired on Israel was an arid, rugged terrain, where the TEL could be hidden easily in ravines or beneath highway underpasses.[63] They moved within a few minutes after the launch, and could be as far as five miles of the launch sites after ten minutes.

Contrary to Soviet doctrine, which calls for employing the Scud in battalions or brigades, the Iraqi Scud units were very small, usually consisting of a single TEL with very few accompanying vehicles. Thus detecting a TEL amounts to detecting a small group of vehicles (or possibly even a single vehicle operating on its own), in a very large area.

The Coalition forces used several types of reconnaissance aircraft to detect the TEL, such as the U-2/TR-1 and RF-4Cs. However, TEL are difficult to locate by aerial or space imagery, because they are not easily distinguishable from other vehicles that might be present in the region; because they can be hidden or camouflaged easily; and because they are constantly on the move. Furthermore, they cannot be detected by signal intelligence equipment (Sigint) because they do not emit electromagnetic energy (like radar transmission).

A launcher is exposed only when it fires a missile. The flames and dust raised during the process are seen from very long distances. The missiles themselves are detectable by radar, by infrared equipment sensors and by digital signal processing satellites. All these types of equipment are able to calculate the location of the launcher itself. As mentioned above, this information is valid for a few moments only.

Due to their mobility, the destruction of a mobile launcher requires a very efficient command, control and communication system. It should be able to transfer data regarding the launchers to the attacking aircraft. It should do so quickly enough for the attacking aircraft to arrive at the site before the detected launcher disappeared. Even when located by the intelligence and by the attacking aircraft, TEL are difficult targets to identify if they move in a group with other vehicles.

Is it worth it?

It is obvious, from what was said above, that very intensive investment is needed in order to succeed in preventing missile attacks by destroying TEL and their infrastructure. It is necessary to invest in intelligence assets, in aircraft, in munitions, in C⁴I systems, and above all, in intensive and continuous training for all the components of this system.

Unlike investments in other methods of defense, this investment is invisible. That is because most of the weapon systems and the doctrines are not specific to combat ballistic missiles. The combat aircraft are those already in service. The munitions are suitable for most other targets (like surface to air missiles, radar, command posts etc.). Every increased investment in these assets would have its benefits in other possible operations. The same is true for any investment in intelligence gathering capabilities, like UAV, and reconnaissance equipment. Even the proposed BLPI system mentioned above, should it materialize, will have inherent capabilities for missions other than countering ballistic missiles. Thus, investing in assets to enhance the capability to fight missile launchers is inseparable from investment in air force capability in general. Any argument for an increase or decrease in this investment should be made with regard to the full spectrum of air force missions. This analysis is well beyond the scope of this study.

DETERRENCE

The Israeli Deterrence Doctrine

Deterrence has been one of the most important elements of Israel's security doctrine for many years. Since the mid-1960s or early 1970s Israel's doctrine relied on two main pillars of deterrence. One is its unique strategy of ambiguous nuclear capability, the other is its conventional capability.

Israel ambiguous deterrence is a doctrine of nuclear deterrence without acknowledging the possession of nuclear weapons.[64] This strategy is highlighted mainly during times of crisis. Another conspicuous element in this strategy is Israel's refusal to join the Non-Proliferation Treaty. This strategy was quite explicit in Israel's refusal to discuss the nuclear issue during the multilateral talks on arms control and regional security (ACRS) between 1992 and 1994.[65] Although this unique form of deterrence was controversial, this strategy is probably going to remain Israel's posture for years to come. In 1998 the Ministry of Defense reviewed Israel's nuclear strategy, but from what was published it seems that Israel's strategy is going to remain as it was.[66]

The other form of deterrence was Israel's conventional capability, and its willingness to use it from time to time to retaliate for actions by its enemies. An example for such an activity was the air raid against the Syrian headquarters in downtown Damascus during the 1973 war, as a retaliation to Syrian rocket attacks on the town of Migdal Ha-Emek. Even activities like the June 1981 raid on Iraq's nuclear reactor, which was a preemptive attack rather than a retaliation, contribute to Israel's image of resilience.

Israeli leaders are aware of the deterring value of Israel's conventional might, and from time time they stress the strategic capabilities of its arsenal. Thus, for example, when the first F-15I combat aircraft arrived in Israel, their strategic role was emphasized in the press.[67] It should be added that many scholars argued that Israel's real deterrence was its conventional capability, much more than its nuclear. Evron concludes in his analysis of Israel nuclear and non-nuclear options that Israel does not need nuclear weapons and nuclear strategy, and can maintain its security by relying on conventional might.[68]

Israeli leaders regard their deterrence as specific deterrence, too. That is to say, they try to signal Israel's enemies that some actions on their part are unacceptable, and will be punished. For example, Israeli leaders hinted in 1990 that Israel would retaliate should Saddam Hussein use his chemical weapons against Israel.[69] After the Gulf War it was argued that Israel's nuclear deterrence prevented Saddam Hussein from using chemical warheads on the missiles fired on Israel. Recently, most of the Israeli warnings were directed at Tehran. For example, former Israeli Minister of Defense, Major General (ret.) Yitzhak Mordechai, said in October 1997: 'The other side must expect, that in case of an attack on the rear we shall inflict on him a heavy toll.'[70] This is a clear example of a perceived, specific threat (of an Iranian non-conventional missile strike on Israel), and a specific response.

Another indication of the use Israeli leaders make of specific deterrence messages took place during the crisis in Iraq in January–February 1998. Israeli leaders turned again to declarative acts. Thus, Minister of Defense Mordechai warned Iraq that Israel 'reserves the right to defend itself'. The event highlighted another important element of Israeli deterrence: its reliance on the USA, as well as its own might. Israeli declarations were supported by American declarations, that promised a tough American response against Iraq, and called Israel to refrain from reaction.[71]

The events of 1998 raised another issue in Israel's deterrence policy. As mentioned above, during the crisis the Israeli public nearly panicked. As some analysts were quick to notice, the situation and the government reaction could have undermined Israel's deterrence.[72]

Deterrence Theory and Israel

Classical deterrence theory refers to deterrence as a way to dissuade the opponent from attacking, by the threat of inflicting a damage that is unacceptable by the potential aggressor.[73]

Deterrence theory was developed around the threat of nuclear weapons.[74] When nuclear weapons are taken out of the picture it becomes much more complicated. Today, there is no nuclear threat on Israel, yet. The threat is that of ballistic missiles, armed with conventional or chemical weapons. It is a far cry from the threat of nuclear weapons. The imbalance between the severity of this threat and Israel's ambiguous nuclear option raises the question of the credibility of Israel's nuclear deterrence: would Israel retaliate with nuclear weapons if it is attacked by missiles armed with conventional warheads? Furthermore, because of its doctrine of ambiguity, Israel has never threatened to use nuclear weapons.[75]

Assessing the credibility of Israel's conventional deterrence is far more complicated. The question is not only one of Israel's readiness to retaliate or the severity of its retaliation. It has also to do with the aggressor's perception of the punishment it might face. Would an aggressor be deterred from firing ballistic missiles on Israel, if he assesses that Israel's response would be a conventional air raid on targets in the center of its capital? On one hand, Israel has done so in the past (in October 1973). On the other hand, in 1991 Israel did not retaliate when it suffered Iraqi ballistic missile attacks during the Gulf War. Although there were many good reasons for Israel's reaction, it was argued that it did affect the credibility of its deterrence.

The Effect of Defensive Measures on Deterrence

It has been argued that the other layers of defense, like the passive defense and the Arrow system, would undermine Israel's deterrence. Opponents of the Arrow argued that deploying the system would jeopardize the credibility of Israel's deterrence. The main thrust of the argument is that deploying a ballistic missile defense (BMD) system would communicate the message that Israel is expecting a ballistic missile attack and preparing for it.

The same argument applies, even more forcefully, to the distribution of protective gear to the population. The events of January–February 1998 were condemned as a severe blow to Israel's deterrence. Deterrence, it was argued, relies among other things on resilience. The message that should be transmitted is that Israel is not willing to accept any kind of threat as a legitimate aspect of the game. Distributing protective gear signals that we are preparing for a blow. It also signals that the Israeli population is weak and not resolute, and therefore is susceptible to pressure.[76]

This argument, however, is problematic. Deterrence is based on the capability to inflict a heavy damage on the potential aggressor. Deterring messages should convey the ability to retaliate and the willingness to retaliate. Acts designed to diminish the damage in case of an attack are by no means a message that this attack is acceptable. Nor do they convey a signal that there would be no retaliation, or that the probability of such a retaliation decreases. Only if Israel had a system that gives an invincible defense, this argument could have applied. Only then one could argue that deploying a defensive system would convey the message that Israel does not really care if it was attacked. But this is not the case. No defensive system gives full protection. In fact, they are designed to decrease the damage in case of an attack, and nothing more.

An important argument raised against defensive systems during the Cold War was that deploying BMD system destabilizes the international system. This is a strong argument in the context of a bipolar system stabilized by mutually assured destruction (MAD). But the applicability of this argument to the Middle East is not clear-cut. Today, only Syria has a substantial capability to inflict a chemical attack on Israel. Egypt might have this capability too, but its strategic posture, as an ally of the United States prevents it from threatening with ballistic missiles or chemical weapons. This situation might well change if and when Iran acquires nuclear capability. Only then, the argument against BMD might become relevant.

THE UNITED STATES AND ISRAELI BALLISTIC MISSILE DEFENSE

Israeli BMD strategy is tightly linked with the United States. Although Israel enjoys a considerable level of independence, all the layers of Israel's strategy are connected to the USA and dependent to some extent on its capability. Thus, the Arrow will be handicapped without satellite early warning, and so will the other programs be, when they materialize.

Operationally, it is hard to envisage today a situation of war with states of the second circle (like Iran or Iraq) without having the USA involved. This will have implications on the usage of any level of defense. The Arrow units will have to work in conjunction with American BMD systems on land and sea. The IBIS operations will have to be coordinated with US forces, which will be scattered in the region. Likewise, any air strike operation against launchers or other assets will have to be coordinated. The lessons of the 1991 Gulf War show that the presence of American (or other foreign) forces might prevent any offensive action altogether. Of course, if there is a war with countries of the first circle, like Syria or Egypt, it is less likely that US forces will be involved directly. This will free Israel from the need to coordinate its offensive actions.

As for Israel's deterrence, experience has shown that Israel is dependent on American deterrence. It was argued that Iraq did not use chemical missiles against Israel during the 1991 Gulf War, thanks to Israeli deterrence.[77] But arguably, the American presence in the region, and the American deterring messages were important as well, if not overwhelming. Israel's dependence on the United States in almost anything that has to do with BMD, raises another factor in the decision-making process on BMD issues: the need to tune Israel's efforts with the American efforts.

It should be said that American BMD programs are designed to mitigate a very different kind of threat: the need to protect US forces outside the homeland against theater ballistic missile and the need to protect the continental USA against long-range ballistic missiles from 'rogue states'. Both efforts are highly controversial in the United States, and are major point of political rivalry.[78] Naturally, officials are searching for allies, both inside the American political system and abroad. This was the background of the offer to join the SDI in 1985. These efforts continue today, when American officials try to persuade many of its allies to join and take part in BMD programs.[79] So far, many of America's allies were not convinced that ballistic missiles are a real national threat for them. But as far as Israel is concerned, the wishes of the great ally add another element to consider.

This argument can be taken one more step further. The American influence is not one-sided, and goes both ways. On both sides of the ocean there are defense establishments that work together and influence each other's thinking. Israeli threat perceptions and experience are learnt by the American defense establishment. These influences its thinking, mainly on the importance of theater ballistic missiles, and are used as arguments in the American internal debate. Likewise, American perceptions are read in Israel and influence the way the Israeli defense establishment thinks about the threat and the ways to mitigate it.[80]

THE POLITICAL OPTION

The International Conventions

There are several international treaties that try to address the problem of weapons of mass destruction: there are the nonproliferation treaty (NPT) and comprehensive test ban treaty (CTBT) that addresses the problem of nuclear proliferation. There are the biological weapons convention (BWC) and the chemical weapon convention (CWC) that address the problem of biological and chemical weapon proliferation. The missile technology control regime (MTCR) is a supplier-side mechanism that addresses the problem of ballistic and cruise-missile technology proliferation. Recently the conference on disarmament in Geneva discussed the future fissile material cutoff treaty (FMCT).

Israel usually refrained from joining these treaties. It sees its security position in the Middle East as unique. Treaties like the NPT jeopardize Israel's security, especially when other countries in the region do not comply even when they join treaties. Israel also fears that verification activities associated with these treaties might compromise its security.

The exceptions were the CWC that Israel signed in 1993 but did not yet ratify, and the CTBT. Israel also promised the United States to comply with the MTCR. Israel usually regards these treaties as a threat to its security, and was wary of the various verification measures that were included in them.[81]

The Regional Process

Israel always favored bilateral processes to the international process, but agreed to join a regional process within the framework of the Madrid process. The arms control and regional security (ACRS) talks were an interesting experience for Israel, and some had high hopes in this process until it was stopped by Egypt's demand to put the Israeli nuclear option on the table from the beginning. In early 2000 there were efforts to revive the Madrid multilateral process but it is still hard to assess the prospects for the renewal of the ACRS talks.

Israel sees several advantages in the regional process. It perceives the process as a mean of building trust and confidence among countries in the region. It is preferred over global processes because in the larger framework it would be more difficult to alleviate Israel's special security concerns.[82]

The regional process still holds a great promise for the future of the region, and would contribute to the security of all the participating parties. There are many obstacles, especially since there are still no peace agreements between Israel and some of the key participants in the region (Syria, Iraq and Iran are the most important).

CONCLUSION

The political avenue is the ultimate answer for addressing the threat facing Israel. Once there is a political solution for the conflict, the weapons themselves would cease to be a problem. Even a partial political arrangement would contribute to the security of Israel, more than any protective measure. Until such a political arrangement is reached, Israel is expected to rely on itself.

Deterrence will remain Israel's best strategy against WMD. The proliferation of weapons of mass destruction changes the ways in which wars are fought. On one hand the probability that future wars would involve massive armor battles is slim. On the other hand there is a growing probability that future wars would be fought by long-range delivery systems, often aimed at civilian targets. In this scenario Israel's security should rely more and more on deterrence. Should another state in the region become nuclear, deterrence and 'mutually assured destruction' seem almost the only way to prevent large-scale destruction in the region.

Yet other means of defense, though costly and of low effectivity, are not to be excluded. The multiple layered defense is, in the final analysis, a sound policy. It is true that the Arrow is costly, and cannot provide total defense. It is useless against nuclear warheads, and would only help to reduce the damage, in case of conventional or chemical attack. The same is also true for the passive defense measures. It is true also that the cost of these systems might be higher than the value of property which can be saved But there are other considerations to be taken into account. External politics (the strategic relations with the USA), internal politics, and bureaucratic politics dictate further investments. Canceling a project like the Arrow is a political decision that no prime minister in Israel can take without fear of political implications. He or she would be blamed for neglecting the population's security. Canceling the project would also mean a loss of large investment in the defense industry. Much more so when a large proportion of these allocations come from the United States. And on top of that, canceling such a program might jeopardize an American interest, and damage the good relations with an ally.

The political implications of canceling an active defense system apply to the protective measures as well. Once the protective equipment was distributed, there would always be demand for more, and the political opposition would always be able to cry that it is not enough. Thus as long as the threat perceptions in the public and among the policy-makers are the way they are, Israel will invest more in these systems.

Finally, the offensive layers of Israel's doctrine, like the BPI or the BLPI contribute to Israel's deterrence. Deployment of a BPI system may convey a message of resolve. BPI systems do not yet exist, and developing them would require large investment over a long period of time. They, too, cannot give an invincible defense, and can be counted on only to control the damage in case of an attack.

To sum up, what is argued here is a paradox. Cost effectiveness alone cannot justify development any type of BMD system. These systems are technically and economically inefficient. But other considerations, like the contribution to the hi-tech industry, internal politics and the effect on the strategic relations with the USA overweigh considerations of efficiency alone and justify the development of the systems.

Thus, it can be predicted that the Arrow system is here to stay. Further investments are expected, for upgrades already planned in the existing system and for acquisition of more batteries. The same is true for the defensive measures. It can be predicted that the sealed rooms and the gas masks will continue to be a part of everyone's life in Israel in the years to come.

On the other hand BPI and BLPI systems are still in their infancy. Should the technical and political obstacles be solved, they might become an important element in Israel's defense doctrine. Yet, it is too early to predict whether BPI or BLPI systems are going to have any significant role in Israel's future defense.

NOTES

1. Ed Blanche, 'Mordechai warned that Israel will strike', *Jane's Defence Weekly*, 5 Nov. 1997.
2. For quantitative data on the various weapons systems in the Middle East see Shlomo Brom and Yiftah Shapir (eds.) *'The Middle East Military Balance 1999–2000'*, The Jaffee Center for Strategic Studies, Tel Aviv Univ (Cambridge, MA: MIT Press 1999) pp.139–412.
3. Maj. Gen. (ret) Yitzhak Mordechai, then Minister of Defense, in a lecture given at a conference in Ef'al. For a summary of his speech see: Amnon Barzilai, 'Mordechai: Should the rear be attacked by missiles Israel would inflict a heavy price', *Ha'Aretz* 28 Oct. 1997. See also Amnon Barzilai, 'From the three M's to C4', *Ha'Aretz* (special supplement on security), 20 Sept. 1998.
4. This essay was written before Israel's withdrawal from Lebanon in May 2000.
5. Amnon Barzilai, 'The crater near building number 5', *Ha'Aretz*, 20 Sept. 1998 (in Hebrew).
6. David Eshel, 'Israel's future forces', *Jane's Defence Weekly* 23/8 (25 Aug. 1999) p.21.
7. Ze'ev Schiff, 'a change in the definition of the threats', *Ha'Aretz*, 5 May 1999 (in Hebrew).
8. Aluf Ben, 'Terrorism is merely a slight headache', *Ha'Aretz*, 7 Sept. 1999 (in Hebrew).
9. See note 3.
10. For a comprehensive discussion of the IDF civil defense forces since 1948, see Natan Roi, 'Haga' (the Civil defense), in Ilan Kfir and Ya'akov Erez (eds.) *'Tzahal Be'Heylo (The IDF's might)*: an encyclopedia of military affairs and security' (Tel Aviv: Revivim 1982) Vol. 16, pp.134–67 (in Hebrew).
11. 'Shelters for the civilian population' in the State Comptroller of Israel, Report no. 44 for 1993 (and for fiscal year 1992), (In Hebrew). (Jerusalem: the Official Publisher, 21 April 1994) pp.956–63.
12. The problem is the different, even contradicting nature of the correct measures one should take in the two different situations. During a chemical agent attack, underground shelters might prove a very dangerous place, if they are not properly sealed and have no filtering system. That is because most CW agents are heavier than air. On the other hand, during a conventional bomb attack, underground shelters may give good protection, but standard apartment houses might collapse. Another problem is the time needed to go to a shelter. When the threat is a ballistic missile attack, there might not be enough time to go to a shelter. In this case it would be reasonable to stay in one's apartment rather than risk being caught in the street, on the way to a shelter. It should be added that the average Israeli building is constructed with a reinforced concrete beams, and is relatively resistant to bombs.
13. See for example: Asher Wallfish, 'The Comptroller eases criticism of army on gas masks, but IDF blasts her report', *Jerusalem Post*, 15 April 1991.
14. 'Protective gear for the civilian population' in the State Comptroller of Israel, Report no. 44, ibid. pp.948–56.
15. Orit Reuveni, *Ba-Mahane*, 3 Nov. 1993 (in Hebrew).
16. Sharon Sade, *Ha'Aretz*, 26 April 1994 (in Hebrew).
17. Reuven Pedatzur, *Ha'Aretz*, 31 Oct. 1996 (in Hebrew).
18. *Follow up report on sheltering* in the State Comptroller of Israel, Report No. 48 for 1997 (9 April 1998) pp.1099–108. The press reported that 500,000 apartments were built since the new law entered force. See Amnon Barzilai, 'on pigs, people and missiles', *Ha'Aretz*, 4 Feb. 1998 (in Hebrew).
19. Ed Blanche, 'Israel seeks protection from chemical attack', *Jane's Defence Weekly*, 18 Feb. 1998.
20. Israel Budget Law No.129 for FY 2000, published 20 March 2000, article 16 (in Hebrew). Expenditure in previous years was similar: 215,264,000 NIS for 1999; 248,167,000 NIS for 1998 (all in current prices).
21. For a list of the various protective kits see the official Homefront Command's website, at www.idf.il/english/organization/homefront/index.stm.
22. Amnon Barzilai, 'What would happen should the batteries run out', *Ha'Aretz*, 5 April 1998 (in Hebrew).
23. Ze'ev Schiff 'The protective gear sets do not assure enough protection for youth', *Ha'Aretz*, 9 Feb. 1998 (in Hebrew).

24. State Comptroller of Israel, report No. 44, p.952 (in Hebrew).
25. Amos Harel, 'Quarter of the population have no protective gear', *Ha'Aretz*, 12 Nov. 1998 (in Hebrew).
26. Blanche (note 19).
27. Amnon Barzilai, 'Operation Panic', *Ha'Aretz*, 24 Feb. 1998 (in Hebrew).
28. The two cases were:
    A. *Ha-Rav Hayim Miller and others vs. the Minister of Defense* (Bagatz 4919/90, Israeli Supreme court decisions, Vol.45, Part II, 1991, pp.293–4). The plaintiff argued that the protective gear was unsuitable for bearded men. This appeal was rejected because the Ministry of Defense argued that by the time the case came up before the court, a suitable technological solution was found. In essence, the plaintiffs' demands were satisfied.
    B. *Miladi Morkus vs. the Minister of Defense* (Bagatz 168/91, Israeli Supreme Court decisions, Vol.45, Part I, 1991, pp.467–8). The plaintiff, an Arab living in the West Bank, demanded that protective gear should be handed to the inhabitants of the West Bank. The Supreme Court endorsed the appeal and ordered the Ministry of Defense to hand out 173,000 sets of protective gear that existed in storage to the adult inhabitants of the region close to Jerusalem. Furthermore, it ordered the ministry to acquire sets for the children of those who get the sets. Third, it ordered the ministry to hand out protective gear sets to the whole population of the region as soon as these are acquired. The court rejected the argument that the decisions to hand out protective gear was a matter of political, military and security decisions that cannot be subjected to a trial by a court of law, and stressed the fact that the legal issue was one of discrimination.
29. The Israeli national health law sets a ceiling for the cost of a medical action to save a human's life See the National Health Insurance law 1994 (Hok Bituah Bri'ut Mamlachti, Tashnad 1994, Sefer Ha-Hukim tashnad, 1469, on 26 June 1994, p.156). Article 19(a) of the law requires the Minister of Health to prepare a list of severe diseases, and sets the maximum cost of annual medical services for an insured citizen who suffers from that particular disease. For example, a person who suffers from HIV is entitled for medical service that would cost no more than 48,000 NIS a year. (Kovetz ha-Takanot Tashnah 5649, 1 Jan. 1995, p.492).
30. Amnon Barzilai, 'A missile is Born', *Ha'Aretz*, 4 Oct. 1998 (in Hebrew).
31. I use here the official name. For some odd reasons the name in English is slightly different from the name in Hebrew: 'Etrog Zahav' actually means 'Golden Citron'.
32. 'Washington Outlook: The Israeli air force took over operational control of...' *Aviation Week and Space Technology*, 20 March 2000. All earlier official estimates ranged between $1.6 and 1.9 billion. See Amnon Barzilai, '$700 millions invested in the Arrow Program', *Ha'Aretz*, 16 Dec. 1996 (in Hebrew).
33. David A. Fulghum and John D. Morrocco, 'First Arrow battery deployed near Tel Aviv', *Aviation Week and Space Technology*, 10 April 2000.
34. Reuven Pedatzur, 'Virtual intercept', *Ha'Aretz*, 24 Sept. 1998 (in Hebrew). Pedatzur cites Col. Butler, the chief of the program within the US Army, who estimates the program at more than $3 billion.
35. 'USA to finance a third Arrow battery for Israel', *Jane's Defence Weekly*, 29 April 1998.
36. 'The Arrow System' in Arieh Stav and Baruch Koroth (eds.) *Ballistic Missiles: the threat and response* (Tel Aviv: Yedioth Aharonoth Chemed books 1999) (in Hebrew) pp.125–30.
37. Tony Cullen and Christopher F. Foss, *Land Based Air Defence 1999–2000* (London: Jane's Information Group 1999) pp.261–3.
38. For a thorough analysis of the lessons of the Patriot deployment to Israel see: Anthony H. Cordesman and Abraham R. Wagner, *The Lessons of Modern War, Vol. IV: the Gulf War* (Boulder, CO: Westview Press 1996) pp.867–72.
39. David Eshel, 'Israel's future Forces', *Jane's Defence Weekly*, 25 April 1999, p.21.
40. Assume a Scud warhead with a mass of 1,000 kg coming at a speed of 1,500 m/sec, hitting head on an interceptor with a mass of 150 kg (approximately the mass of the Erint interceptor) and flying at 2,500 m/sec. According to the law of conversion of momentum, and assuming a perfect inelastic collision, the combined body weighing 1150 kg will be slowed down to 978 m/sec. ($1000 \times 1500 - 150 \times 2500)/1150 = 978$m/sec). Now one has to calculate the

kinetic energy of each of the bodies before the collision and the kinetic energy of the combined body after the collision:

½ 1000x15002 = 1.125x10^9 joules; ½ 150x25002 = 4.68x10^8 joules; ½ 1150x978^2 ~ 5.5x10^8 joules; the difference is the energy that was converted into heat: 1.04 x 10^9 joules.

Assuming that an explosion of 1 kg of TNT produces 4.18 x 10^6 joules (10^6 Calories, which is the standard measure for nuclear explosions)–we get the equivalent of approximately 250 kg of TNT! This is of course a very rough calculation that assumes a perfect collision and ignores many aspects of the dynamics of an actual collision.

41. The exact figures are classified. Unconfirmed reports put it at 14 targets, but it is not clear whether this is the number of targets the system can track or the number of targets it can intercept simultaneously.

42. For a different approach see Reuven Pedatzur *The Arrow System* Memorandum No.42 (in Hebrew) (Jaffee Center for Strategic Studies, Tel Aviv Univ. 1993) p.51.

43. Shlomo Gazit, 'Political and Military developments', in *War in the Gulf, implications for Israel* (JCSS report Tel Aviv Univ. (1992) pp.39–40.

44. See for example: William Saffire, 'The Great Scud-Patriot mystery', *New York Times*, 7 March 1991, p.25.

45. Bradley Burston, 'With the help of friends and foes', *Jerusalem Post*, 15 March 1991; Reuven Pedatzur, 'The Repression Syndrome', *Ha'Aretz*, 4 Aug. 1991 (in Hebrew).

46. Reuven Pedatzur, 'The illusion of perfect defense', *Ha'Aretz*, 7 May 1998 (in Hebrew); see also 'The Fox is Saddam', *Ha'Aretz*, 10 Jan. 1999. Dr Pedatzur published scores of articles in *Ha'Aretz* opposing the deployment of the Arrow system.

47. The Lavi combat aircraft was cancelled in 1985. It was too ambitious, too expensive, and probably was an inferior solution for the Israeli Air Force needs, compared with the F-16 or F-15. But I argue that the project was important in terms of the push it gave the Israeli industry.

48. For Turkey's interest in BMD see for example: David Eshel, 'Turkey and Israel will cooperate on missile defence systems', *Jane's Defence Weekly*, 29 April 1998; Lale Sariibrahimoglu, 'USA and Turkey will talk on Arrow 2 missile', *Jane's Defence Weekly* 32/20, 17 Nov. 1999, p.3. For attempts to sell the Arrow see for example: Frank Wolfe, 'IAI plans to pick US company for arrow co-production', *Defense Daily* 205/44, 8 March 2000; Barbara Opall-Rome, 'Israel MOD opens door to export of Arrow missile', *Defense News* 15/4, 31 Jan. 2000, p.4; Steve Rodan, 'Israel seeks US partner for Arrow', *Jane's Defense Weekly* 33/9, 1 Jan. 2000, p.3.

49. For a technical description of the principles of BPI see Dan Rosen, 'Boost Phase Intercept of Ballistic missiles' and Moshe Guelman, 'IBIS a general introduction', both in Stav and Koroth (note 36) pp.193–203 and pp.204–10.

50. The Talon/Raptor system was to fly at 65,000 feet, for 50 hours. The Talon UAV was to carry 6 Raptor missiles. The missile was designed to be a kinetic kill vehicle, weighing 20 kg, and capable of intercepting targets between 50 and 200 km, at 3,300 m/sec. See Guy Norris, *Flight International*, 20 Oct.1993; James Hacket, *Defense News*, 30 Aug. 1993.

51. Barbara Opall-Rome, 'Israel pushes its BPI project', *Defense News*, 2 Nov. 1998. The HA-10 was offered to the USA, but was rejected as too small. See also David Fulghum, 'Reconnaissance, missile defense deemed most crucial Israeli needs', *Aviation Week and Space Technology*, 1 Feb. 1999, p.64.

52. David Eshel, 'in search of an effective defence', in *Jane's Defence Weekly* 31/10, 10 March 1999, p.71.

53. Barzilai, 'a Missile is Born' (note 30).

54. Steve Rodan, 'BPI future in debate', *Jane's Defence Weekly* 32/19, 10 Nov. 1999, p.27.

55. Opall-Rome (note 51).

56. David Fulghum and John D. Morrocco, 'Israel Air Force to grow', *Aviation Week and Space technology*, 10 April 2000. Hints about it were published earlier. See Barbara Opall-Rome 'Israel proposes mission to target missile launchers', *Defense News* 14/12, 29 March 1999, p.1. See also Amnon Barzilai, 'Israel develops a UAV that would attack launchers', *Ha'Aretz*, 25 Dec. 1998 (in Hebrew).

57. For technical analysis of the problems of intercepting ballistic missiles in their boost phase

see David Vaughan *et al.* 'Developing BPI/API capability' in Stav and Koroth (note 36) pp.47–267. For a technical analysis of the use of lasers for boost phase intercept see Geoffrey E. Forden 'the Airborne Laser', in ibid. pp.227–46.

58. For the sake of comparison – the THAAD is designed to intercept at 2,000 m/sec. The American program for BPI – the Talon (now cancelled) was projected to intercept at 3,000–4,000 m/sec

59. Reuven Pedatzur, 'the advantages of Moab', *Ha'Aretz*, 8 Nov. 1998 (in Hebrew).

60. *Conduct of the Persian Gulf War – Final report to Congress*, US Department of Defense (April 1992) pp.165–8. See also Cordesman and Wagner (note 38) pp.860–7.

61. Amnon Barzilai, 'In Middle East, more missiles, same old threats', *Ha'Aretz*, 22 Dec. 1999 (in Hebrew). For tunnels in Libya see Joshua Sinai, 'Ghadaffi's Libya: the patient proliferator', *Jane's Intelligence Review* 10/12 (Dec. 1998) pp.27–30. For tunnels in Syria see Harold Hough 'Viewing Syria's strategic missile infrastructure from space', *Jane's Intelligence Review* 10/4 (April 1998) pp. 24–25. For tunnels in Iran see Barbara Starr; 'USA moves to block weapon danger', *Jane's Defence Weekly* 12 April 1997.

62. It was estimated at the time of the Gulf War that Iraq had 36 mobile launchers, but the largest number of missiles fired within one day was 10 missiles. (*Conduct of the Gulf War*, note 60 p.165) thus it is possible that a smaller number was active during the war itself.

63. *Conduct of the Gulf War* (note 60) p.167.

64. For a comprehensive analysis of Israel's nuclear deterrence see Shai Feldman, *Israeli Nuclear Deterrence* (NY: Columbia UP 1982). Feldman argued in his book for a shift to open deterrence.

65. Nitzan Hurvitz, 'Peres dismisses the value of the NPT', *Ha'Aretz*, 19 Feb. 1995 (in Hebrew). Peres is quoted as telling Mr Musa that Israel has no intention of joining the NPT as long as it is threatened by Iran and Iraq. See also Ze'ev Schiff, 'An Egyptian wall', *Ha'Aretz*, 27 Jan. 1995 (in Hebrew).

66. Barbara Opall-Rome, 'One on one: Interview with Maj. General Yitzhak Ben-Yisrael', *Defense News*, 17 Aug. 1998. General Ben-Yisrael discussed the paradox between the need to deter and the secrecy, and claimed that all the options will be reviewed. Brig. Gen. (ret) Ephraim Sneh, who became in 1999 Deputy Minister of Defense argued then for the continuation of the nuclear ambiguity: see Ephraim Sneh, 'Dimona sacrificed for Yitzhar', *Ha'Aretz*, 13 Aug. 1998 (in Hebrew).

67. Amos Harel, 'Minister of defense in the ceremony for the arrival of the new planes: a leap in the deterring capability of the air force', *Ha'Aret*, 20 Jan. 1998 (in Hebrew).

68. Yair Evron, *Israel's Nuclear Dilemma* (Ithaca, NY: Cornell UP 1994).
For thorough analysis of the aspects of Israel's conventional deterrence see Uri Bar-Joseph, 'Variations on a theme: the conceptualization of deterrence in Israeli strategic thinking', *Security Studies* 7/3 (Spring 1998) pp.145–81. See also Ellie Lieberman, 'What makes Deterrence Work? Lessons from the Egyptian-Israeli Enduring Rivalry', *Security Studies* 4/4 (Summer 1995) pp. 851–910. Bar-Joseph distinguishes between four types of deterrence according to the goals of the deterrence. An analysis of the relevance of each type of deterrence in countering nonconventional threats to Israel is beyond the scope of this essay.

69. For an analysis of Israeli leader's messages, see Shai Feldman, 'Israel's deterrence and the Gulf War' in *War in the Gulf* (note 43) pp.184–208. Prof. Feldman argues that Israeli leaders failed in implementing a coherent policy of deterring messages, but he thinks that this had little effect on the Arab perceptions of Israel's strength.

70. Amnon Barzilai, 'Mordechai: Israel shall inflict a high cost if the rear would be attacked with ballistic missiles', *Ha'Aretz*, 28 Oct. 1997 (in Hebrew).

71. Yerah Tal, 'USA promises a tough response to an Iraqi attack on Israel', *Ha'Aretz*, 6 Feb. 1998 (in Hebrew).

72. 'The correct response for a threat', *Ha'Aretz*, editorial (unsigned) 12 Feb. 1998 (in Hebrew).

73. Thomas C. Schelling *Arms and Influence* (New Haven, CT: Yale UP 1966) pp.1–18. See also Bernard Brodie, *Strategy in the Missile Age* (Princeton UP 1959) p.273, See also Patrick Morgan, *Deterrence* (Beverly Hills and London: Sage 1977); Kenneth N. Waltz, *The Spread of Nuclear Weapons: More may be Better* Adelphi Papers No. 171 (London: IISS 1981) pp.28–30.

74. Feldman, *Israeli Nuclear Deterrence* (note 64) pp.42–3.

75. For an analysis of the Arabs perceptions of Israel's nuclear deterrence see Emili B. Landau and Ariel E. Levite, *Israel's Nuclear Image: Arab Perceptions of Israel's Nuclear Posture* (Tel Aviv: Jaffee Center for Strategic Studies and Papirus Books 1994) pp.165–7 (in Hebrew).
76. Reuven Pedatzur, 'A Severe Blow to deterrence', *Ha'Aretz*, 24 Feb. 1998 (in Hebrew).
77. Feldman, 'Israel's deterrence and the Gulf War' (note 69) pp.184–208.
78. To name just a few examples of the debate see: Michael O'Hanlon 'Star wars strike back', *Foreign Affairs* 78/6 (Nov.–Dec. 1998); John Steinbrunner, 'National missile defense: collision in progress', *Arms Control today* 29/7 (Nov. 1999) pp.3–6; Lisbeth Gronlund and George Lewis, 'How a limited national missile defense would impact the ABM treaty', *Arms Control Today* 29/7 (Nov. 1999) pp.7–13; Paul Mann, 'Missile defense gains political favor amid rifts', *Aviation Week and Space Technology*, 1 March 1999, p.51; David Smith, 'Has time come to throw ABM to the dustbin', *Jane's Intelligence Review* 10/12 (Dec. 1998); Michael A. Dornheim, 'Missile defense soon, but will it work?', *Aviation Week and Space Technology*, 24 Feb. 1997.
79. Alcibiadis Thalassocrates, 'NATO opens up a TMD effort', *Military Technology* 22/8 (Aug. 1998); Nick Cook, 'Europe's missing Shield', *Jane's Defence Weekly* 31/17, 28 April 1999; Philip Finnegan, 'Politics hinders joint Gulf missile defense', *Defense News* 14/11, 22 March 1999; John Morrocco, 'Allies pursue few indigenous projects', *Aviation Week and Space Technology* 151/7, 16 Aug. 1999, pp.76–7.
80. One important report issued in the United States was the 'Rumsfeld report', which reassessed the threat of ballistic missiles. The report influenced both the debate in the United States, giving much support to the proponents of BMD, and in other countries: in Europe and of course in Israel. On the American debate see: Richard Garwin 'What have we done', and Lisbeth Gronlund and David Wright, 'What they haven't done', both in *Bulletin of the Atomic Scientists* (Nov. 1998).
81. For a statement of Israel's policy regarding arms control regimes see: Eytan Bentsur (the Director General of the Ministry of Foreign Affairs), 'Israel's Approach to Regional Security, Arms Control and Disarmament', Statement before the Conference on Disarmament in Geneva on 4 Sept. 1997.
82. Bentsur, ibid.

6

Israeli War Objectives into an Era of Negativism

AVI KOBER

It has often been claimed that Israel has never had well-defined war objectives and that its political war objectives have been overshadowed by military considerations – attaining the *military* war objectives and achieving battlefield decision. The Israeli Cabinet has also been criticized for having failed in adjusting war objectives to developments on the battlefield during the course of war. Many have also believed that, as a declared 'status-quo state', Israel's war objectives have been of a thwarting nature, focusing on negating the other side's aggressive intentions rather than achieving 'positive' gains in war. Yet, when one studies the nature of Israeli war objectives and the role they have played in the conduct of the Arab–Israeli Wars, one finds that many of these claims are not empirically supported.

In the wake of the 1967 Six Day War, a new strategic reality evolved in the Middle East. Subsequent to the 1973 October War, the region underwent dramatic political changes. Both wars gradually changed how Israel addressed its security problems. Militarily stronger but affected by an environment of new political and military constraints, Israel has also revisited its attitude towards its war objectives. What course have these developments taken, and how have they affected Israeli war objectives?

In this contribution I will put forward the following arguments:

(a) Whereas in the pre-1967 period there existed a non-linear, asymmetrical relationship between Israeli political and military war objectives – the former tending to be 'defensive' and the latter 'offensive' – starting in the late 1960s, this relationship came to be more linear and symmetrical, due to political and military constraints. Israeli political and military war objectives since the 1970s have gradually become more 'defensive' in nature, with the phenomenon intensifying in the 1980s and 1990s. Four main factors account for the strengthening of a defensive approach: superpower constraints, difficulty in gaining public legitimization for initiating war, the peace process, and the spread of surface-to-surface missiles in the Middle East.

(b) In recent years, the value of battlefield decision has been diminishing, while the weight of victory – the achievement of the war objectives – has been growing. Among the factors responsible for this trend, the following seem to have affected it more than others: the strengthening of firepower relative to maneuver on the battlefield, difficulty in translating battlefield decision to political achievements, and growing political constraints on freedom of action on the battlefield.

In the ensuing discussion, I will first refute some of the images related to Israeli war objectives before 1967. I will then analyze the changes they underwent from the late 1960s through the mid-1970s. Finally, I will try to extrapolate the nature of Israeli war objectives into the next millennium.

ISRAELI WAR OBJECTIVES – IN RETROSPECT

Is it True that Israel has Never Clearly Defined its War Objectives?

It has more than once been argued that the Israeli political echelon used to refrain from defining clear war objectives, whether before or in the course of the Arab–Israeli wars. Two explanations were offered for this phenomenon: first, lack of consensus with regard to national goals, from which war objectives were supposed to be drawn;[1] second, the predominance of the defense establishment in shaping Israeli strategic thinking at the expense of the political echelon.[2] Neither claim or explanation is supported by empirical evidence. As I will show below, not only have war objectives existed in each of the Arab–Israeli wars, but they also were defined by the political rather than the military echelon.

True, for Israel, security has always come first. As Ben-Gurion once put it, 'I cannot help seeing things through security glasses [...] If there is security, there is everything. If there is no security – there is nothing.'[3] Yet, it is only natural that the minister in charge of defense would be so deeply involved in the decision-making process with regard to war objectives. It seems that the predominance of the relatively vaguely defined 'defensive' war objectives over the more specifically defined 'offensive' ones has been the reason for the feeling of many, especially in the military, that as far as the political war objectives are concerned they have often operated in vacuum.

The Primacy of Politics: Have Israeli War Objectives Reflected the Ascendancy of the Political Rationale over the Military?

In principle, war ought to be the instrument of politics.[4] Both military victory, defined in terms of the fulfillment of the military war objectives,[5] and battlefield decision, defined in terms of denying the enemy the will and/or ability to carry on the fight,[6] are, in that sense, the servants of the political war objectives. While the political war objectives are expected to be looking beyond the horizon of a particular war, the military war objectives are usually confined to the horizon of the particular war. Their realization, through missions fulfilled by the military, is supposed to serve the attainment of the political objectives. Given the complexities and sensitivities entailed in the use of force in modern times, however, a two-way relationship between ends and means is in place. It is important that the political and the military echelons cooperate and take into account their respective views as to how the military can best serve the political war objectives, without necessarily doing so at the expense of combat effectiveness.[7]

There have been events in Israeli military history wherein over-enthusiasm on the part of the military, representing the ascendancy of the expressive element in war over rational calculation,[8] created tension and, sometimes, incompatibility between the political and military war objectives. During the early 1950s, it was common knowledge among military commanders that Chief of Staff Major General Moshe Dayan preferred 'noble stallions' to 'reluctant mules', to the point of almost encouraging 'positive' indiscipline and treating it as a consequence of high morale and fighting spirit.[9] This attitude applied to both 'current security' and 'basic security' operations.[10] For example, at the initial stages of the 1956 Sinai War, Brigadier General Assaf Simhoni, OC Southern Command, took the Israeli 7th Armored Brigade into action 24 hours ahead of schedule, ignoring a clear instruction not to do so. The political logic behind this instruction was that, should the French and the British fail to live up to their commitment to join the war and strategically cooperate with Israel, Israel could still claim the operation was nothing but a reprisal. Unaware of the political complexity of the situation, Simhoni considered that instruction to be politically unwise and militarily too costly.[11] Dayan took no disciplinary action. In 1967, Defense Minister Moshe Dayan rejected the idea that Israeli troops should advance to the Suez Canal. He thought the war objectives could be achieved without an Israeli presence on the bank of the canal and that it would be reasonable to allow the Egyptians to maintain normal life along the Suez Canal, so as to create strategic stability once the war was over.[12] But Israeli forces did advance to the canal, because senior officers, such as Deputy Chief of Staff General Haim Bar-Lev, felt that the military accomplishment would be incomplete if Egyptian troops were allowed to stay east of the canal.[13]

However, cases of disobedience on the part of the military in general and with regard to war objectives in particular have been very rare. Even when the political instructions were considered by the military to be heavily constraining its freedom of action – sometimes to the extent of threatening to deny it combat effectiveness and military achievements – it eventually subordinated its missions and objectives to the political war objectives.

To mention only few examples: in the early stages of the 1948 War of Independence, Ben-Gurion, as simultaneous Prime Minister and Defense Minister, instructed the GHQ to open the blocked road to besieged Jerusalem. Outspoken reservations on the part of the military, based on operational grounds, were of no avail. Ben-Gurion's instructions subsequently led to the Nahshon operation (April 1948) and the Latrun operations (May 1948) which, despite great difficulties, eventually enabled the IDF to connect Jerusalem to the rest of the territories under Israeli control.[14]

In autumn, 1948, Ben-Gurion ordered the mass of most of Israeli ground forces to the Egyptian front, so as to effectively confront the Egyptian army and win the entire war. The GHQ protested, claiming that this would expose Israel's soft underbelly (the Jordanian front), but complied with the order.[15]

At the end of that war, during Operation 'Horev' on the southern front (December 1948), Israeli forces were operating in Egyptian territory. An ultimatum was delivered by Britain and the United States, demanding that Israel withdraw its forces at once. As Ben-Gurion thought that the military objective of pulling the Egyptians back to the international border could be achieved while operating east of it, and that operational convenience did not justify risking a conflict with the great powers, he ordered limiting the territorial scope of the operation. Again, the military tried to dissuade him, but ultimately complied with the political instruction to withdraw.[16]

At times, the IDF has been too passive in everything regarding the political war objectives. For example, prior to the 1982 Lebanon War, Israeli senior officers, including Chief of Staff Major General Raphael Eytan – who, in principle, supported the war – voiced their doubts regarding the chances of both achieving the ambitious political war objectives and avoiding confrontation with the Syrian army in Lebanon, basing their assessments on a wargame ('Shoshanim') that had been played only few months before the war broke out. Unfortunately, they refrained from making any serious attempt to talk Defense Minister Ariel Sharon out of going to that war or at least reconsidering its objectives.[17]

The obedience of the Israeli military can be attributed to three foundations on which civil-military and political-military relations are based: normative, legal, and practical. The principle of the subordination of war to politics had been a deeply rooted norm since the days of the inter-community struggle between the 'Yishuv' and the Palestinians and the struggle against British rule. It has only strengthened ever since. As Ben-Gurion put it, 'It is not for the army to decide anything related to policy, regime, law, or governance. The army does not even determine its own structure, organization, and operations. Of course, it is not for the army to decide anything related to war and peace. It is merely an executive arm [...]. [The aforesaid] are solely determined by the civil authorities.'[18] On another occasion, Ben-Gurion said that 'military matters, as any other practical matter, ought to be determined by those who have open eyes and common sense, and not by technicians, though the latter's advice is vital'.[19]

Two basic laws, established by the Israeli legislature during the 1960s and the 1970s – 'Basic law: the Cabinet', 1968, and 'Basic Law: the Army', 1975 – have constitutionally regulated and institutionalized that norm. Finally, at the practical level, the political and the military echelon have from time to time agreed upon unwritten rules of cooperation that would enable them to work together with the lowest friction possible. Where chemistry existed between key political and military figures, as in the case of Ben-Gurion and Dayan or Dayan and Bar-Lev, cooperation became even smoother.[20]

Have Israeli War Objectives been Static or Dynamic?

Statesmen and senior officers are tested, among other criteria, by their ability to define realizable war objectives or update them during the war, if the political or the military conditions either force them to give up objectives they have adopted prior to the war or enable them to achieve new ones in its course.[21] For example, Egypt's war objectives in the 1973 October War were tailored to its military capabilities;[22] and Israeli objectives in the 1967 Six Day War were expanded as a result of new opportunities that had opened up, as will be elaborated below.

During the Arab–Israeli wars, conditions and situations developed from time to time that required either extending the objectives beyond their original formulation or redefining them in a more limited fashion. The 1967 War provides us with the best example of extending objectives. Before Dayan came to office as Defense Minister, less than a week before the war broke out, the military war objectives were confined to the destruction of the Egyptian air force and Egyptian ground forces deployed close to the Israeli-Egyptian border, so as to acquire bargaining chips for the sake of lifting the blockade of the Straits of Tiran.[23] But, once Dayan assumed office, the military war objectives were reshaped under his supervision. They were now to include the destruction of the Egyptian army in the entire Sinai and the occupation of the peninsula.[24]

During the war, the objectives were stretched even further, as it became clear that Israel could achieve more, thanks to its military superiority and unexpected passivity on the part of the Soviet Union, the patron of Egypt and Syria. The political and military war objectives were consequently extended so as to include Jordan and Syria. On the Jordanian front, the Israelis had first thought merely of the liberation of the Old City of Jerusalem, but were soon tempted to occupy the entire West Bank. On the Syrian front, it now became both desirable and feasible to relieve the settlements in the Jordan Valley from Syrian fire on their homes and fields and solve the water problem – which had been a source of many incidents between Israel and Syria since the early 1950s but particularly during the early and mid-1960s – by occupying the Golan Heights.[25]

The War of Attrition (1969–70) is another example of the elastic nature of Israeli war objectives. In that war, Israel shifted its operations from the area along the Suez Canal to grand-strategic bombing in the heart of Egypt, with the intention of bringing about the collapse of Nasser's regime. Such collapse, it was believed, would not only put an end to the war, but might also create favorable conditions for peace between the two countries. However, once the Soviets escalated their involvement in the conflict and decided to intervene in the war, following a desperate visit by Nasser to Moscow in January 1970, Israel had to readjust its war objectives. It thus returned to more limited objectives and operations which were similar to those that had characterized the earlier stages of the war.[26]

Have Israeli Political War Objectives really been of a Thwarting Nature?

During the first half of the twentieth century, the Zionist movement had been torn between two competing ethos: defensive and offensive. The defensive ethos reflected basic, moral resentment of the idea of violence and treated war as a necessary evil, or an act of no alternative, imposed on the Jewish community in Palestine by the Arab community's aggression. It was

rooted in basic Jewish rejection of violence, not only for practical reasons –
the Jews being a minority everywhere in the Diaspora – but also on moral
grounds: violence was perceived as contradictory to Jewish values. The
offensive ethos, on the other hand, was inspired by Zionism being a national
movement. As such, it bought land from Palestinian Arabs, built new
settlements, and fought in order to establish a territorial base for
independence.[27]

Since the establishment of the State of Israel, the tension between these
two approaches has, to a great extent, been reflected in Israeli strategic
thinking in general and the Israeli attitude to war objectives in particular.
One could quite easily identify two main schools of thought among Israel's
defense elite with regard to how far Israel could afford to go with its
political war objectives. The 'positive' school, for one, has advocated the
adoption of 'offensive' political war objectives. By contrast, the 'negative'
school, represented by most of the political decision-makers, has preferred
war objectives of a thwarting nature, such as denying the enemy any
political, military, or territorial gains from its use of force.

The positive school has argued that a threatened nation has the right to
initiate war and capture new territories, if necessary, so as to create a more
favorable strategic environment.[28] Both the 1956 Sinai War and the 1982
Lebanon War were presented by the 'positivists' as a proof that the
implementation of such war objectives was feasible. Positive political war
objectives were also believed by their proponents to be a prerequisite for
efficiently operating and building up the armed forces, as compatible with
the principle of the economy of force,[29] and as saving casualties.[30] The
positive approach was identified with Clausewitz's notion of war being the
continuation of politics,[31] ignoring the fact that, for Clausewitz, the nature –
or content – of the objective had not really mattered, as long as one existed,
irrespective of whether 'positive' or 'negative'. Prominent 'positivists' have
been General (res.) Rehav'am Ze'evi, General (res.) Benjamin Peled, and
Colonel (res.) Emanuel Wald.

'Soft' positivists have rejected the idea of initiating war, but, on the other
hand, have justified the adoption of positive – sometimes extremely
ambitious – political war objectives, in case a large-scale war was forced
upon Israel. For example, Yigal Allon thought that, in 1967, Israel missed
the opportunity to reach Cairo, Damascus, and Amman and put an end to
the bloody Arab–Israeli conflict.[32] Meanwhile, Professor Yuval Ne'eman, a
reserve colonel, has argued that, in the case of an Arab attack, Israel should
feel free to consider the possibility of shattering the Syrian state,
establishing an independent Druze state in the Horan, encouraging the

establishment of a Kurdish state in northern Iraq, and annexing southern Lebanon and the strategically important Edom mountains.[33]

The competing, 'negative' school has emphasized the need to safeguard the territorial integrity of Israel and protect the homeland. Israel, according to this school, has no aspirations to expand. Consensus in the Israeli society could be created only with regard to the direct defense of Israel. Both the nature of the Arab–Israeli strategic balance and superpower involvement in the Arab–Israeli conflict would not allow Israel to achieve objectives beyond those of a thwarting nature, such as forcing the Arabs to surrender or dictating peace.[34] However, should the opportunity arise to achieve positive political objectives in the event a war of no choice breaks out, such option ought to be seriously considered, as long as vital security interests are at stake.[35] On this point, the gap between the negativists and the soft positivists becomes almost negligible. Finally, 'negative' objectives would encourage, and even oblige, the military to prepare for a variety of modus operandi, thereby lending the political echelon freedom of choice under the greatest possible range of circumstances. A representative of this school has been General (res.) Israel Tal.[36]

One would quite reasonably expect that a state like Israel, that basically sees itself as a 'status quo state', would adopt war objectives of a 'negative', or thwarting nature. Indeed, such an approach has often been attributed to it.[37] If one studies Israeli political war objectives over the years, however, one discovers – perhaps surprisingly – that the objectives have rather constituted a combination of both negativism and positivism. In 1948, Israel was preoccupied with thwarting the Arab states' invasion, the purpose of which had been to deny Israel the right to exist as an independent state. But, alongside this negative objective, there could easily be detected both political and military positive objectives.

In February 1948, three months before the Arab invasion took place, the Haganah (the main Jewish defense organization) formulated 'Plan D', which was issued as an order in March. The plan postulated the need to create territorial congruity between the various Jewish settlements throughout Palestine. Such congruity was meant to serve the political objective of establishing a territorial infrastructure as solid as possible for the new Jewish state.[38] Indeed, once the war ended, Israel found itself with a territory greater than the one the 'Yishuv' (pre-State Jewish community) leadership had agreed to in November 1947, when it accepted the United Nations partition resolution.

Before the 1956 Sinai War, too, Israel perceived a serious threat stemming from the Egyptian-Czech arms deal that had been signed in 1955.

Under those circumstances, the Sinai War was a preventive war.[39] Additional threats had been the closing of the Straits of Tiran by Egypt, and the 'current security' problems stemming from Palestinian infiltration of Israeli territory. Chief of Staff Dayan tried to convince Prime Minister Ben-Gurion that the insecurity along the border in itself deserved to be dealt with by going to war, but Ben-Gurion hesitated. The rare opportunity to strategically cooperate with France and Britain against Egypt infused new self-confidence into Israeli veins. Thanks to the coalition with the two great powers, it unexpectedly seemed possible to at least play with the idea of achieving far-reaching positive political war objectives. The positive objectives – possibly the most ambitious Israel has ever wished to achieve – were, in fact, a scheme of a new regional order. Provided that Nasser's regime could be toppled, Israel wished to bring about the disintegration of Jordan and its partition between Israel and Iraq (a pro-Western monarchy at the time) and the disintegration of Lebanon and its partition between Syria, Israel, and an independent Christian state. Israel also wished the Suez Canal to be under international control and the Straits of Tiran under Israeli control.[40]

The 1967 crisis started when Egypt massed its forces in the Sinai and again closed the Straits of Tiran. Coping with these serious threats became Israel's first priority. Israeli decision-makers made great efforts to prevent Jordan from joining the war and refrained from attacking Syria. But, in light of the overwhelming military success on the Egyptian front, they started thinking in terms of positive political war objectives vis-à-vis Jordan and Syria. This resulted in the occupation of the entire West Bank and the seizure of the Golan Heights.

The 1967 War was certainly a watershed in Israeli political and military thinking. Following this war, Israel felt very safe, thanks to its achievements on the battlefield and the perception that, for the first time, it enjoyed 'defensible borders'.[41] Particularly notable among the expressions of Israeli self-confidence were the changes in Israeli deterrence policy, such as the diminishing value of *casi belli* and the willingness to make do with red lines, instead,[42] or the emphasis put on deterrence-by-denial, instead of deterrence-by-punishment. This satisfaction with the new situation, on the one hand, and the belief that the world would not tolerate any further Israeli territorial expansion, on the other, led Israel into the most 'negative' era in the history of its war objectives. As early as 31 July 1967, less than two months after the war, the Israeli Cabinet, under Prime Minister Eshkol, stressed its commitment to maintaining the territorial, political, and military new status quo as long as the Arabs were unwilling to negotiate with

Israel.[43] 'Positivism', however, did not completely disappear. In the 1969/70 War of Attrition, which had been initiated by Egypt, Israel escalated its military operations and started attacking counter-value targets in the Egyptian rear, attempting to overthrow Nasser's regime.[44]

The October 1973 Yom Kippur War was the war with the most 'negative' war objectives. True, in discussions that had been held during April–May, 1973, in Israeli GHQ and the Ministry of Defense on future war objectives, Defense Minister Dayan expressed his view that should Egypt and Syria attack Israel, Israel would be free to achieve positive war objectives on both fronts.[45] However, it had been generally accepted that the main objective should be denying the enemy any military achievement. This objective was reaffirmed once the 1973 War started.[46] Both Israeli policy and military operations focused on thwarting the Egyptian and Syrian offensives and pushing the attackers back to the 1967 ceasefire lines. However, this did not prevent Israel from eventually occupying territory on the west bank of the Suez Canal and additional territory on the Golan Heights.

The 1982 Lebanon War can be considered a 'positive' episode, or a temporary deviation from negativism. Ariel Sharon, who had assumed office as Israel's new Defense Minister in August 1981, brought with him a forgotten spirit of activism. His activism expressed itself, among other things, in the reintroduction of *casi belli* to Israeli defense policy, including, for the first time, a *casus belli* that for many in Israel related to 'current security' threats – insurgency from Lebanon.[47] This could, to a large extent, be interpreted as an act of preparing the ground for the upcoming Israeli initiation of war.

In 1982, Israel faced no existential threat. Under the pretext of defending northern Israel and Israeli troops in southern Lebanon from Palestinian terrorists, Israel, under Begin and Sharon, aimed at establishing a friendly, Christian regime in Lebanon that would not only sign a peace treaty with Israel, but also expel the Palestinian Liberation Organization (PLO) from Lebanon. Some Israeli decision-makers, such as Sharon and Chief of Staff Eytan, also toyed with the possibility that the PLO would return to Jordan, from which it had been driven in 1970. There it would, hopefully, topple the monarchy and create a Palestinian state. Assuming that the transformation of Jordan into a Palestinian state would satisfy Palestinian national aspirations, Israel would be able to keep the West Bank for itself.[48]

NEGATIVE POLITICAL WAR OBJECTIVES, POSITIVE MILITARY WAR OBJECTIVES

It is only natural that states with revisionist values, translated into positive (offensive) political war objectives, would adopt positive (offensive) military war objectives, as well as offensive doctrines and strategies. But, negative *political* war objectives, too, can be translated into positive *military* war objectives and offensive doctrine and strategy, as exemplified by the Israeli case. Strategic concepts such as prevention and preemption are representative of the combination of negative political war objectives and positive military war objectives carried out through offensive strategy.

This combination has been characteristic of Israel for many years and has been considered compatible with the above dialectic relationship between the defensive and offensive ethos, as well as with the notion of: 'he who rises to kill you, rise to kill him first.'[49] True, the Israeli army was given the name *Israel Defense Forces*, but 'defense', in this context, stands for the *objective*, not the strategy. Israel's strategy, from the second truce in the 1948 War of Independence and through all the Arab–Israeli wars has been rather offensive.[50] There are two possible explanations for the tendency to assign a defensive nature to Israeli strategy and ascribe offense only to the operational level:[51] a confusion between (war) objectives and strategy, on the one hand and, on the other, a need to reconcile, with the actual offensive nature of the IDF's strategy, the mistaken belief that defense will be the stronger form of waging war, as argued by Clausewitz and Liddell Hart.[52]

Israel preferred offense to defense for three main reasons. The inability to absorb enemy attack, for one, has been a constraint that has accounted for the relative importance of both offense and positive military war objectives. When there is an absence of strategic depth,[53] there is a need to transfer the war to enemy territory as rapidly as possible.[54] Such a situation is likely to dictate preference for positive military war objectives and offense.[55]

The obverse is equally true: where one is capable of absorbing enemy offensive during the initial stages of a war, this will facilitate the adoption of negative war objectives and a defensive strategy.[56] In the wake of the 1967 War, Israel felt it had gained strategic depth for the first time. This could enable it to at least consider the possibility of changing its military doctrine and strategy from offensive to defensive and adopting war objectives of a thwarting nature. In practice, no change in Israeli doctrine ever took place.

The second reason for the offensive approach has not been explicitly acknowledged by Israeli strategic thinkers but has intuitively existed in the backs of their minds. Offense has been considered a 'force multiplier', enabling the few to compensate for their quantitative inferiority by initiating the war and choosing the place and time of the confrontation, where they could mass enough forces so as to outnumber the enemy and inhibit casualties.[57] The third reason is related to the linkage between offense and battlefield decision: offense, either at the strategic or the operational level, has always been regarded as the only form of war by which it is possible to obtain battlefield decision.[58]

Both the 1956 and 1967 wars were, from the Israeli point of view, acts of self-defense; in other words, wars of no choice. Yet, in both cases it was Israel that delivered the first strike and acted upon positive military war objectives, such as driving the Egyptian army out of the Sinai Peninsula.[59] In 1956, in light of the Czech-Egyptian arms deal of 1955, Israel felt that, by initiating a war imminently, it would have a chance of preventing an attack by a well-equipped Egyptian army, probably within months, which Israel might otherwise not be able to cope with. In 1967, Israel decided to launch a preemptive attack, as, by the time the war started, the Egyptians had deployed forces along the Israeli border, after having violated the demilitarization of the Sinai and having closed the Straits of Tiran. The Israeli positive military war objectives in this case included the destruction of the Egyptian air force, the destruction of the ground forces in the Sinai, and the occupation of the peninsula, including Sharm Al-Sheikh, so as to remove both threats. As far as Jordan and Syria were concerned, since both states attacked Israel once the war with Egypt broke out – though it was a small scale and, to a great extent, reluctant attack – Israel took advantage of the circumstances and launched a large-scale counter-attack on the West Bank and the Golan Heights.[60]

Has Commitment to Battlefield Decision really Overshadowed the Achievement of the War Objectives?

It might be useful, at this stage, to differentiate between two concepts that are usually regarded and employed as synonyms: battlefield decision and victory. As has already been mentioned, whereas battlefield decision can be defined in terms of negating the other side's combat capability, victory can be defined in terms of the correlation between what each adversary defines as its political and military war objectives, before and during a war, and what it actually succeeds in achieving during that war. These definitions suggest: (a) that victory ought to be treated as a more subjective concept than battlefield decision: whereas only one side can decide, there may be more than one victor; and (b) that victory is amenable to manipulation by decision-makers.

Battlefield decision has been a central component of Israel's security doctrine. The assumption has been that since deterrence is bound to fail sooner or later, there will eventually be a need to recourse to battlefield decision. In turn, the ability to achieve a battlefield decision has been supposed to rehabilitate Israel's failed deterrence, to significantly prolong the lulls between wars, and over the long term, even to bring about peace with the Arabs.[61] The perceived need to achieve battlefield decision in and of itself, by virtue of its centra, has been considered as a war objective and as standing at the very foundation of Israeli strategic and operational planning. From the Israeli standpoint, therefore, battlefield decision has become, at one and the same time, both an end and a means to that end.[62] Paradoxically, Israel's difficulty in translating its military achievement into political gains has encouraged it to achieve battlefield decision, because only on the battlefield could it demonstrate relative advantage over its enemies. Thus, while the Arabs have focused on political achievements out of military weakness, Israel has been pushed to focus on battlefield decision out of political weakness.[63] This preference of battlefield decision over victory has, however, gradually changed since the late 1970s, for reasons that will be discussed below.

ISRAELI WAR OBJECTIVES AT THE CROSSROADS

Is There Any Future for Positive War Objectives?

Israeli war objectives since the 1970s have gradually become more negative in nature, with the phenomenon intensifying in the 1980s and 1990s. Four main factors account for the strengthening of negativism: superpower constraints, difficulty in gaining public legitimization for initiating war, the peace process, and the proliferation of surface-to-surface missiles in the Middle East.

SUPERPOWER CONSTRAINTS

The principle of self-reliance has always been one of the foundations upon which Israeli national security has been based, but Israel has never been sure of its ability to cope independently with the challenges to its security. Its dependence on superpowers for the sake of defense, on the one hand, and superpower involvement in the Middle East during the Cold War, on the other, have made it imperative for Israel to take superpower constraints into account in everything related to war. It, therefore, concentrated a great deal of diplomatic efforts in gaining the support of the great powers before, during, and after any particular war. In 1956, it cooperated with France and Britain, while, in 1967, it permitted itself to deliver the first strike only after it had become quite clear that the United States would support the initiative, or at least not object to it. In 1982, also, Israel had reached a tacit understanding with Secretary of State Alexander Haig before it attacked in Lebanon. But, no other example demonstrates superpower constraints better than the 1973 case.

Once the 1973 war broke out, the Israeli cabinet decided to refrain from any occupation of territories beyond those that had been occupied in 1967. The logic behind that decision, as explained by Defense Minister Dayan, was that 'we are not popular in the world with anything related to territories. Should we nevertheless occupy additional territories, we would not be able to keep them for long, because of political reasons.'[64] In the mid-1970s, Prime Minister Yitzhak Rabin, Foreign Minister Yigal Allon, Defense Minister Shimon Peres and Chief of Staff General Mordechai Gur all publicly ruled out the possibility that Israel would, in the future, initiate a war against the Arabs. The main reasons for this were Israel's delicate diplomatic situation in the international arena and its growing dependence on the United States.[65]

Such considerations have not become less weighty in the post-Cold War era. True, the United States has become the only superpower in the region, and, unlike the Soviet Union in its time, it has never supported any aggression against Israel. On the other hand, however, henceforth, the United States is not likely to support Israeli war initiative, either. Furthermore, in recent years, Israel has been facing severe security challenges, stemming from the spread of surface-to-surface missiles and weapons of mass destruction within range of its entire territory (see below). Countries located at a distance from Israel, for example, Iraq and Iran, have become real or potential threats. Thus, cooperation with the United States has become crucial to coping with these challenges, making Israel even more dependent on the United States than in the past.

Consequently, Israel's future ability to gain the sympathy and assistance of the United States in the event of crisis or war will require both the adoption of negative political war objectives and a higher level of restraint in all matters related to the use of force. Defense is likely to be perceived by the Israeli political and military elite as serving that cause much more effectively than offense, if applied at least at the strategic level. Unfortunately, this may mean the absorption of a costly first strike initiated by the Arabs, just for the sake of justifying active and direct US assistance to Israel, as was the case in 1973. Israeli readiness to absorb attack due to superpower constraints was demonstrated during the 1991 Gulf War, when Israel refrained from any response to Iraqi attacks.

NATIONAL CONSENSUS

National consensus has become a factor that might affect any decision regarding war and peace in the future. The mass media have brought war to every citizen's home in near-real time, making it impossible for the leadership to ignore the public's attitudes toward a war, particularly its objectives and the way it is conducted. As de Tocqueville learned from his studies of American democracy, once a democracy has been induced, however reluctantly, to wage a war believed to be just, it will be ready to sacrifice a great deal in the effort to win it.[66] It is easier to forge positive political war objectives in a society that exhibits widespread consensus over values and political objectives. The reverse is equally true: society is reluctant to sacrifice once it perceives of the war as being a 'war of choice'.

The reservations expressed by some 400,000 Israelis with regard to the positive war objectives adopted by the Israeli Cabinet during the 1982 Lebanon War constituted a watershed in the linkage between war and society in Israel. They made it clear even to right wing circles that, where a war by choice is concerned, there will be no alternative but to ensure that the national consensus is as widespread as possible in everything associated with the war's justification and public legitimization for the manner in which it is being conducted.[67] Since 1982, decision-makers in Israel have become aware of the fact that the Israeli public is reluctant to sacrifice, unless the defense of the homeland is at stake; in other words, it is ready to fight only a war of no choice. Societal cost tolerance tends to be very low, particularly in circumstances where the war is considered to be a war of choice.

In post-heroic war, one is often not allowed to kill and almost always not supposed to get killed.[68] Such a climate also goes against the likelihood of conducting a war by choice. In the post-heroic era, if a power finds itself at war, and provided that it enjoys technological superiority, it may be tempted to use massive fire, instead of maneuvering for the sake of inflicting heavy casualties on the enemy and avoiding casualties to its own troops, as was the case with US and British operations against Saddam Hussein in 1998 and NATO's operations in Kosovo. The IDF has adopted such modus operandi since the late 1970s. Before Defense Minister Ezer Weizman approved the Litani Operation of March 1978, he instructed Chief of Staff Gur that '[the operation] should be conducted very carefully. Ten Fatah [Arab fighters] are not worth even the hand of one of our soldiers. The more lives of our guys we can save, the better. [...] As a pilot, my ideal is that the ground forces should be able to move without shooting even one bullet.'[69]

When Chief of Staff General Ehud Barak explained why Israel preferred using massive fire instead of maneuvering forces on the ground during

Operation 'Accountability' (1993), he stressed the fact that '[during the operation] only one Israeli soldier was killed, whereas the Hizballah suffered heavy damage'. 'This kind of operation reflects our relative advantage over the Hizballah', he added.[70] A senior commander elaborated on this during the operation, saying that 'the less casualties we suffer on our side, the more successful we consider the operation to be. [...] We have methods by which we can inflict intolerable damage on the other side, while minimizing the casualties on our side.'[71]

The same logic applied to Operation 'Grapes of Wrath' (1996). But, whereas in Operation 'Litani' and the 1982 Lebanon War, maneuver still played a significant role, in the more limited military operations in Lebanon during the 1990s – 'Accountability' and 'Grapes of Wrath' – it almost disappeared. In late 1999, Chief of Staff General Shaul Mofaz admitted that the IDF now leaned on air activity against the Hizballah, rather than activities on the ground, so as to reduce casualties.[72]

WAR OBJECTIVES IN A TIME OF PEACE

In the world of today, conflict reduction, conflict resolution, and preservation of the status quo are cherished. Defensive postures and elusive concepts such as deterrence, early warning, and arms control[73] are highly regarded. In the Middle East, the peace process, backed by security and arms control arrangements, has been accelerating since the early 1990s. Under such conditions, for Israel to initiate a war against an Arab state so as to achieve positive war objectives, such as changing the territorial or political status quo, would be extremely difficult. Particularly constraining might be both the danger that, unlike the case of the 1982 Lebanon War,[74] a crisis or war with one Arab state would spill over to confrontation with other Arab states, out of inter-Arab solidarity, and the difficulty of proving to the world that the enemy had been about to attack in the short or long term, a difficulty that Israel has had to cope with for years. Challenges that might accompany the peace process or characterize the new era of peace between Israel and its neighbors include, for instance, attempts to bring deadlocked negotiations back on track, coping with violations of agreements either by coercive diplomacy or limited engagements, and support for friendly regimes in jeopardy.[75]

THE PROLIFERATION OF SURFACE-TO-SURFACE MISSILES IN THE MIDDLE EAST

The reality that the entire Middle East is saturated with 369 ballistic missile launchers[76] and some 2,000 SSMs with various kinds of warheads,[77] most of which are aimed at the civilian rear, is strengthening the deterrent posture of those possessing such capabilities at the expense of their military freedom of action. Such reality, too, is likely to decrease war proneness and the readiness to use force for positive war objectives. States in general and status quo states in particular will think twice before they decide to go to war, and, should they eventually resort to use of force for positive war objectives, they are likely to fight for very limited political and military objectives, so as to prevent escalation.

Victory Instead of Battlefield Decision?

In recent years, the value of battlefield decision has been diminishing, while the weight of victory – the achievement of the war objectives – has been strengthening. Among the factors responsible for this trend, the following seem to have affected it more than others: the strengthening of firepower relative to maneuver, difficulty in translating battlefield decision to political achievements, and growing political constraints on freedom of action on the battlefield.

THE STRENGTHENING OF FIREPOWER RELATIVE TO MANEUVER

The stronger firepower becomes, the more difficult it is to achieve battlefield decision, especially within a short period of time. One of the prominent examples of this phenomenon in the twentieth century is that of the 1973 October War. In this war, the battlefield was saturated with both forces and fire, along with natural or artificial obstacles. Improved Arab anti-tank and anti-aircraft capability, both quantitative and qualitative, which had been developed between 1967 and 1973, posed a threat to the until-then unchallenged dominant weapon systems on the battlefield – aircraft and tanks – which both combined firepower and mobility. The challenge to Israeli freedom of action on the ground and in the air became significant.[78] On such a battlefield, it became very difficult to maneuver and, consequently, less possible to attack, reach battlefield decision, and achieve positive war objectives. Only when Israeli forces crossed the Suez Canal and reached maneuver space, thanks to crucial Egyptian mistakes (the Egyptian army had reinforced its forces on the east bank of the canal with the intention of delivering a counter-attack there, leaving a gap between its Second and Third Armies on the west bank, which enabled the IDF to break through), could they achieve battlefield decision on the Egyptian front and occupy territory on the west bank of the Suez Canal. Similar obstacles occurred in 1982.[79]

Firepower is likely to become even stronger in the foreseeable future. On a battlefield saturated with precise, long-range, and destructive fire, it will be more difficult to maneuver, attack, and achieve positive war objectives. Under such circumstances, Israel might adopt a defensive approach, founded on its increasing superiority in long-range precision-guided munitions. In the initial stages of the war, Israel might transfer the war to enemy territory via fire, instead of maneuver, destroy enemy forces, and only thereafter consider the political and military conditions for launching a counter-attack on the ground, with the aim of achieving positive war objectives.

DIFFICULTY IN TRANSLATING BATTLEFIELD DECISION TO POLITICAL ACHIEVEMENTS

In the wars of the past, there used to be a high correlation between battlefield decision and the attainment of the war objectives. Today, however, that linkage has been disconnected. War objectives can nowadays be achievable merely by using force, short of battlefield decision. Military superiority can no longer guarantee political victory, while military inferiority does not exclude the possibility of achieving victory.

These changes were reflected in discussions on Israeli war objectives held in Israeli GHQ and the Ministry of Defense in the spring and summer of 1973. Chief of Staff Lieutenant General David Elazar and his deputy Major General Israel Tal expressed different views on the linkage between military and political achievements in war. Whereas Elazar believed that Israel could not only destroy enemy forces and defeat them on the battlefield but also impose on them political concessions and acceptable solution to the conflict, Tal was very skeptical with regard to Israel's ability to translate military achievements into political gains. He therefore recommended that, in case of war, Israel confine itself to grand strategic bombing (aimed at economic and military infrastructure) and refrain from carrying out large-scale offensive plans.[80] Tal seems to have understood the non-linear nature of war and peace much better than Elazar.

And, indeed, when one studies the Arab–Israeli wars, one finds that, while Egypt translated its defeats on the battlefield in both 1956 and 1973 into political victory, Israel failed to translate its overwhelming military achievements in 1967 into a peace process with the Arabs. It was only after the 1973 War, with its debatable outcomes, that the peace process could be moved forward. It appears that it is the use of force in itself that often proves to be more effective, politically, than the achievement of battlefield decision. This reality, too, has brought even right-wing Israeli politicians like former Defense Minister Moshe Arens to conclude that, under such circumstances, it would be reasonable to set negative war objectives.[81]

One important reason for the disconnection between battlefield decision and victory is the complicated balance between enemies in our time. That balance no longer reflects only their relative destructive power, but also their relative cost tolerance.[82] In other words, one can be militarily strong but socially weak, and vice versa. In low-intensity conflicts in particular, the small military achievements amassed by the militarily weaker side during the protracted confrontation are often more important and feasible than the attempt to obtain rapid and unequivocal military achievements on the battlefield. Where guerrillas, terrorists, and civil resistance are concerned, battlefield decision is an almost irrelevant notion. Achieving political and military objectives (victory), on the other hand, has become the central criterion for determining the results of conflicts of that nature. Wearing out not only the military forces of the enemy, but also its society, is often believed to be most effective, though battlefield decision cannot be ruled out.[83]

During the past 25 years, low-intensity conflicts have become Israel's most frequent type of confrontation with its enemies. Hizballah is an example of an organization confronting Israel which, despite its extreme military inferiority, has managed to compensate by demonstrating both reasonable loss ratios and stronger societal perseverance.[84] According to former Israeli Defense Minister Yitzhak Mordechai, from his very first day in office, in mid-1996, he appreciated that terrorism and guerrilla actions could not be defeated militarily.[85] In February–March 1998, the Israeli government agreed to implement UN Security Council Resolution 425 of 1978 and withdraw from Lebanon, provided that such withdrawal be accompanied by security arrangements. In 1999, Prime Minister Barak announced his government's intention to withdraw Israeli troops from Lebanon by July 2000. Since Hizballah's main war objective has been to drive Israel out of southern Lebanon, this can undoubtedly be considered a political victory for Hizballah over Israel, at least in Hizballah's eyes. It appears that Israel's experience with both high-intensity and low-intensity conflicts has strengthened its feeling that, should a war erupt, it would be more reasonable to place less emphasis on battlefield decision and more emphasis on victory, instead.

GROWING POLITICAL CONSTRAINTS ON THE FREEDOM OF ACTION ON THE
BATTLEFIELD

As a result of both great sensitivities entailed in the use of force in our time, and the existence of much more effective technological means of command and control, the political echelon nowadays often feels that it must, and can be more deeply involved in the military aspects of the conduct of war, including the shaping of the military war objectives and even the missions. This was very clearly demonstrated during the 1982 Lebanon War, and is likely to typify almost any future war or operation.

According to General Amir Drori, OC Northern Command, the 1982 War 'was characterized, much more than previous wars, by the intervention of the political echelon in all the stages of the battle. [...] There was even some pullback of [our] forces because of the political echelon's decision [...].'[86] The Israeli high command focused on the achievement of the war objectives rather than attaining battlefield decision. Once the war had spilled over and become an Israeli–Syrian confrontation, Israeli decision-makers were mostly interested in creating a situation that would not allow the Syrians to maintain their military and political control of Lebanon. Although this did not rule out the possibility of defeating the Syrians on the battlefield, it most certainly required that the IDF achieve control of the Beirut–Damascus highway, which was believed to be the key to politically controlling Lebanon.[87] When the Israeli high command decided, on 10 June, to unilaterally ceasefire at noon on the following day, it did so not only because it felt that it had to comply with American pressures to stop the war. It decided to comply only after the military had promised that, by the time of ceasefire, the military war objectives would have been achieved, and once a feeling had spread among members of the Cabinet that the war had already exceeded its original objective of assuring that northern Israel be out of Katyusha rocket range.[88]

CONCLUSION:
INTO AN ERA OF BOTH POLITICAL AND MILITARY NEGATIVISM

Israeli war objectives in the past were, at least to some extent, different from how they were generally perceived. Not only have there existed Israeli war objectives in each of the Arab–Israeli wars, but they have also been defined by the political, rather than by the military, echelon and have even proven to be relatively dynamic in nature. The impression that Israel has failed to formulate war objectives can, to a large extent, be attributed to the relatively vague definition of its negative objectives. The subordination of war to politics has been deeply rooted in Israeli civil-military and political-military relations. It has expressed itself not only in principle, but also in practice. It is, however, true that the perceived need to achieve battlefield decision, so deeply embedded in Israeli strategic thinking, has created a strong commitment to its achievement at the expense of the commitment to achieve the war objectives. Battlefield decision has often taken on the meaning of an objective, rather than a means.

Finally, Israeli political war objectives throughout the years have comprised a combination of both negativism and positivism. Due to Israel's narrow security margins, negative *political* war objectives have often been translated into, or accompanied by, positive *military* war objectives, carried out by attack and battlefield decision.

From the late 1960s through the mid-1970s, a new military and political reality developed in the Middle East. From the perspective of Israeli war objectives, the period since then can be characterized by a gradual shift to negativism: deterrence-by-denial and war objectives of a thwarting nature. The strong sense of self-confidence in the wake of the 1967 War, thanks to the so-called defensible borders, perceived superpower constraints by Israeli decision-makers, unwillingness on the part of large portions of the Israeli society to wage war by choice, and the developing reality of peace between Israel and the Arab world as of the mid-1970s have all played a significant role in the shaping the new attitude.

The process was, at first, mainly affected by a combination of military self-confidence and political awareness of superpower constraints: Israel felt that, under the new conditions, it would be neither militarily necessary nor politically feasible to occupy more territories. Later, however, Israel also gradually withdrew from its unequivocal commitment to the achievement of battlefield decision, putting more emphasis on victory; that is, the achievement of the war objectives, which, as noted, have become more negative than ever before.

The main reasons for the declining value of battlefield decision, as opposed to the rising value of victory, have been the strengthening of firepower relative to maneuver on the battlefield, the difficulty in translating battlefield decision to political achievements, and the growing political constraints on the freedom of action on the battlefield.

Since the late 1980s, the volume of the voices calling for the introduction of more defensive elements into the Israeli security conception has amplified considerably. Senior Israeli politicians on both sides of the political spectrum, such as Yitzhak Rabin on the one hand and Ariel Sharon on the other, have delivered themselves of the view that Israel was neither interested in going to war in order to achieve positive gains from the other side nor willing to pay the price for it. In his capacity as Defense Minister Rabin rejected the idea that Israel would attack the Arabs and postulated that Israel's main political war objective was to force the enemy to ask for ceasefire, without having been able to capture any territory under Israeli control.[89] On another occasion he explained why Israel had no reason to adopt a policy that involved the initiation of war for far-reaching, positive political and territorial objectives. First, Israel cannot impose peace agreements on its enemies; second, Israel has no need of any more land.[90] As for Sharon, he surprisingly presented views that, in the past had been characteristic of the negativists, in Israeli strategic thinking.[91]

These trends are only going to intensify in the foreseeable future. It will be difficult, in the future, for Israel to achieve positive war objectives for both military and political reason. At the same time, victory, defined here in terms of the achievement of the war objectives, will become more central in Israeli strategic thinking and practice than the achievement of battlefield decision. These two seemingly contradictory trends are likely to lead Israel towards placing greater emphasis on victory which, at least in the initial stages of a future war, will take on a negative, rather than positive, meaning. Mainstream thinking on war objectives in the future is likely to be more negative than ever.

NOTES

I wish to thank Uri Bar-Joseph, Stuart A. Cohen, and Efraim Inbar for their useful comments on an earlier draft.

1. Israel Tal, Lecture, Israeli National Defense College, 25 March 1978.
2. Emanuel Wald, *Kilelet Hakelim Hashvurim*]The Curse of the Broken Vessels] (Tel Aviv: Shoken 1987) [Hebrew].
3. Zehava Ostfeld, *An Army Is Born* (Tel Aviv: Ma'arachot 1994) [Hebrew] p.755.
4. Carl von Clausewitz, *On War* [1833] (Princeton UP 1976) pp.86–7. For a comparative analysis of Sun Tzu, Clausewitz and Jomini with regard to 'the primacy of politics and the military commander', see Michael I. Handel, *Masters of War: Classical Strategic Thought* (London and Portland, OR: Frank Cass 1996) Ch.6.
5. For victory defined in terms of the relationship between war objectives and war outcomes, see for example: Raymond G. O'Connor, 'Victory in Modern War', *Journal of Peace Research* 4 (1969) p.367; Berenice Carroll, 'How Wars End: An Analysis of Some Current Hypotheses', ibid. p.305.
6. Clausewitz (note 4) pp.90, 77; B.H. Liddell Hart, *Thoughts on War* (London: Faber 1943) p.20; Avi Kober, 'Military Decision in War: A Framework for Research', *Armed Forces & Society* 22/1 (Fall 1995) pp.66–82.
7. Clausewitz (note 4) p.87.
8. On 'self-destructive persistence', see Fred C. Iklé, *Every War Must End* (NY: Columbia UP 1971) p.34. On the tension between the expressive and instrumental elements in war, see: C.R. Mitchell, *The Structure of International Conflict* (London: Macmillan 1981) p.26; Yehoshfat Harkabi, *War and Strategy* (Tel Aviv: Ma'arachot 1990) [Hebrew] pp.46–50.
9. Edward Luttwak and Dan Horowitz, *The Israeli Army* (London: Allen Lane 1975) p.160.
10. Israelis have traditionally considered 'current security' – their name for 'low-intensity conflicts' – to be a minor challenge relative to the 'basic security' challenges posed by the regular armies of Arab states. For the distinction between current and basic security, see Shimon Peres, *The Next Phase* (Tel Aviv: Am Hasseffer 1965) pp.9–15.
11. Luttwak and Horowitz (note 9) pp.151–3; Moshe Dayan, *Story of My Life* (Jerusalem:

Edanim 1976) [Hebrew] p.277; Motti Golani, *There Will Be War Next Summer: The Road to the Sinai War, 1955–1956* (Tel Aviv: Ma'arachot 1997) [Hebrew] pp.456–60.

12. Dayan (note 11) p.471.

13. Carmit Gai, *Bar-Lev: A Biography* (Tel Aviv: Am Oved 1998) [Hebrew] p.140.

14. On the tension between Ben-Gurion and the military during the initial stages of the War of Independence, see Anita Shapira, *The Army Controversy, 1948: Ben-Gurion's Struggle for Control* (Tel Aviv: Hakibbutz Hame'uhad 1985) [Hebrew].

15. Dan Schueftan, *A Jordanian Option* (Tel Aviv: Hakibbutz Hame'uhad 1986) [Hebrew] pp.81, 96; Gershon Rivlin and Elhanan Oren (eds.) *The War of Independence: Ben-Gurion's Diary* (Tel Aviv: Ministry of Defence 1982) [Hebrew] p.900.

16. *Ben-Gurion's Diary* (note 15) pp.914–18; John and David Kimche, *Both Sides of the Hill: Britain and the Palestine War* (London: Secker & Warburg 1960); Netanel Lorch, *Israel in the Grip of Superpowers* (Tel Aviv: Ma'arachot 1990) [Hebrew] pp.17–147.

17. Zeev Schiff, 'A Moment before the Fatal Snow', *Ha'aretz*, 20 June 1997. The Hebrew initials of the Peace for Galilee Operation create the Hebrew word 'snow'.

18. David Ben-Gurion, *Tzava Uvittahon* [Army and Security] (Tel Aviv: Ma'archot 1955) [Hebrew] p.151.

19. Shapira (note 14) pp.36–7.

20. For an excellent analysis of civil-military and political-military relations in Israel, see Yoram Perri, *Between Battles and Ballots: Israeli Military in Politics* (Cambridge: Cambridge UP 1983). See also Yehuda Ben-Meir, *Civil-Military Relations in Israel* (NY: Columbia UP 1995).

21. Iklé (note 8) pp.1–16.

22. Avi-Shai, 'Egypt's War Objectives and Offensive Plan for the Yom Kippur War', *Ma'arachot* 250 (July 1976) p.33.

23. Zeev Schiff, *A History of the Israeli Army* (NY: Macmillan 1985) p.132; Luttwak and Horowitz (note 9) pp.231–3.

24. Yitzhak Rabin, *Pinkas Sherut* (Tel Aviv: Ma'ariv 1979) p.182.

25. Dayan (note 11) pp.474–5; Rabin (note 24) pp.191, 194, 200; Eytan Haber, *Mahar Tifrotz Milhama* [Tomorrow a War Will Break Out] (Tel Aviv: Edanim 1987) [Hebrew] p.250; Aharon Yariv, 'Strategic Decisions in War', in *Cautious Assessment: Writings by Aharon Yariv* (Tel Aviv: Ma'arachot 1999) [Hebrew] pp.139–47.

26. Jonathan Shimshoni, *Israel and Conventional Deterrence: Border Warfare from 1953 to 1970* (Ithaca, NY: Cornell UP 1988) p.152; Rabin (note 24) p.261. For the Egyptian perspective, see: Dan Schueftan, *Attrition: Egypt's Post-War Political Strategy, 1967–1970* (Tel Aviv: Ma'arachot 1989) [Hebrew] pp.245–52.

27. The tension between the defensive and the offensive ethos is analyzed in-depth in Anita Shapira, *Land and Power: The Zionist Resort to Force, 1881–1948* (NY: Oxford UP 1992).

28. Yehezkel Dror, *A Grand Strategy for Israel* (Jerusalem: Academon 1989) [Hebrew] p.165–73.

29. Benjamin Peled, 'Security Without Limits', in Zvi Ofer and Avi Kober (eds.) *The Price of Power* (Tel Aviv: Ma'arachot 1984) [Hebrew] pp.75–80.

30. This point was made by Menachem Begin and Raphael Eytan. See Efraim Inbar, *The Outlook on War of the Political Elite in the Eighties* (Jerusalem: Leonard Davis Inst. for Int. Relations 1988) pp.17, 24.

31. Zvi Lanir, 'Political and Military Objectives in Israeli Wars', in idem, *War by Choice* (Tel Aviv: Jaffee Center for Strategic Studies 1985) [Hebrew] pp.117–56.

32. Yigal Allon, *Kellim Shluvim* (Tel Aviv: Hakibbutz Hame'uhad 1980) [Hebrew] p.111.

33. Inbar (note 30) p.23.

34. Both left-wing and right-wing figures in Israel have expressed themselves on the limits to Israeli use of force and its inability to force its will on the Arabs. For expressions made to this affect by Yitzhak Rabin, Shimon Peres, Hayim Bar-Lev, Mordechai Gur, Moshe Arens, and Mordechai Zippori, see Inbar (note 30) pp.14–15, 22.

35. Rabin (note 24) p.22.

36. Israel Tal, *National Security: The Few Against the Many* (Tel Aviv: Dvir 1996) [Hebrew] pp.54–6.

37. Uri Dromi, 'Reflections on Israeli Use of Force', *Skira Hodshit* Nos. 2–3 (1986) pp.38–47.
38. Israel Bär, 'The War of Independence: Operational Aspects', *Ma'arachot* 62-63 (July 1950) p.63; Elhanan Oren, 'The War of Independence: Objectives and Results', *Ma'arachot* 118–19 (1959) p.53.
39. For a detailed and thorough study of the processes that preceded the Sinai War from the Israeli perspective, see Golani (note 11).
40. Ibid, pp.401–5; Michael Bar-Zohar, *Ben-Gurion* (Tel Aviv: Am Oved 1977) [Hebrew] pp.1234–1235. Ben-Gurion had toyed with the idea of annexing the West Bank since the early 1950s. He considered Jordan to be an unstable and unnatural entity that might disintegrate due to internal or external developments. See Moshe Zak, 'The Corridor to Gaza Separated between Ben-Gurion and Abdallah', *Ma'ariv*, 17 Oct. 1986.
41. Dan Horowitz, *Israel's Concept of Defensible Borders* (Jerusalem: Leonard Davis Inst. for Int. Relations 1975); Yigal Allon, 'Israel: The Case for Defensible Borders', *Foreign Affairs* 55/1 (Oct. 1976) pp.38–53.
42. I distinguish between *casi belli* and red lines per the severity of the threats involved and the means used to cope with them. According to these criteria, *casi belli* refer to situations that severely threaten the state's national security, let alone existence, and therefore need to be coped with by an a priori commitment to go to war should such threats materialize. Red lines, on the other hand, represent threats of a less severe nature that can be handled first with easier means than war, such as diplomatic or economic pressures. For an approach that prefers to treat *casi belli* as types of red lines, in general, and in the Israeli case in particular, see Micha Bar, *Red Lines in Israel's Deterrence Strategy* (Tel Aviv: Ma'arachot 1990) [Hebrew] pp.103–119.
43. Shimshoni (note 26) p.132.
44. Schueftan, *Attrition* (note 26) pp.246–8.
45. Dayan raised the idea of occupying the city of Port Sa'id, on the north-eastern corner of the Suez Canal. He also spoke about the need to establish a bridgehead on the western bank of the canal in order to destroy Egyptian surface-to-air missile bases and regain command of the air over the Bar-Lev line. Another objective mentioned by Dayan was gaining control of oil production sites in the Gulf of Suez in case of an Egyptian attempt to deny Israel free passage of oil through the Gulf of Eilat. Finally, Dayan referred to the need to occupy territory in Lebanon and the Golan Heights so as to drive a wedge between Syria and Lebanon and between Syria and Jordan, and would improve Israeli radar control capability in the vicinity of Mount Hermon. Uri Bar-Joseph, *The Way to Israel's Pearl Harbor* (forthcoming).
46. Ya'acov Hisdai, *Be'et Barzel* (Jerusalem: Laor 1983) [Hebrew] p.46; Dayan (note 11) pp.578, 601.
47. *War by Choice* (note 31) pp.157–163.
48. Ehud Ya'ari and Zeev Schiff, *Milhemet Sholal* (Jerusalem: Shoken 1984) [Hebrew]; Arye Naor, *Cabinet at War* (Tel Aviv: Lahav 1986) [Hebrew] pp.48–49; Shai Feldman and Heda Rechnitz-Kijner, *Deception, Consensus and War: Israel in Lebanon* (Tel Aviv: Jaffee Center for Strategic Studies 1984); Raphael Eytan, *Story of a Soldier* (Tel Aviv: Ma'ariv 1985) p.286; Inbar, *The Outlook on War* (note 30) pp.24–25; Gad Barzilai, 'Democracy in War'(Jerusalem: PhD Dissertation 1987) p.198; Reuven Avi-Ran, *The War of Lebanon – Arab Documents: The Road to War* (Tel Aviv: Ma'arachot 1987) [Hebrew] p.152; Avigdor Ben-Gal, 'Military Operations and Lessons of War', in Shmuel Meir (ed.) *The Lebanon War: A View from 1987* (Tel Aviv: Jaffee Center for Strategic Studies 1988) [Hebrew] p.57.
49. On these concepts, see for example: Glenn H. Snyder, *Deterrence and Defense* (Princeton UP 1961) pp.104–5; Robert Harkavy, *Preemption and Two-Front Conventional Warfare* (Jerusalem: Leonard Davis Inst. for Int. Relations 1977) pp.6–11. For Israeli conception of prevention and preemption, see: Avi Kober, *[Battlefield] Decision in the Arab-Israeli Wars, 1948-1982* (Tel Aviv: Ma'arachot 1995) [Hebrew] pp.168–71.
50. Kober, ibid.
51. Dan Horowitz, 'The Israeli Concept of National Security and the Prospects of Peace in the Middle East', in Gabriel Sheffer (ed.) *Dynamics of a Conflict* (Atlantic Highlands, NJ: Humanities Press 1975) pp.235–75.
52. Clausewitz (note 4), p.358; B.H. Liddell Hart, *Strategy* (London: Faber 1967) p.163.

53. For a discussion on the meaning of strategic depth in general and in Israel in particular, see: Aharon Yariv, 'Strategic Depth', *The Jerusalem Quarterly* 17 (Fall 1980) pp.3–12.
54. David Ben-Gurion, *Behilahem Israel* (Tel Aviv: Mapai 1952) [Hebrew] p.90.
55. Robert Jervis, 'Cooperation Under the Security Dilemma', *World Politics* 30/2 (Jan. 1978) p.203.
56. Ibid. p.187.
57. Kober, *[Battlefield] Decision* (note 49) pp.162–6. For a detailed analysis of the logic of Israeli traditional offensive approach, see Ariel Levite, *Offense and Defense in Israeli Military Doctrine* (Jerusalem Post 1989).
58. See Avi Kober, 'A Paradigm in Crisis? Israel's Doctrine of Military Decision', *Israel Affairs* 2/1 (Autumn 1995) pp.195–7.
59. Dayan (note 11) p.242.
60. Ibid. p.444.
61. Moshe Arens, 'Ending Wars', *Ma'arachot* 292-3 (March–April 1984) p.3; Avner Yaniv, 'Deterrence and Defense in Israel's Strategy', *Medinah, Mimshal Ve-yahasim Benle'umiyim* 24 (Summer 1985) pp.53–4; Lanir (note 31) p.129.
62. Chief of Staff Elazar defined Israel's war objectives in terms of battlefield decision in a discussion held at the IDF's GHQ, 16 April 1973, see Bar-Joseph (note 45). For Defense Minister Rabin's definition of Israel's military war objectives in terms of battlefield decision, reached through the destruction of enemy forces and occupying enemy territory, see *Ha'aretz*, 29 Sept. 1989.
63. For a detailed discussion of Israeli battlefield decision conception, see Kober, *[Battlefield] Decision* (note 49) Ch.6.
64. Dayan (note 11) p.578.
65. Efraim Inbar, 'Israel's Strategy Since the Yom Kippur War', *Ma'arachot* 289–90 (Oct. 1983).
66. Alexis de Tocqueville, *Democracy in America* [1835, 1840] (NY: Vintage Books 1954) pp.292–293.
67. Ben-Gurion, *Behilahem Israel* (note 54) pp.14, 127, 132, 244, 289; Peres, *Tomorrow is Now*, pp.249–50; Avner Yaniv, *Dilemmas of Security* (NY: Oxford UP 1987) p.103; Israel Tal, 'Offense and Defense in the Wars of Israel', *Ma'arachot* 311 (March 1988) p.6; Moshe Bar Kochva, 'Changes and Trends in the IDF's Structure', *Skirah Hodshit* 3–4 (1988) p.24.
68. Edward N. Luttwak, 'Where Are the Great Powers?' *Foreign Affairs* 73/4 (July/Aug. 1994) pp.23–8; 'Toward Post-Heroic Warfare', ibid. 74/3 (May/June 1995) pp.109–22; 'A Post-Heroic Military Policy', ibid. 75/4 (July/Aug. 1996) pp.33–44.
69. Mordechai Gur, *Chief of the General Staff, 1974–1978* (Tel Aviv: Ma'arachot 1998) [Hebrew] p.404.
70. An interview with Barak, *Ha'aretz*, 30 July 1993.
71. Press conference with the Northern Command's Chief of Staff, Brigadier R., *Ha'aretz*, 29 July 1993.
72. Interview to Israeli Radio, Channel 2, 6 Oct. 1999.
73. Deterrence is elusive because it depends very heavily on psychology; early warning at the national level is elusive, due to its dependence on the intellectual skills of a few intelligence evaluators; arms control is elusive because it is strongly based on mutual confidence.
74. In 1982, Egypt refrained from coming to Syria's help. In its peace agreement with Israel it had undertaken not to give its inter-Arab obligations priority over its commitment to peace with Israel. It was also unwilling to either risk its new territorial achievements as a result of the peace process or jeopardize the prospects of economic recovery. Its army was still in a process of modernization, and its relations with Syria and the PLO – two of the most outspoken radical rejectionists in the Arab world – were tense. It also realized that any hostility against Israel would harm its close relations with the United States, the political, military and economical support of which was considered to be vital. Dan Schueftan, 'The Lebanon War and the Arab World', *Ma'arachot* 284 (Sept. 1982) p.64; Itamar Rabinowitz, 'The Arab World in the Lebanon War', in Meir, *The Lebanon War* (note 48) p.11; Chaim Herzog, *The Arab-Israeli Wars* (Jerusalem: Edanim 1983) [Hebrew] pp.291–2.
75. See Yehezkel Dror, 'Modern Technology as a Basis for a War Doctrine', paper presented at

a conference on *Technology and War*, BESA Center for Strategic Studies, 27 Jan. 1998.
76. Shlomo Brom and Yiftah Shapir (eds.) *The Middle East Military Balance, 1999–2000* (Cambridge, MA: Jaffee Center for Strategic Studies & MIT Press 1999) p.414.
77. Interview with Uzi Rubin, head of Israeli program of defense against ballistic missiles, *Ha'aretz*, 28 Oct. 1997.
78. Kober, *[Battlefield] Decision* (note 49) pp.369–72.
79. Ibid. pp.411–17.
80. Hanoch Bartov, *Dado* (Tel-Aviv: Ma'ariv, 1978) [Hebrew] Vol. I, pp.266–7.
81. Arens (note 61) p.3.
82. Stephen P. Rosen, 'War and the Willingness to Suffer', in Bruce M. Russett (ed.) *Peace, War and Numbers* (Beverly Hills, CA: Sage 1972) pp.167–83.
83. Mao Tse-Tung, *Selected Works* (London: Lawrence & Wishart 1954), 'Strategic Problems of China's Revolutionary War', Ch. 2; Che Guevara, *On Guerrilla Warfare* (NY: Praeger 1961) p.11; Vo Nguyen Giap, *People's War, People's Army* (Hanoi: Foreign Languages Publishing House 1961) pp.28–30.
84. In this particular case, the loss ratios do not include civilians, since both sides have agreed to refrain from attacking civilian targets. In 1995 the loss ratios (human casualties) were 3.9 to 1 in Israel's favor; in 1996, they declined to 2.3 to 1; and, in 1997, they declined even further to 1.7 to 1, only (the helicopter crashes of Feb. 1997 excluded). The above figures are based on the IDF Spokesman and Hizballah Internet sites (www.israel-mfa.gov.il/idf; www.moqawama.org), and the Lebanese newspaper *Al-Hayat* (*Ha'aretz*, 26 Dec. 1997).
85. *Ha'aretz*, 15 Sept. 1998.
86. Feldman and Rechnitz-Kijner (note 48) p.33.
87. Kober, *[Battlefield] Decision* (note 49) pp.420–2.
88. Naor (note 48) p.82; Yehuda Ben-Meir, Lecture, Symposium on 'Strategic Decisions in War', Jaffee Center for Strategic Studies, 1985; Ariel Sharon (with David Chanoff), *Warrior* (Tel Aviv: Steimatzky 1989) pp.468–9.
89. *Ha'aretz Supplement*, 29 Sept. 1989.
90. Address by Yitzhak Rabin at the Begin-Sadat Center for Strategic Studies, Bar-Ilan University, 10 June 1991.
91. See Ariel Sharon's lecture at Jaffee Center for Strategic Studies, Tel Aviv University, 12 Sept. 1989.

Abstracts

The Concept of Security: Should it be Redefined?
BENJAMIN MILLER

This essay addresses the debate on the expansion of the concept of security, which emerged especially after the end of the Cold War. My argument is based on a distinction between the phenomenon to be explained and the explanations, which include all the relevant competing causal factors affecting the explained phenomenon. The subject matter, that the security field addresses, is the threat of organized inter-group violence, and the ways to manage and to prevent it. Here a somewhat broadened version of the traditionalist security concept is in order, which should treat peace as a central element of the field alongside war. Yet, regarding the competing explanations of war and peace, the door should be kept wide open to a great variety of causal factors, theories and explanations, on the condition that they logically and empirically affect war and peace.

New Threats, New Identities and New Ways of War:
The Sources of Change in National Security Doctrine
EMILY O. GOLDMAN

Incremental adaptations in national security doctrines are part of the normal course of events, but rarely do states dramatically alter their national security doctrines or adopt a new national security identity. Dramatic discontinuities in the strategic, technological, and domestic environments, such as those ushered in by the end of the Cold War and the onset of the information age, can alter the foundations of long-standing national security doctrines and produce dissension over the precepts and policies that should replace them. This essay provides a framework for understanding 'national security uncertainty', its causes, and the consequences for diplomatic postures, resource allocation, military mission priorities, and domestic mobilization.

Technology's Knowledge Burden, the RMA and the IDF: Organizing the Hypertext Organization for Future 'Wars of Disruption'?
CHRIS C. DEMCHAK

In modernizing the IDF by adopting many budget-reducing elements of the US-defined RMA model of a modern military, Israeli defense leaders are choosing a path highly problematical for the knowledge-conditions of the nation. Even in selected pieces, the RMA model remains a socio-technical arrangement most appropriate for an expeditionary army of a geographically isolated, wealthy society. This work reviews the RMA model's organizational knowledge requirements and the current knowledge conditions facing the IDF. The discussion addresses the RMA implications for Israel's conventional deterrence; the role of surprise in future conflicts; and the possible transformation of the IDF into a non-RMA knowledge-centric organization more congruent with Israeli geostrategic and internal knowledge conditions.

Non-Conventional Solutions for Non-Conventional Dilemmas?
YIFTAH S. SHAPIR

This study surveys Israel's doctrine of multi-layered defense against the threat of ballistic missiles. It describes the nation's unique combination of deterrence, passive defense, active defense, and offensive tactics against this threat and analyzes the technical, tactical, and political arguments for and against each layer of defense. The analysis concludes that deterrence is likely to be Israel's most effective strategy to forestall this threat in the future. Nevertheless, it also argues that although other methods might be technically less efficient, domestic and external political considerations may justify them and render them a sound strategy.

Israeli War Objectives into an Era of Negativism
AVI KOBER

Israeli war objectives since the 1970s have gradually become more 'defensive' in nature. Four main factors have accounted for it: superpower constraints, difficulty in gaining public legitimization for war, the peace process, and the spread of surface-to-surface missiles in the Middle East. At the same time, Israel has gradually withdrawn from its unequivocal commitment to the achievement of battlefield decision, putting more emphasis on the achievement of the political war objectives. The main reasons for this have been the strengthening of firepower relative to maneuver on the battlefield, the difficulty in translating battlefield decision to political achievements, and the growing political constraints on the freedom of action on the battlefield.

About the Contributors

Uri Bar-Joseph is a Senior Lecturer at the division of International Relations at Haifa University. He is the author of *The Watchman Fell Asleep: The Surprise of Yom Kippur and Its Sources* (Hebrew 2001), *Intelligence Intervention in the Politics of Democratic States: The United States, Britain, and Israel* (1995), and *The Best of Enemies: Israel and Transjordan in the War of 1948* (1987).

Benjamin Miller is Senior Lecturer in International Relations at the Hebrew University of Jerusalem. He is the author of *When Opponents Cooperate: Great Power Conflict and Collaboration in World Politics* (1995) and he has published numerous articles on international relations theory and international security. Miller's current work focuses on constructing a theory of regional war and peace and applying it to the Balkans, South America, Western Europe and the Middle East in the nineteenth and twentieth centuries.

Emily O. Goldman is Associate Professor of Political Science at the University of California, Davis. She co-directs the Joint Center for International and Security Studies (JCISS), a research partnership between UC Davis and the Naval Postgraduate School in Monterey. Professor Goldman is the author of *Sunken Treaties: Naval Arms Control Between the Wars* (1994) and has published numerous articles on US foreign and national security policy, and military affairs.

Chris C. Demchak is an Associate Professor in the University of Arizona. Focusing on the implications of new organizational structures/ capabilities given new IW and network complex systems, she is the author of *Military Organizations, Complex Machines: Modernization in the US Armed Services* (1991) and articles on comparative militaries and policies. A US Army Reserve officer, Demchak also has regional expertise in Europe, Africa and the Middle East, and speaks five languages.

Yiftah S. Shapir is a Researcher at the Jaffee Center for Strategic Studies (JCSS), Tel Aviv University. He is responsible for the quantitative part of the *Middle East Military Balance* – the annual publication of the Jaffee Center, and specializes in proliferation of weapons of mass destruction.

Avi Kober lectures at the Department of Political Studies at Bar-Ilan University (Israel) and is a Research Associate at BESA Center for Strategic Studies. He is the author of *Battlefield Decision in the Arab-Israeli Wars, 1948–1982* (Hebrew 1995) and has published numerous articles on military thought, Israeli security conception, Arab–Israeli wars, and low-intensity conflicts. He also edited and co-edited books on Israeli national security.

Index

Significant information in notes is indexed as 172n31, i.e. note 31 on page 172

For Product Safety Concerns and Information please contact our EU
representative GPSR@taylorandfrancis.com Taylor & Francis Verlag GmbH,
Kaufingerstraße 24, 80331 München, Germany

Printed and bound by CPI Group (UK) Ltd, Croydon, CR0 4YY
08/06/2025
01896991-0009